# BLACK
# WOMEN WRITERS
# AT WORK

# BLACK WOMEN WRITERS AT WORK

*Edited by*
· CLAUDIA TATE ·

CONTINUUM · NEW YORK

The Continuum Publishing Company
575 Lexington Avenue
New York, New York 10022

Printed in the United States of America

*Library of Congress Cataloging in Publication Data*

Main entry under title:

Black women writers at work.

1. Afro-American authors—Interviews.   2. Women
authors, American—Interviews.   3. Authors, American—
20th century—Interviews.   4. American literature—
Afro-American authors—History and criticism.
5. American literature—Women authors—History and
criticism.   6. American literature—20th century—
History and criticism.   7. Authorship.   I. Tate,
Claudia.
PS153.N5B56      1983      810′.9′9287         82-23546
   ISBN 0-8264-0232-1         0-8264-0243-7 pbk

Grateful acknowledgment is made to the following for permission to reprint:
lines from "Note on Commercial Theatre" is from *Selected Poems of Langston
Hughes* by Langston Hughes, copyright 1948 by Alfred A. Knopf, Inc., reprinted
by permission of Random House, Inc.; lines from "And Still I Rise" is from *And
Still I Rise* by Maya Angelou, copyright 1978 by Maya Angelou, reprinted also
by permission of Random House, Inc.; lines from "Short Poem" is from *I've Been
A Woman* by Sonia Sanchez, reprinted by permission of The Black Scholar Press;
and from *The World of Gwendolyn Brooks,* excerpts from "The Sundays of Satin-
Legs Smith" and "at the hairdresser's," copyright 1945 by Gwendolyn Brooks
Blakely, and the excerpt from "XV," copyright 1949 by Gwendolyn Brooks Bla-
kely, are reprinted by permission of Harper & Row, Publishers, Inc.

*For my parents*
*and grandmother,*
*and for Harold, Read, and Jerome*

# CONTENTS

# · FOREWORD ·

*I*nterviews with writers, that most recent of literary genres, have become a staple in our time.

All that makes the best of such collections fascinating, useful, distinguishes this one. These fourteen writers, each in their own way and voice, take us into the heart of the creative process.

With an accuracy, clarity, often musicality, that in themselves exemplify the writer's love, care, for language, they illuminate origins, motive springs; how these become substance, vision; varying ways of working, of being productive. Uses of autobiographical materials are discussed; influences, predecessors; place and power of imagination; the self-critical faculty; criticism. The larger questions are here too: why and for whom do I write? What is the writer's responsibility to one's work, to others, to society? Towards what do I aspire?

The result is one of those rare, rich sourcebooks for writers, readers, teachers, students—all who care about literature and the creation of it.

Yet—as if this were not ample—this collection transcends its genre. It becomes a harbinger book, a book of revelation, of haunting challenge, opening on to central concerns not only of writing, but of life, of living, today.

Each and all of these writers would honor any collection using the all-embracing word: "writer" without qualification in its title; each of these fourteen are passionately individual, complex, original; of diverse backgrounds, cultures. Yet they are fit, gathered here into what is considered a reductive, a lesser category: *black* writers, *women* writers, *black women writers.*

It is an unhappy fact that association with a category: Native-American, Asian-American, *any* hyphenated American, working class, black, women, ethnic, minority, "sub-culture"—U.S.A. American all—has, with occasional exception, relegated a writer to less than full writer's status; resulted as well in ignorance of or lack of full recognition to a writer's work and achievement.

But it is this very grouping, the very juxtaposition of these distinctly individual writers who *are* black, who *are* women, that enlarged, transformed this collection.

Women of color, daughters and granddaughters—often blood kin still—of working people whose lives were, are, consumed mostly by the struggle for maintaining human life, they have a based closeness to what is called the human condition, to what Toni Cade Bambara calls "the truth about human nature, about the human potential."

As in their work, we are wrenched into comprehensions significantly, crucially different from that which prevail in most of our country's literature and social attitude today. Human functioning is revealed in its evil or in its true, experienced worth; value is attributed to where it humanly belongs; great capacities are recognized, traced in everyday use. They make us profoundly conscious of what harms, degrades, denies development, destroys; of how much is unrealized, unlived; instead of "oppressed victims," they tell of the ways of resistances, resiliences.

As was said of Chekhov, they see and write with love and anguish of their human beings not only as their lives have made them (and they make their lives), but also as they might have been, might be, if circumstances were other. In a more painful sense than Emily Dickinson, they "dwell in possibility, a fairer house than prose."

This vision remains the healing, life-affirming vision writers can give in our time when most of us are less than is in us to be, for inherent in it is the need to act to transform common circumstances so they do not injure; the belief that this is possible as well as necessary. It enables us to comprehend, shape, change reality, and the human destiny.

For the life of what I began to say here, turn to these pages on which these writers limn themselves and so much else; and from these pages—you readers who have not yet the fortune of knowing their work—turn to their way-opening work, as surely you will.

TILLIE OLSEN

# · ACKNOWLEDGMENTS ·

*I* would like to thank Howard University's Faculty Research Program in the Social Sciences, Humanities, and Education, administered by Dr. Lorraine A. Williams, vice president for academic affairs, and Mr. Vernon Jones, research analyst for the vice president's office; Dr. Estelle W. Taylor, chairman of the English department, who understood the demands of full-time research and who encouraged me during moments of uncertainty; Mrs. Constance Stokes, Janet Sims, the entire staff of the Moorland-Spingarn Research Center, and E. Ethelbert Miller and Curvin Simms of the Afro-American Resource Center for their research assistance; Dr. Stephen Henderson, director of the Institute for the Arts and the Humanities, and his administrative assistant, Juliet Bowles; Michael Miller and Harold Washington of Audio-Visual Aids; my friends and colleagues at Howard, especially Professors Paul Logan, Al Frost, Pat Jackson, Christian Filistrat, and Beverlee Bruce, who all convinced me that the end was in sight even when they could not see it for themselves; and Professors Michael S. Harper of Brown University, Alan Heimert of Harvard University, and Arthur P. Davis of Howard University for their support of my work.

I would also like to express my appreciation to my typists Ann Goldman, Cynthia Parker, Linda Jabari, Karen Murdock, Sally McCoy, and particularly Alice Snead who typed the bulk of this manuscript; my research assistants Wahneema Lubiano and Reginald Robinson for their outstanding hard work; my babysitters Kay Oyarzo, Catherine Gibbs, and Liza Samuels; and to Mary Helen Washington, editor of *The Black-Eyed Susans* and *Midnight Birds*, for her advice at the project's inception.

I am indebted to the National Endowment for the Humanities, and especially Mary Jaffe, for providing the means for carrying out this project. I am most indebted to the women in this volume, for without their cooperation and encouragement there would not have been this collection of interviews.

My expression of gratitude would be incomplete were I not to mention my parents, Harold and Mary Tate, my brother Harold, my grandmother Mozella Austin, who lived through this project with me and whose faith in me was unwavering, even though mine was not; and my sons, Read and Jerome.

This project is made possible with partial support from the Faculty Research Program in the Social Sciences, Humanities, and Education of the Office of the Vice President for Academic Affairs at Howard University, and with partial support from the National Endowment for the Humanities.

# · INTRODUCTION ·

*B*lack Women Writers At Work is not a collection of disrobing exposés revealing the personal lives of black women writers. Neither is it so purely literary in its focus that the writers' experiences and interests are divorced from their works. Extraliterary concerns—social and political issues as well as intimate aspects of their personal lives—do, indeed, have direct bearing on the creative process. This viewpoint is by no means new and startling. As long as critics have been around, they have insisted that the artist's life and art are inextricably linked. This rather predictable relationship, however, takes on especially vibrant technical and thematic forms when an artist is creating within an environment of diverse, and often conflicting, social traditions. And nowhere else in America is the social terrain more complex, controversial, and contradictory than where a racial minority and the "weaker" gender intersect.

This book builds its literary foundation on this notion of linkage. The interviews are fashioned so that the writers share their conscious motives for selecting particular characters, situations, and techniques to depict their ideas. For example, Toni Morrison describes the inspiration for her stories as commonplace ideas—familiar platitudes and warmed-over sentiments—in short, as clichés.

Gwendolyn Brooks explains the rage that dominates "The Ballad of Pearl May Lee" [*A Street in Bronzeville*] in terms of her own anger toward those Afro-Americans who prefer light-skinned black people:

> I hope you sense some real rage in "The Ballad of Pearl May Lee." The speaker is a very enraged person. I know because I consulted myself in how I have felt. Why in the world . . . has

it been that our men have preferred for some time now that pigmentation which is as close to white as possible?*

The interviews are also designed for the writers to comment on how aspects of their personal lives find their way into the work. Moreover, they provide a platform on which the writers play a seldom seen role—that of critic of their own work, including both criticism of their critics and the conventional practices of literary criticism. The interviews, therefore, are a direct means for each writer to share her own assessment of her work and the criticism that it has engendered, and to understand the assessment in the context of contemporary literature.

By virtue of their race and gender, black women writers find themselves at two points of intersection: one where Western culture cuts across vestiges of African heritage, and one where male-female attitudes are either harmoniously parallel, subtly divergent, or in violent collision. Their work addresses what it means to be human, a condition not entirely determined by genetic makeup but is also comprised of conscious volition. As a result, their fictional characters engage in perplexing struggles to maintain their human dignity and emotional sensitivity in an impersonal, alien, and frequently threatening world. Being both black and female, these writers write from a unique vantage point. They project their vision of the world, society, community, family, their lovers, even themselves, most often through the eyes of black female characters and poetic personae. Their angle of vision allows them to see what white people, especially males, seldom see. With one penetrating glance they cut through layers of institutionalized racism and sexism and uncover a core of social contradictions and intimate dilemmas which plague all of us, regardless of our race or gender. Through their art they share their vision of possible resolution with those who cannot see.

In setting up as a basis of this study a correspondence between life and art, I am not suggesting that there is a simple one-to-one correspondence between a story, poem, or play and the real-life situations out of which these might have originated. In fact, art seldom mimics life. An intermediary process involving reflection, distillation, organization, and most of all imagination, separates the two realms. The

* All excerpts in the introduction, unless otherwise indicated, are from the interviews in this book.

writer projects her understanding of life, her vision as it were, into an imaginary world. She may, if she so chooses, tap the reservoir of personal experience as an aid in depicting a scene. Whether the personal or imaginary ingredient is predominant in the finished product depends entirely on the individual artist. Toni Morrison, for instance, says that her stories take shape in the depths of her imagination rather than in real-life situations. She says: "Writing has to do with the imagination. It's being willing to open a door or think the unthinkable, no matter how silly it may appear."

When autobiographical content is used as the basis for an imaginative piece, it generally assumes a very different and sometimes unrecognizable configuration. Hence, no clear correspondence can be said to exist between the actual details of an artist's life and a depicted incident. So when Alice Walker says that " 'To Hell with Dying' . . . is [her] most autobiographical story . . . though in fact, none of it happened," we understand that the term "autobiographical" is redefined to indicate some aspect of the origin of the work, but is by no means a substantial or total account of it. Nikki Giovanni emphatically denies that experience is the basis for art: "We cheapen anything written when we consider it an experience. Because if it's someone else's experience, we don't have to take it seriously. . . . Writers write because they empathize with the general human condition."

Ntozake Shange, on the other hand, acknowledges that her poetry reflects an intense awareness of herself:

> I see my self-consciousness in terms of battling with myself to let go of something. . . . I had fought through very difficult emotional tasks in order to allow myself to say: "Okay, as weird as *this* is, *this* is truly how I feel. Therefore, if I write anything else, it would be a lie.". . . In other words, my self-consciousness has nothing really to do with other people. It has to do with whether or not I'm going to confront what I'm feeling.

Shange's approach to her work is highly personal. However, this only indicates that her work originates from self-encounter, not that it actually portrays personal experiences.

Although the terms "self-conscious," "personal," and "autobiographical" have similar meanings in ordinary usage in that they indicate a common point of origin, these terms also have, as these writers insist, distinct meanings as they pertain to artistic creation. This is important to keep in mind especially when one examines critically works by women writers, inasmuch as two fallacies seem to be prevalent in criticism. On the one hand the writers are often identified, or more accurately misidentified, with their female characters. On the other hand, the works themselves are frequently overlooked in favor of rather blasé, and often presumptuous discussions of the writers' personal lives. As a result, these works usually do not receive genuine critical notices.

Whether the subject of a book originates in personal experience, in observation, empathy, or imaginative projection is not nearly so important as the degree of truthfulness and sincerity with which a book is rendered. If a writer honestly depicts what he or she *really* feels, sees, and believes, rather than merely to portray what might please a specific audience or what might be financially rewarding, then a work breathes with its own self-sustaining vitality. It then possesses a truth that exceeds the limited experience that is depicted and is, therefore, applicable to life in general. The work, despite of or perhaps precisely because of its unique and particular details of race and gender, achieves universality. It is the critic's responsibility to determine its degree of achievement.

By and large black women writers do not write for money or recognition. They write for themselves as a means of maintaining emotional and intellectual clarity, of sustaining self-development and instruction. Each writes because she is driven to do so, regardless of whether there is a publisher, an audience, or neither.

*Black Women Writers At Work* does not simply address itself to the subject of the writer's vision and its vantage point, and then suggest the fictional application of the vision or state in complex terms "the moral of the story." To do so would isolate a work within the general purview of social and psychological concerns or within the personal sphere of the writer's consciousness. Certainly, these are important aspects of writing and literary criticism, and the interviews address them. This study also analyzes and evaluates the quality of this artistic sight—its clarity, exactness of hue, and fineness of texture. Consequently, each interview is a carefully controlled dialogue fashioned to engage the writer in an analytical discussion of her work with regard to theme and technique, as well as the intellectual and social climates from which the work arose. Each writer presents an understanding of her own sensibility, and explains aspects of her craft that are rendered in particular rhetorical, dramatic, and lyrical details. As a result, the interviews provide firsthand accounts for appreciating a specific body of literature and the creative process in general.

For this purpose, I have selected two basic types of questions. The first is a group of core questions addressing some generic issues. For example, how being black and female constitute a particular perspective in their work; for whom they write; what determines their interest as writers; and whether there is a difference between the types of events, characters, themes, etc., that male and female writers, black and white, select in order to dramatize their stories.

The second type addresses specific aspects of an individual writer's vision and style. For instance, Nikki Giovanni goes into why she felt an urgency to change her tone from an outspoken black militant to a private, introspective individual who gives lyrical analyses of subjects ranging from intimate relationships to international events. Kristin Hunter identifies the source of her unfailing humor. Alexis DeVeaux relates the impact her lesbian lifestyle has on her selection of theme and event.

My questions concerning Ntozake Shange's *For Colored Girls Who Have Considered Suicide When the Rainbow Is Enuf* are not meant to suggest that this work is some kind of literary touchstone for black women writers. They only reflect the undeniable fact that this work attracted a great deal of attention, and as a result had serious effects on the literary media as it affected blacks and women. Therefore I wanted to discuss its social and literary impact.

My findings about the characteristics of writing by black women, which I outline in the following paragraphs, stem from two sources—from a survey of much of the imaginative writing by black women and from the information provided in the interviews. Both indicate a preponderance of certain themes, many of which are typical of American literature in general and Afro-American literature in particular, and some seem to be unique to the writings of black women. A case in point is the quest theme—a character's personal search for a meaningful identity and for self-sustaining dignity in a world of growing isolation, meaninglessness, and moral decay. This theme assumes a special dimension when it is depicted by black

American writers, inasmuch as their sense of isolation and moral hypocrisy has always been qualified by racial prejudice. Black women writers, of course, are confronted with the same racial climate as their male counterparts, but by virtue of their gender their depictions of it often reflect differences—sometimes subtle and sometimes obvious—in tone, in character selection, setting, and plot.

Black women writers usually project their vision from the point of view of female characters. Regardless of the genre, these writers' imaginative embodiment of the female perspective in "the black heroine" has distinct characteristics, some of which originate in gender and its associated sex roles, while others reflect the process of observation from a vantage point other than that determined by sex. For example, the black heroine seldom elects to play the role of the alienated outsider or the lone adventurer in her quest for self-affirmation. This does not mean that she is unconcerned about her self-esteem and about attaining a meaningful social position, but rather that her quest of self-discovery has different priorities and takes place in a different landscape. She does not, for instance, journey across the Northeast like Richard Wright's Cross Damon in *The Outsider,* nor does she explore the underground regions of urban civilization like Ralph Ellison's invisible man. On the contrary, she is usually literally tied down to her children and thus to a particular place. Or, she is ensconced in her community, dependent on friends and relatives for strength during times of hardship and for amusement during times of relaxation. The most memorable black heroes, on the other hand, are not generally encumbered with the weight of dependents or with strong ties to the community; as a result, they are either free to begin with or free themselves so as to travel light.

Because of the restrictions placed on the black heroine's physical movement, she must conduct her quest within close boundaries, often within a room as in the case of Sula Peace in Toni Morrison's *Sula,* or within the borders of two nearby towns as is the case of Ursa Corregidora in Gayl Jones's novel *Corregidora.* Even when she does actually cover a lot of territory as Meridian Hill does in Alice Walker's *Meridian,* it is not her physical movement that demands our attention since this is not of primary importance. It is more important for us to know that Meridian lives in the Deep South and, like the four walls of a room, geographical boundaries merely represent the physical limits of her quest. Meridian's destination, like that of her sister heroines, is not a place but a state of mind. In this regard, the black heroine and the black hero share the same quest in that both seek increasingly higher levels of emotional and intellectual awareness of the self and the outside world. The hero's destination is often an actual place, and is an external projection of his growing awareness. The heroine's emerging awareness takes the form of conceptual abstractions, which are frequently embodied in and communicated through symbols. Thus, her quest does not terminate with her arrival at a new destination; in fact, she remains stationary. Her journey is an internal one and is seldom taken on land.

Inasmuch as physical limitations confine the black heroine's quest within a given area, her strong inclination for forming complex personal relationships add depth to her identity quest in lieu of geographical breadth. These relationships, which should not be mistaken for ordinary contact among people based on superficial familiarity, fall into two fundamental categories—those in which the heroine is a confused or troubled participant, and those which occur after she has achieved some understanding of herself and of others, thus making the relationship mutually beneficial. The first type of relationship may not mature into the second type, since it may be terminated because it was exploitative. Or it may terminate in an emotional impasse and as a result disintegrate if the heroine is unable to resolve the central conflict of her relationship. If she is to meet the quest objective, she must attain an understanding and awareness of herself and of the other.

In work after work we see the heroine as a participant in these two basic types of relationships—rather than as an outsider plotting out her destiny in isolation. This is not to suggest that her self-awareness and destiny are controlled by or subordinated to other people; on the contrary, she is aware that she alone must be determined to understand the conditions of her life, first by means of intense introspection, before she can move on to establish meaningful relationships with other people. Alexis DeVeaux calls attention to the black heroine's fulfillment of this requirement precisely by these means:

> I see a greater and greater commitment among black women writers to understand self, multiplied in terms of the community, the community multiplied in terms of the nation, and the nation multiplied in terms of the world. You have to understand what your place as an individual is and the place of the person who is close to you. You have to understand the space between you before you can understand more complex or larger groups.

If the relationships are beneficial, the likelihood increases for the affirmation of her self-esteem, but if they are exploitative, she faces extreme peril.

Self-esteem is so primary an issue in writings by black women that it deserves special attention. Many heroines suffer from a loss of pride and personal worth. In most cases it is difficult to know the origin of this loss, that is to say whether it resulted first from her forming destructive relationships or whether it caused her to form such relationships. But once these two lethal forces are linked, the heroine becomes entangled in an ever-worsening situation. A chain reaction is set into motion: as her self-esteem deteriorates, she becomes more and more trapped in destructive relationships, which erode her self-esteem still further. She becomes increasingly desperate to the point where she can either summon enough spiritual energy and exert a furious effort to sever the destructive relationship and restore her self-esteem, or she can continue in the downward spiral to utter wretchedness. The latter situation is dramatized in Sonia Sanchez's "After Saturday Night Comes Sunday." In this short story, the heroine deteriorates until she arrives at the threshold of insanity, where she must either regain control of her life or possibly lose control forever. Sanchez further elaborates on this situation in the interview and points out that people in general and women especially tend to lose sight of themselves in a bad relationship. But this does not mean that they must see themselves as victims: "They must see what must be done and they must move on it because it's beyond their power to change the situation." Ntozake Shange in *For Colored Girls* calls attention to how male-oriented black women are, how all women in general are. The level of self-esteem of many of the personae in the choreopoem is a direct result of whether the man-woman relationship is exploitative. In the end the women realize that their sense of pride and well-being must first emanate from within themselves before it can be shared with another person. Shange is adamant about this point in all of her work: "When I die, I will not be guilty of having left a generation of girls behind thinking that anyone can tend to their emotional health other than themselves."

To base one's self-esteem on self-sacrifice by caring exclusively for others, whether it be one's mate, children, or one's extended family, and not to care for one's spiritual well-being is a self-destructive proposition. By no means are the women in this volume advocating that women be egocentric and live in isolation, or only amongst themselves—in short without men, as some of their critics have suggested. This interpretation is not merely myopic, but borders on the ridiculous. What these writers are saying is that women must assume responsibility for strengthening their self-esteem by learning to love and appreciate themselves—in short, to celebrate their womanhood. Only then will they be able to become involved in mutually fulfilling relationships.

Another characteristic of the black heroine is that she, like her counterparts in real life, not only carries the double burden of racism and sexism, but must also stand erect under their weight, must also walk, run, and even fight. She is a guerilla warrior, "fighting," as DeVeaux insists, "the central oppression of all people of color as well as the oppression of women by men." She wages this struggle with self-confidence, with courage and conviction, and her principal strategy is her self-conscious affirmation of black womanhood. Her battle cry gives pitch and timber to the countless unheard voices of armies of black women. We hear her words rise from the centermost region of individual consciousness and gather into the collective chorus of self-proclaimed sisterhood. The words may vary but the meaning is singular—survival with dignity.

Typically, the black heroine lives each day believing that life ought not be seen as a problem to be solved, for often there are no answers. She insists that life is an experience to be lived, a process; as a result, she learns that conflicts are often resolved but are seldom solved. Frequently, her resolution is nothing more than to change.

There are two kinds of change. One is the result of willful decision and consequent action, and the other is, as Audre Lorde defines it, "[c]hange ris[ing] endemically from the experience fully lived and responded to." Thus, the latter does not occur as the direct result of deliberate decision; it is not precipitated by the exertion of power and dominion over another person. This type of change, which is just as valid as that arising from willful action, occurs because the heroine recognizes, and more importantly respects her inability to alter a situation. However, this is not to imply that she is completely circumscribed by her limitations. On the contrary, she learns to exceed former boundaries but only as a direct result of knowing where they lie. In this regard, she teaches her readers a great deal about constructing a meaningful life in the midst of chaos and contingencies, armed with nothing more than her intellect and emotions.

The black heroine's awareness of herself, first as a human being and second as a woman, is firmly secured in her psychological makeup. Her quest for self-affirmation almost always begins with this point of awareness and develops as she qualifies her individual character, nurtures her self-esteem, recognizes her desires, and defines the nature of her relationships with other people. In so doing the black heroine must relate to herself, others, and the world around her with increasing clarity. This may appear to be simple and ordinary, but is actually quite complex and demands intense introspection. These are the subjects depicted in the works by black women writers—conflicts and ambitions which constitute the black heroine's struggle to map out her destiny and to give it meaning.

While many black writers, male and female, fit into the general tradition in Afro-American literature of celebrating black survival by overcoming racial obstacles, other writers give their attention to those who fall in battle, insisting that their fight, though unsuccessful, is valiant and therefore merits artistic attention. By and large black women writers have this distinctive voice in the literature. Pecola in Toni Morrison's *The Bluest Eye;* DeWitt Williams in Gwendolyn Brooks's *A Street in Bronzeville;* Eva in Gayl Jones's *Eva's Man;* Beau Willie in Ntozake Shange's *For Colored Girls* all remind us that for every victor in the American racial wars there is the vanquished, who is too easily forgotten.

Black women writers do, indeed, celebrate racial victory, but they also acknowledge defeat, not for the purpose of reinforcing a sense of defeat or victimization but to insure that we all learn to recognize what constitutes vulnerability in order to avoid its consequences in the future. This recognition originates in acknowledging the source of one's pain and reconciling oneself to bearing, in some measure, responsibility for it. Hence, we find as a recurring theme in the works of black women that black people must assume ultimate responsibility for their behavior, despite the racial and social contingencies they face. Racism does not alleviate their responsibility to maintain their sense of human dignity, and they can either protect or exploit those around them.

Black women writers did not suddenly begin to write in the 1970s in the wake of the women's movement, as too many are eager to believe. There has been continuous literary activity among black American women ever since Phillis Wheatley in the eighteenth century. What is true is that most of the work, like that by women in general, has remained in attic trunks, hidden away from the world by both choice and fortune. Many writers have not sought to share their innermost thoughts with the world because they felt that their efforts were too private or that they might be misunderstood. Others felt their work exceeded the boundaries of traditional social or moral propriety, or of acceptable racial content. Still others feared encountering the male-dominated press or hostile critics. All of these reasons pertain to Audre Lorde's work, but she had decided to place her work before the public anyway. By and large, the results were predictable: "Black writers, of whatever quality, who step outside the pale of what black writers are supposed to write about, or who black writers are supposed to be, are condemned to silences in black literary circles that are as total and as destructive as any imposed by racism. This is particularly true for black women writers who have refused to be delineated by male-established models of femininity."

Even when their works are published, these writers still remain obscure since they seldom receive the same marketing attention or support of the academic community their male counterparts do. It is only a recent phenomenon that books by black women writers have been appearing in numbers greater than a couple a year. This has prompted a few people to believe that they are witnessing some kind of conspiracy on the part of black women writers to overshadow black male writers, or to undermine the celebratory tradition in Afro-American literature. Neither assumption is true, of course. What we are witnessing, in fact, is black women gaining access to the publishing industry in increasing numbers and, as a result, more and more works by and about black women are appearing in print.

Black women writers and critics are acting on the old adage that one must speak for oneself if one wishes to be heard. They are realizing that no one else can or will say what she has to say, and that silence condemns the silent to misrepresentation and neglect. Langston Hughes immortalized this idea in verse, and his words are most appropriate for the black heroine, her creators and critics:

> . . . someday somebody'll
> Stand up and talk about me,
> And write about me—
> Black and beautiful—
> And sing about me,
> And put on plays about me!
> I reckon it'll be
> Me myself!
>
> Yes, it'll be me.
> —"Note on Commercial Theatre"
> *Selected Poems of Langston Hughes*

This book originates in this belief, that no one can promote the black woman writer's literary well-being better than she can herself.

# · MAYA ANGELOU ·

*M*aya Angelou, author, poet, playwright, stage and screen per-
former, director, and former nightclub singer, was born Marguerite Johnson in 1928 in St. Louis, Missouri. She attended public
schools in Arkansas and California, later studied dance with Martha
Graham and drama with Frank Silvera.

She began her literary career as a poet. Her published collections
include Just Give Me a Cool Drink of Water 'Fore I Die *(1971)*; Oh
Pray My Wings Are Going to Fit Me Well *(1975)*; *and* And Still I
Rise *(1976)*. These are characterised by a spontaneous joyfulness and
an indomitable spirit to survive and succeed.

Angelou's four autobiographical works depict sequential periods of
her early life. I Know Why the Caged Bird Sings *(1970) is about
Marguerite Johnson and her brother Bailey, growing up in Arkansas,
Missouri and California. It is the story of a black girl stumbling about
in a society that devalues her beauty and her ambition.* Gather Together In My Name *(1974) covers the period after the birth of Marguerite's son Guy and her courageous struggle as a single parent to
provide for him.* Singin' and Swingin' and Gettin' Merry Like
Christmas *(1976) describes Maya's stage debut, concluding with her
return from the international tour of* Porgy and Bess. The Heart of
Woman *(1981) has a more mature Maya becoming more comfortable
with her creativity and her success.*

◆  ◆  ◆

MAYA ANGELOU:   Image making is very important for every
human being. It is especially important for black American women
in that we are, by being black, a minority in the United States, and
by being female, the less powerful of the genders. So, we have two

1

areas we must address. If we look out of our eyes at the immediate world around us, we see whites and males in dominant roles. We need to see our mothers, aunts, our sisters, and grandmothers. We need to see Frances Harper, Sojourner Truth, Fannie Lou Hammer, women of our heritage. We need to have these women preserved. We need them all: . . . Constance Motley, Etta Motten. . . . All of these women are important as role models. Depending on our profession, some may be even more important. Zora Neale Hurston means a great deal to me as a writer. So does Josephine Baker, but not in the same way because her profession is not directly related to mine. Yet I would imagine for someone like Diahann Carroll or Diana Ross, Miss Baker must mean a great deal. I would imagine that Bessie Smith and Mammie Smith, though they are important to me, would be even more so to Aretha Franklin.

If I were a black male writer, I would think of Frederick Douglass, who was not just a politician, but as a writer was stunning. In the nineteenth century I would think of William Wells Brown, Martin Delaney, and certainly David Walker, who showed not only purpose but method. In the twentieth century I would think of Richard Wright, Jean Toomer, and so on. They mean a great deal to me. I'm black, and they experienced America as blacks. These particular writers may mean more to the black male writer, just as I imagine Jack Johnson would mean a great deal to Jesse Owens, and Jesse Owens a great deal to Arthur Ashe.

CLAUDIA TATE:   When you write, are you particularly conscious of preserving certain kinds of images of black people?

ANGELOU:   Well, I am some time, though I can't actually say when this happens in the creation of the work. I make writing as much a part of my life as I do eating or listening to music. Once I left church, and as I walked down the street, three young black women stopped me and asked if I would have a glass of wine with them. I said, "Yes." One is a painter; one is an actress, and one a singer. We talked, and when I started to leave, I tried to tell them what it means to me to see young black women. I tried to tell them, but I could hardly explain it. My eyes filled with tears. In one way, it means all the work, all the loneliness and discipline my work exacts, demands, is not in vain. It also means, in a more atavistic, absolutely internal way, that I can never die. It's like living through children. So when I approach a piece of work, *that* is in my approach, whether it's a poem that might appear frivolous or is a serious piece. In my approach I take as fact that my work will be carried on.

C.T.: Did you envision young Maya as a symbolic character for every black girl growing up in America?

ANGELOU: Yes, after a while I did. It's a strange condition, being an autobiographer and a poet. I have to be so internal, and yet while writing, I have to be apart from the story so that I don't fall into indulgence. Whenever I speak about the books, I always think in terms of the Maya character. When I wrote the teleplay of *I Know Why the Caged Bird Sings,* I would refer to the Maya character so as not to mean me. It's damned difficult for me to preserve this distancing. But it's very necessary.

C.T.: What has been the effect of the women's movement on black women?

ANGELOU: Black women and white women are in strange positions in our separate communities. In the social gatherings of black people, black women have always been predominant. That is to say, in the church it's always Sister Hudson, Sister Thomas and Sister Witheringay who keep the church alive. In lay gatherings it's always Lottie who cooks, and Mary who's going over to Bonita's where there is a good party going on. Also, black women are the nurturers of children in our community. White women are in a different position in their social institutions. White men, who are in effect their fathers, husbands, brothers, their sons, nephews and uncles, say to white women, or imply in any case: "I don't really need you to run my institutions. I need you in certain places and in those places you must be kept—in the bedroom, in the kitchen, in the nursery, and on the pedestal." Black women have never been told this. Black women have not historically stood in the pulpit, but that doesn't undermine the fact that they built the churches and maintain the pulpits. The people who have historically been heads of institutions in black communities have never said to black women—and they, too, are their fathers, husbands, brothers, their sons, nephews and uncles— "We don't need you in our institutions." So there is a fundamental difference.

One of the problems I see that faces black women in the eighties, just as it has in the past two decades, has been dealt with quite well in Michele Wallace's *Black Macho and the Myth of the Superwoman.* A number of black men in the sixties fell for a terrible, terrible ploy.

They felt that in order to be total and free and independent and powerful, they had to be like white men to their women. So there was a terrible time when black men told their women that if you really love me, you must walk three steps behind me.

I try to live what I consider a "poetic existence." That means I take responsibility for the air I breath and the space I take up. I try to be immediate, to be totally present for all my work. *I try.* This interview with you is a prime example of this. I am withdrawing from the grief that awaits me over the death of someone dear so that I can be present for you, for myself, for your work and for the people who will read it, so I can tell you exactly how I feel and what I think and try to answer your questions as cheerfully—if I feel cheerful—as I can. That to me is poetic. I try for concentrated consciousness which I miss by more than half, but I'm trying.

C.T.:  How do you fit writing into your life?

ANGELOU:  Writing is a part of my life; cooking is a part of my life. Making love is a part of my life; walking down the street is a part of it. Writing demands more time, but it takes from all of these other activities. They all feed into the writing. I think it's dangerous to concern oneself too damned much with "being an artist." It's more important to get the work done. You don't have to concern yourself with it, just get it done. The pondering pose—the back of the hand glued against the forehead—is baloney. People spend more time posing than getting the work done. The work is all there is. And when it's done, then you can laugh, have a pot of beans, stroke some child's head, or skip down the street.

C.T.:  What is your responsibility as a writer?

ANGELOU:  My responsibility as a writer is to be as good as I can be at my craft. So I study my craft. I don't simply write what I feel, let it all hang out. That's baloney. That's no craft at all. Learning the craft, understanding what language can do, gaining control of the language, enables one to make people weep, make them laugh, even make them go to war. You can do this by learning how to harness the power of the word. So studying my craft is one of my responsibilities. The other is to be as good a human being as I possibly can be so that once I have achieved control of the language, I don't force my weaknesses on a public who might then pick them up and abuse themselves.

During the sixties some lecturers went to universities and took thoughtless liberties with young people. They told them "to turn on, tune in and drop out." People still do that. They go to universities, and students will ask them, "Mr. So-and-So, Ms./Miss/Mrs./Brother/Sister So-and-So, these teachers here at this institution aren't happening, like what should we do?" Many lecturers have said, "Don't take it! Walk out! Let your protest be seen." That lecturer then gets on a plane, first-class, with a double scotch on-the-rocks, jets off to San Juan, Puerto Rico for a few days' rest, then travels to some other place where he or she is being paid two to three thousand dollars to speak. Those young people risk and sometimes lose their scholastic lives on that zoom because somebody's been irresponsible. I loathe that. I will not do it. I *am* responsible. I *am* trying to be responsible.

So first, I'm always trying to be a better human being, and second, I continue to learn my craft. Then, when I have something positive to say, I can say it beautifully. That's my responsibility.

C.T.:   Do you see any distinctions in the ways black male and female writers dramatize their themes and select significant events? This is a general question, but perhaps there is some basis for analysis. Gayl Jones responded to this question by saying she thought women tended to deal with events concerning the family, the community, personal events, that were not generally thought to be important by male writers. She said that male writers tended to select "representative" events for the significant events in their works. Toni Bambara said she thought women writers were concerned with developing a circumscribed place from which the story would unfold. Have you observed such patterns in your reading?

ANGELOU:   I find those observations interesting. In fact, the question is very interesting. I think black male writers do deal with the particular, but we are so conditioned by a sexist society that we tend to think when they do so that they mean it representationally; and when black females deal with the particular they only mean it as such. Whether we look at works by Richard Wright, James Baldwin, or John Killens—I'm thinking of novelists—we immediately say this is a generalization; this is meant as an overview, a microcosmic view of the world at large. Yet, if we look at works by Toni Morrison or Toni Bambara, if we look at Alice Walker's work or Hurston's, Rosa Guy's, Louise Meriwether's, or Paule Marshall's, we must say that these works are meant as general statements, universal statements. If *Daddy Was a Numbers Runner* [by Louise Meriwether] is not a microcosm of a macrocosm, I don't know what it is. If Paule Marshall's *Chosen Place and Timeless People* is not a microcosm, I don't know what it is. I don't know what *Ruby* [by Rosa Guy] is if it is not a microcosm of a larger world. I see everybody's work as an example of the particular, which is indicative of the general. I don't see any difference really. Whether it's Claude Brown's or Gayl Jones's. I can look at *Manchild in the Promised Land* and at *Corregidora* and see that these writers are talking about particular situations and yet about the general human condition. They are instructive for the generalities of our lives. Therefore, I won't indulge inherent distinctions between men and women writers.

C.T.:   Do you consider your quartet to be autobiographical novels or autobiographies?

ANGELOU:   They are autobiographies. When I wrote *I Know Why the Caged Bird Sings,* I wasn't thinking so much about my own life or identity. I was thinking about a particular time in which I lived and the influences of that time on a number of people. I kept thinking, what about that time? What were the people around young Maya doing? I used the central figure—myself—as a focus to show how one person can make it through those times.

I really got roped into writing *The Caged Bird.* At that time I was really only concerned with poetry, though I'd written a television series. Anyway, James Baldwin took me to a party at Jules Feiffer's house. It was just the four of us: Jimmy Baldwin and me, Jules Feiffer and his wife, at that time Judy Feiffer. We sat up until three or four o'clock in the morning, drinking scotch and telling tales. The next morning Judy Feiffer called a friend of hers at Random House and said, "You know the poet, Maya Angelou? If you can get her to write a book. . ." Then Robert Loomis at Random House phoned, and I said, "No, I'm not interested." I went out to California and produced my series for WNET. Loomis called two or three times, and I said, "No, I'm not interested. Thank you so much." Then, I'm sure he talked to Baldwin because he used a ploy which I'm not proud to say I haven't gained control of yet. He called and said, "Miss Angelou, it's been nice talking to you. I'm rather glad you decided not to write an autobiography because to write an autobiography as literature is the most difficult thing anyone could do." I said, "I'll do it." Now that's an area I don't have control of yet at this age. The minute someone says I can't, all my energy goes up and I say, what? What? I'm still unable to say that you may be wrong and walk away. I'm not pleased with that. I want to get beyond that.

C.T.: How did you select the events to present in the autobiographies?

ANGELOU: Some events stood out in my mind more than others. Some, though, were never recorded because they either were so bad or so painful, that there was no way to write about them honestly and artistically without making them melodramatic. They would have taken the book off its course. All my work, my life, everything is about survival. All my work is meant to say, "You may encounter many defeats, but you must not be defeated." In fact, the encountering may be the very experience which creates the vitality and the power to endure.

C.T.: You are a writer, poet, director, composer, lyricist, dancer, singer, journalist, teacher and lecturer. Can you say what the source of such creative diversity is?

ANGELOU: I don't do the dancing anymore. The rest I try. I believe talent is like electricity. We don't understand electricity. We use it. Electricity makes no judgment. You can plug into it and light up a lamp, keep a heart pump going, light a cathedral, or you can electrocute a person with it. Electricity will do all that. It makes no judgment. I think talent is like that. I believe every person is born with talent. I believe anyone can learn the craft of painting and paint.

I believe all things are possible for a human being, and I don't think there's anything in the world I can't do. Of course, I can't be five foot four because I'm six feet tall. I can't be a man because I'm a woman. The physical gifts are given to me, just like having two arms is a gift. In my creative source, wherever that is, I don't see why I can't sculpt. Why shouldn't I? Human beings sculpt. I'm a human being. I refuse to indulge any man-made differences between myself and another human being. I will not do it. I'm not going to live very long. If I live another fifty years, it's not very long. So I should indulge somebody else's prejudice at their whim and not for my own convenience! Never happen! Not me!

C.T.: How do you integrate protest in your work?

ANGELOU:   Protest is an inherent part of my work. You can't just not write about protest themes or not sing about them. It's a part of life. If I don't agree with a part of life, then my work has to address it.

I remember in the early fifties I read a book, *Dom Casmurro*. It was written by Machado De Assis, a nineteenth-century Brazilian. I thought it was very good. A month later I thought about the book and went back and reread it. Two months later I read the book again, and six months later I realized the sensation that I had had while reading the book was as if I had walked down to a beach to watch a sunset. I had watched the sunset and turned around, only to find that while I had been standing there the tide had come in over my head. I decided to write like that. I would never get on a soapbox; instead, I would pull in the reader. My work is intended to be slowly absorbed into the system on deeper and deeper levels.

C.T.:   Would you describe your writing process?

ANGELOU:   I usually get up at about 5:30, and I'm ready to have coffee by 6, usually with my husband. He goes off to his work around 6:30, and I go off to mine. I keep a hotel room in which I do my work—a tiny, mean room with just a bed, and sometimes, if I can find it, a face basin. I keep a dictionary, a Bible, a deck of cards and a bottle of sherry in the room. I try to get there around 7, and I work until around 2 in the afternoon. If the work is going badly, I stay until 12:30. If it's going well, I'll stay as long as it's going well. It's lonely, and it's marvelous. I edit while I'm working. When I come home at 2, I read over what I've written that day, and then try to put it out of my mind. I shower, prepare dinner, so that when my husband comes home, I'm not totally absorbed in my work. We have a semblance of a normal life. We have a drink together and have dinner. Maybe after dinner I'll read to him what I've written that day. He doesn't comment. I don't invite comments from anyone but my editor, but hearing it aloud is good. Sometimes I hear the dissonance; then I'll try to straighten it out in the morning. When I've finished the creative work and the editing and have six hundred handwritten pages, I send it to my editor. Then we both begin to work. I've kept the same editor through six books. We have a relationship that's kind of famous among publishers, since oftentimes writers shift from one publisher to another for larger advances. I just stay with my own editor, and we'll be together as long as he and I are alive. He understands my work rhythm, and I understand his. We respect each other, but the nit-picking does come. He'll say, "This bothers me—on page twelve, line three, why do you have a comma there? Do you mean to break the flow?"

C.T.:   How do you feel about your past works?

ANGELOU:   Generally, I forget them. I'm totally free of them. They have their own life. I've done well by them, or I did the best I could, which is all I can say. I'm not cavalier about work anymore than I am about sitting here with you, or cooking a meal, or cleaning my house. I've tried to be totally present, so that when I'm finished with a piece of work, I'm finished. I remember one occasion when we were in New York City at the Waldorf Astoria some years ago. I think I was with my sister friends—Rosa [Guy], Paule [ Marshall] and Louise [Meriwether]. We were sitting at a table near the bandstand during some tribute for someone, and I felt people staring at me. Someone was singing, say, stage left, and some people were performing a dance. It was very nice, but I felt people staring; so I turned around, and they were. My sister friends were all smiling. I wondered what was happening. I had been following the performance. Well, it turned out that the singer was doing a piece of mine, and they had choreographed a dance to it. I had forgotten the work altogether. The work, once completed, does not need me. The work I'm working on needs my total concentration. The one that's finished doesn't belong to me anymore. It belongs to itself.

C.T.:   Would you comment on your title selections?

ANGELOU:   As you probably know, the title *I Know Why the Caged Bird Sings* is from [Paul Lawrence] Dunbar's "Sympathy." *Gather Together in My Name,* though it does have a biblical origin, comes from the fact I saw so many adults lying to so many young people, lying in their teeth, saying, "You know, when I was young, I never would have done.... Why I couldn't.... I shouldn't..." Lying. Young people know when you're lying; so I thought for all those parents and non-parents alike who have lied about their past, I will tell it.

*Singin' and Swingin' and Gettin' Merry Like Christmas* comes from a time in the twenties and thirties when black people used to have rent parties. On Saturday night from around nine when they'd give these parties, through the next morning when they would go to church and have the Sunday meal, until early Sunday evening was the time when everyone was encouraged to sing and swing and get merry like Christmas so one would have some fuel with which to live the rest of the week.

*Just Give Me a Cool Drink of Water 'Fore I Die* refers to my belief that we as individuals in a species are still so innocent that we think we could ask our murderer just before he puts the final wrench upon the throat, "Would you please give me a cool drink of water?" he would do so. That's innocence. It's lovely.

The tune of *Oh, Pray My Wings Are Gonna Fit Me Well* originally comes from a slave holler, and the words from a nineteenth-century spiritual:

> *Oh, pray my wings are gonna fit me well.*
> *I'm a lay down this heavy load.*
> *I tried them on at the gates of hell.*
> *I'm a lay down this heavy load.*

I planned to put all the things bothering me—my heavy load—in that book, and let them pass.

The title poem of *And Still I Rise* refers to the indomitable spirit of black people. Here's a bit of it:

> *You may write me down in history*
> *With your bitter, twisted lies,*
> *You may trod me in the very dirt*
> *But still, like dust, I'll rise.*

C.T.:  Can black women writers help clarify or help to resolve the black sexist debate that was rekindled by Ntozake Shange's *For Colored Girls Who Have Considered Suicide When the Rainbow Is Enuf* and Michele Wallace's *Black Macho and the Myth of the Superwoman*?

ANGELOU:  Neither Miss Shange nor Miss Wallace started the dialogue, so I wouldn't suggest any black woman is going to stop it. If anything could have clarified the dialogue, Toni Morrison's *The Song of Solomon* should have been the work to do that. I don't know if that is a chore or a goal black women writers should assume. If someone feels so inclined, then she should go on and do it.

Everything good tends to clarify. By good I mean well written and well researched. There is nothing so strong as an idea whose time has come. The writer—male or female—who is meant to clarify this issue will do so. I, myself, have no encouragement in that direction. There's a lot that hasn't been said. It may be necessary to hear the male view of *For Colored Girls* in a book or spoken upon the stage. It may be necessary, and I know it will be very painful.

C.T.: What writers have influenced your work?

ANGELOU: There were two men who probably formed my writing ambition more than any others. They were Paul Lawrence Dunbar and William Shakespeare. I love them. I love the rhythm and sweetness of Dunbar's dialect verse. I love "Candle Lighting Time" and "Little Brown Baby." I also love James Weldon Johnson's "Creation."

I am also impressed by living writers. I'm impressed with James Baldwin. I continue to see not only his craftsmanship but his courage. That means a lot to me. Courage may be the most important of all the virtues because without it one cannot practice any other virtue with consistency. I'm impressed by Toni Morrison a great deal. I long for her new works. I'm impressed by the growth of Rosa Guy. I'm impressed by Ann Petry. I'm impressed by the work of Joan Didion. Her first collection, *Slouching Toward Jerusalem,* contains short pieces, which are absolutely stunning. I would walk fifty blocks in high heels to buy the works of any of these writers. I'm a country girl, so that means a lot.

C.T.: Have any of your works been misunderstood?

ANGELOU: A number of people have asked me why I wrote about the rape in *I Know Why the Caged Bird Sings.* They wanted to know why I had to tell that rape happens in the black community. I wanted people to see that the man was not totally an ogre. The hard thing about writing or directing or producing is to make sure one doesn't make the negative person totally negative. I try to tell the truth and preserve it in all artistic forms.

# · TONI CADE BAMBARA ·

*B*orn *in 1931 in New York City and educated at Queens and City Colleges as well as at several European institutions, Toni Cade Bambara has been, at different stages in her life, a New York City welfare investigator; a free-lance writer; a program director at a New York City community center; an English instructor; a member of several black studies programs, including those at Rutgers and Duke Universities; a consultant in women's studies at Emory and Atlanta Universities; and a writer-in-residence at Spelman College.*

*She was one of the first writers to address the issue of black awareness and feminism, in a book-length anthology which she edited, entitled* The Black Woman *(1970). This was followed by another anthology,* Tales and Stories for Black Folks *(1971), and two collections of her own short stories,* Gorilla, My Love *(1972) and* The Sea Birds Are Still Alive *(1972).* Gorilla, My Love *contains stories about a young black girl, her family and community, told from the girl's point of view.* The Sea Birds Are Still Alive *focuses on the intense psychological interactions among people, especially women, involved in intimate relationships. Bambara's most recent major work and her first novel* The Salt Eaters *(1980) depicts the merging of psychic power and modern technology as a means of confronting complex social and environmental issues, which threaten human survival in the last years of the twentieth century. In addition to these book-length publications, Bambara is a frequent contributor of articles, film and book reviews to newspapers, magazines, and scholarly journals.*

◆ ◆ ◆

Revolution begins with the self, in the self. The individual,
the basic revolutionary unit, must be purged of poison and lies

12

that assault the ego and threaten the heart, that hazard the next larger unit—the couple or pair, that jeopardize the still larger unit—the family or cell, that put the entire movement in peril.

—"On the Issue of Roles,"
from *The Black Woman,* p. 109.

CLAUDIA TATE:    What has happened to the revolutionary fervor of the sixties?

TONI CADE BAMBARA:    The energy of the seventies is very different from that of the previous decade. There's a different agenda and a different mode of struggle. The demystification of American-style "democracy," the bold analytical and passionate attention to our condition, status and process—the whole experience of that era led us to a peculiar spot in time, the seventies. Some say it's been a period of retreat, of amnesia, of withdrawal into narcissism. I'm not so sure. I'd say the seventies is characterized by a refocusing on the self, which is, after all, the main instrument for self, group and social transformation.

I travel around the country a lot, and I am continually struck by the differences between the two decades. There's a difference between the apathy/retreat characterization of the seventies and what's actually going on, at least as I'm experiencing it on campuses, in prisons, in community groups. We didn't *seem* to be in a period of intense political activity as we defined its terms in the sixties. We were trained by the sixties to perceive activity, to assess movement and progress, in particular modes—confrontation, uncompromising rhetoric, muscle flexing, press conferences, manifestoes, visible groups, quasi-underground groups, hitting the streets, singing, marching, etc. On the other hand, the workings of the seventies, while less visible and less audible and less easy to perceive, to nail down and define, were no less passionate and no less significant. People attempted to transform themselves cell by cell, to organize block by block. Both seem to me essential prerequisites to broad-based organizing and clear-headed strategizing.

Unfortunately, we still have not moved toward establishing an independent black political party. We still haven't clarified the issue of alliances or independent struggle. We still haven't identified the social and political imperatives of this moment or gotten a consensus regarding our domestic and foreign policy. And the eighties are now upon us—a period of devastating conflicts and chaos, a period that calls for organizing of the highest order and commitment of the most sticking kind, a period for which the sixties was mere rehearsal and the seventies a brief respite, a breathing space. Most of us are still trying to rescue the sixties—that stunning and highly complicated period from 1954 to 1972—from the mythmakers, still trying to ransom our warriors and theorists from those nuts who would cage 'em all up, crack their bones, and offer us some highly selective media fiction in place of the truth. The eighties . . . a lotta work ahead of us.

You look at what the mythmakers have done in extravaganzas like *Roots* and *King,* playing with people's blood and bones. But you just can't get overwhelmed by the massive ignorance that characterizes this racist, hardheaded, heedless society. It's a tremendous responsibility—responsibility and honor—to be a writer, an artist, a cultural worker . . . whatever you want to call this vocation. One's got to see what the factory worker sees, what the prisoner sees, what the welfare children see, what the scholar sees, got to see what the ruling-class mythmakers see as well, in order to tell the truth and not get trapped. Got to see more and dare more.

I read an awful lot—major-house books, small-press journals, offset manuscripts from local writers' workshops. I don't see the fiercesome fearlessness yet that I'd hoped to see in this period. A lot of talented, brilliant, sharp folks are out there writing. But ah . . . lotta work ahead of us.

C.T.:   How does being black and female constitute a particular perspective in your work?

BAMBARA:   As black and woman in a society systematically orchestrated to oppress each and both, we have a very particular vantage point and, therefore, have a special contribution to make to the collective intelligence, to the literatures of this historical moment. I'm clumsy and incoherent when it comes to defining that perspective in specific and concrete terms, worse at assessing the value of my own particular pitch and voice in the overall chorus. I leave that to our critics, to our teachers and students of literature. I'm a nationalist; I'm a feminist, at least that. That's clear, I'm sure, in the work. My story "Medley" could not have been written by a brother, nor could "A Tender Man" have been written by a white woman. Those

two stories are very much cut on the bias, so to speak, by a seam-
stress on the inside of the cloth. I am about the empowerment and
development of our sisters and of our community. That sense of
caring and celebration is certainly reflected in the body of my work
and has been consistently picked up by other writers, reviewers, critics, teachers, students. But as I said, I leave that hard task of analysis
to the analysts. I do my work and I try not to blunder.

C.T.:    How do you fit writing into your life?

BAMBARA:    Up until recently, I had never fully appreciated the
sheer anguish of that issue. I never knew what the hell people were
talking about when they asked, "How do you manage to juggle the
demands of motherhood, teaching, community work, writing and
the rest?" Writing had never been a central activity in my life. It was
one of the things I did when I got around to it or when the compul-
sion seized me and sat me down. The short story, the article, the
book review, after all, are short-term pieces. I would simply com-
mandeer time, space, paper and pen, close the door, unplug the
phone, get ugly with would-be intruders and get to work for a few
days. Recently, however, working on a novel and a few movie
scripts—phew! I now know what that question means and I despair.
I had to renegotiate a great many relationships that fell apart
around me; the novel took me out of action for nearly a year. I was
unfit to work—couldn't draft a simple office memo, couldn't keep
track of time, blew meetings, refused to answer the door, wasn't interested in hanging out in any way, shape, or form. My daughter
hung in there, screened calls, learned to iron her own clothes and
generally kept out of my sight. My mama would look at me funny
every now and then, finding that days had gone by and I hadn't
gotten around to combing my hair or calling her to check in and just
chat. Short stories are a piece of time. The novel is a way of life.

I began the novel *The Salt Eaters* the way a great many of my
writings begin, as a journal entry. I frequently sit down and give
myself an assignment—to find out what I know about this or that, to
find out what I think about this or that when I am cozy with myself
and not holding forth to a group or responding to someone's position. Several of us had been engaged in trying to organize various
sectors of the community—students, writers, psychic adepts, etc.—
and I was struck by the fact that our activists or warriors and our

adepts or medicine people don't even talk to each other. Those two camps have yet to learn—not since the days of Toussaint* anyway, not since the days of the maroon communities,** I suspect—to appreciate each other's visions, each other's potential, each other's language. The novel, then, came out of a problem-solving impulse—what would it take to bridge the gap, to merge those frames of reference, to fuse those camps? I thought I was just making notes for organizing; I thought I was just exploring my feelings, insights. Next thing I knew, the thing took off and I no longer felt inclined to invest time and energy on the streets. I had to sort a few things out. For all my speed-freak Aries impulsiveness, I am a plodder; actually, my Mercury conjunct with Saturn is in Aries, too, so I like to get things sorted before I leap. I do not like to waste other people's time and energy. I will not waste mine.

I have no shrewd advice to offer developing writers about this business of snatching time and space to work. I do not have anything profound to offer mother-writers or worker-writers except to say that it will cost you something. Anything of value is going to cost you something. I'm not much of a caretaker, for example, in relationships. I am not consistent about giving vibrancy and other kinds of input to a relationship. I don't always remember the birthdays, the anniversaries. There are periods when I am the most attentive and thoughtful lover in the world, and periods, too, when I am just unavailable. I have never learned, not yet anyway, to apologize for or continually give reassurance about what I'm doing. I'm not terribly accountable or very sensitive to other people's sense of being beat back, cut out, blocked, shunted off. I will have to learn because the experience of *The Salt Eaters* tells me that I will be getting into that long-haul writing again, soon and often.

I've had occasion, as you can well imagine, to talk about just this thing with sister writers. How do the children handle your "absence"—standing at the stove flipping them buckwheats but being totally elsewhere? How does your man deal with the fact that you are just not there and it's nothing personal? Atrocity tales, honey, and sad. I've known playwrights, artists, filmmakers—brothers I'm talking about—who just do not understand, or maybe pretend not to

* Toussaint L'Ouverture (1743?–1803) was the black liberator of Haiti.
** Communities of escaped slaves in the Americas.

understand, that mad fit that gets hold of me and makes me prefer working all night and morning at the typewriter to playing poker or going dancing. It's a trip. But some years ago, I promised myself a period of five years to tackle this writing business in a serious manner. It's a priority item now—to master the craft, to produce, to stick to it no matter how many committee meetings get missed.

My situation isn't nearly as chary as others I know. I'm not a wife, and my daughter couldn't care less what the house looks like so long as the hamper isn't overflowing. I'm not a husband; I do not have the responsibility of trying to live up to "provider." I'm not committed to any notion of "career." Also, I'm not addicted to anything—furniture, cars, wardrobe, etc.—so there's no sense of sacrifice or foolishness about how I spend my time in non-money-making pursuits. Furthermore, I don't feel obliged to structure my life in respectably routine ways; that is to say, I do not mind being perceived as a "weirdo" or whatever. My situation is, perhaps, not very characteristic; I don't know. But to answer the question—I just flat out announce I'm working, leave me alone and get out of my face. When I "surface" again, I try to apply the poultices and patch up the holes I've left in relationships around me. That's as much as I know how to do . . . so far.

C.T.:    What determines your responsibility to yourself and to your audience?

BAMBARA:    I start with the recognition that we are at war, and that war is not simply a hot debate between the capitalist camp and the socialist camp over which economic/political/social arrangement will have hegemony in the world. It's not just the battle over turf and who has the right to utilize resources for whomsoever's benefit. The war is also being fought over the truth: what is the truth about human nature, about the human potential? My responsibility to myself, my neighbors, my family and the human family is to try to tell the truth. That ain't easy. There are so few truth-speaking traditions in this society in which the myth of "Western civilization" has claimed the allegiance of so many. We have rarely been encouraged and equipped to appreciate the fact that the truth works, that it releases the Spirit and that it is a joyous thing. We live in a part of the world, for example, that equates criticism with assault, that equates social responsibility with naive idealism, that defines the unrelenting pursuit of knowledge and wisdom as fanaticism.

I do not think that literature is *the* primary instrument for social transformation, but I do think it has potency. So I work to tell the truth about people's lives; I work to celebrate struggle, to applaud the tradition of struggle in our community, to bring to center stage all those characters, just ordinary folks on the block, who've been waiting in the wings, characters we thought we had to ignore because they weren't pimp-flashy or hustler-slick or because they didn't fit easily into previously acceptable modes or stock types. I want to lift up some usable truths—like the fact that the simple act of cornrowing one's hair is radical in a society that defines beauty as blonde tresses blowing in the wind; that staying centered in the best of one's own cultural tradition is hip, is sane, is perfectly fine despite all claims to universality-through-Anglo-Saxonizing and other madnesses.

It would be dishonest, though, to end my comments there. First and foremost I write for myself. Writing has been for a long time my major tool for self-instruction and self-development. I try to stay honest through pencil and paper. I run off at the mouth a lot. I've a penchant for flamboyant performance. I exaggerate to the point of hysteria. I cannot always be trusted with my mouth open. But when I sit down with the notebooks, I am absolutely serious about what I see, sense, know. I write for the same reason I keep track of my dreams, for the same reason I meditate and practice being still—to stay in touch with me and not let too much slip by me. We're about building a nation; the inner nation needs building, too. I would be writing whether there were a publishing industry or not, whether there were presses or not, whether there were markets or not.

I began writing in a serious way—though I can't recall a time when I wasn't jotting stuff down and trying to dramatize lessons learned—when I got into teaching. It was a way to keep track of myself, to monitor myself. I'm a very seductive teacher, persuasive, infectious, overwhelming, irresistible. I worked hard in the classroom to teach students to critique me constantly, to protect themselves from my nonsense; but let's face it, the teacher-student relationship we've been trained in is very colonial in nature. It's fraught with dangers. The power given teachers over students' minds, students' spirits, students' development—my God! To rise above that, to insist of myself and of them that we refashion that relationship along progressive lines demanded a great deal of courage, imagination, energy and will. Writing was a way to "hear" myself, check myself. Writing was/is an act of discovery. I frequently discovered that I was dangerous, a menace, virtually unfit to move the students and myself into certain waters. I would have to go into the classroom and beat them up for not taking me to the wall, for succumbing to mere charm and flash, when they should have been challenging me, "kicking my ass." I will be eternally grateful to all those students at City College and Livingston/Rutgers for the caring and courageous way they helped to develop me as a teacher, a person, a writer . . . and a mother, too. Fortunately, for all concerned, my daughter, a ninety-nine-year-old wise woman who travels under the guise of a young thumb-sucking kid, knows when to walk away from me, close her ears, turn my rantings into a joke, call me on a contradiction. But even after she is grown, and even if I never teach again, I will still use writing as a way to stay on center, for I'll still be somebody's neighbor, somebody's friend, and I'll still be a member of our community under siege or in power. I'll still need to have the discipline writing affords, demands. I do not wish to be useless or dangerous, so I'll write. And too, hell, I'm a writer. I am compelled to write.

C.T.:   Do you see any differences in the ways black male and female writers handle theme, character, situation?

BAMBARA:   I'm sure there are, but I'd be hard pressed to discuss it cogently and trot out examples. It's not something I think about except in the heat of reading a book when I feel an urge to "translate" a brother's depiction of some phenomena or say "amen" to a sister's. There are, I suppose, some general things I can say. Women are less likely to skirt the feeling place, to finesse with language, to camouflage emotions. But then a lot of male writers knock that argument out—James Baldwin trusts emotions as a reliable way to make an experience available; a lot of young brothers like Peter Harris, Melvin Brown, Calvin Kenley, Kambon Obayani have the courage to be "soft" and unsilent about those usual male silences. One could say that brothers generally set things out of doors, on open terrain, that is, male turf. But then Toni Morrison's *Song of Solomon,* angled from the point of view of a man, is an exception to that. I've heard it said that women tend to aim for the particular experience, men for the general or "universal." I don't know about all that. The notion of a street, though, is certainly handled in particular ways. To walk down the street as a woman is a very particular experience. I don't find that rendered in Ralph Ellison, Richard Wright, or John A. Williams the way I *feel* it in Gayl Jones, Sonia Sanchez, etc. But then Ann Petry's *The Street* draws me up short; I don't recognize *anybody* walking down *that* street. I've never been on *that* block; I've not *felt* that kind of out-of-itness. Finally, I guess, I just don't *believe* that woman.

In writing "The Tender Man," I couldn't wait to get Cliff and Aisha off the street and into the restaurant. I kept losing the point of view, kept sliding into the way the street resonates for Aisha, who is not the character over whose shoulder the camera looks. A brother writing that story, I suspect, would have handled the setting very differently. Aisha probably would have been less ambivalent, and Cliff's attitude toward his white wife and his child would have been rendered with a lot less ambiguity, too.

Of course, one of the crucial differences that strikes me immediately among poets, dramatists, novelists, storytellers is in the handling of children. I can't nail it down, but the attachment to children and to two-plus-two reality is simply stronger in women's writings; but there are exceptions. And finally, there isn't nearly as large a bulk of gynocentric writing as there is phallic-obsessive writings. I'll tell you—there was a period, back in 1967 or '68, when I thought I would run amok if I heard one more poem with the unzipped pants or the triggered gun or the cathedral spire or the space-missile thrust or the good f---. I'd love to read/hear a really good discussion of just this issue by someone who's at home with close textual reading—cups, bowls and other motifs in women's writings. We've only just begun, I think, to fashion a woman's vocabulary to deal with the "silences" of our lives. I'd like to see Eleanor Traylor*—to my mind, the best reader/seer we've got—bring her mind to bear on the subject.

C.T.:    Do you attempt to order human experience? Or, do you simply record experience?

BAMBARA:    All writers, musicians, artists, choreographers/dancers, etc., work with the stuff of their experiences. It's the translation of it, the conversion of it, the shaping of it that makes for the

---

* A teacher of literature.

drama. I've never been convinced that experience is linear, circular, or even random. It just is. I try to put it in some kind of order to extract meaning from it, to bring meaning to it.

It would never occur to me to simply record, for several reasons. First, it is boring. If I learn in math class that the whole is the sum of its parts, I'm not interested in recording that or repeating that. I'm more interested in finding out whether it is axiomatic in organizing people, or if, in fact, the collective is more than or different from the mere addition of individuals. If I learn in physics that nature abhors a vacuum, right away I want to test it as a law. If it is law, then my cleaned out pocketbook ought to attract some money. Secondly, mere recording is not only boring, it is impolite and may be even immoral. If I wrote autobiographically, for example, I'd wind up getting into folks' business, plundering the lives of people around me, pulling the covers off of friends. I'd be an emotional gangster, a psychic thug, pimp and vampire. I don't have my mother's permission to turn her into a still life. I wouldn't ask a friend to let me impale her/him with my pen or arrest them in print. I wouldn't even know how to ask permission; it seems so rude. Frequently, when I hear a good story, I will ask, "Hey, mind if I use that?" By the time, though, that I convert it my way, it's unrecognizable. Not only because I do not think it's cool to lock people into my head, my words, the type, but also because a usable truth can frequently be made more accessible to the reader if I ignore the actual facts, the actual setting, the actual people, and simply reset the whole thing. I think I hear myself saying that the third reason is that lessons come in sprawled-out ways, and craft is the business of offering them up in form and voice, a way of presenting an emotional/psychic landscape that does justice to the lesson as quickly and efficiently as possible.

I used to assign my students a writing/thinking exercise: remember how you used to get all hot in the face, slide down in your seat, suddenly have to tie your shoe even though you were wearing loafers back then in the fourth grade whenever Africa was mentioned or slavery was mentioned? Remember the first time the mention of Africa, of Black, made your neck long and your spine straight, made the muscles of your face go just so? Well, make a list of all the crucial, relevant things that happened to you that moved you from hot face to tall spine; then compose a short story, script, letter, essay, poem that make that experience of change available to the young brothers and sisters on your block.

Oh, the agony, the phone calls I got in the middle of the night, the mutterings for days and days, the disrupted whist games, the threats to my life and limb. It was hard. The notes, the outlines, the rough drafts, the cut-downs, the editing, the search for form, for metaphor. Ah, but what wonderfully lean and brilliant pieces they produced. And what they taught themselves and each other in that process of sifting and sorting, dumping, streamlining, tracing their own process of becoming. Fantastic. And I'm not talking about seasoned writers or well-honed analysts. I'm talking about first-year students from non-writing background at the City College of New York, at Livingston/Rutgers, folks who were not college-bound since kindergarten, folks who had been taught not to value their own process, who had not been encouraged, much less trained, to keep track of their own becoming. Ordering is the craft, the work, the wonder. It's the lifting up, the shaping, the pin-point presentation that matters. I used to listen to those folks teaching younger kids at the campus or at neighborhood centers, giving those kids compact, streamlined "from point A (hot face) to point B (proud)" lessons. Fantastic.

I'm often asked while on the road, "How autobiographical is your work?"—the assumption being that it has to be. Sometimes the question springs from the racist assumption that creative writing and art are the domain of white writers. Sometimes the question surfaces from a class base, that only the leisured and comfortable can afford the luxury of imagination. Sometimes it stems from the fact that the asker is just some dull, normal type who cannot conceive of the possibility that some people have imagination, though they themselves do not, poor things. I always like to dive into that one. It was once argued, still argued, that great art is the blah-blah of the white, wealthy classes. Uh huh. And what works have survived the nineteenth century? The landed-gentry tomes or Frederick Douglass's autobiography? The gentle-lady romances or the slave narratives? After I climb all over that question and try to do justice to those scared little creative writers asking out of sincere concern and confusion, I usually read my "Sort of Preface" from *Gorilla, My Love*, which states my case on autobiographical writing; namely, I don't do it . . . except, of course, that I do; we all do. That is, whomsoever we may conjure up or remember or imagine to get a story down, we're telling our own tale just as surely as a client on the analyst's couch, just as surely as a pilgrim on the way to Canterbury, just as surely as the preacher who selects a particular text for the sermon, then departs from it, pulling Miz Mary right out of the pew and clear out of her shouting shoes. Can I get a witness? Indeed. But again, the tales of Ernest J. Gaines, of Baldwin, of Gwen Brooks, whomever—the particulars of the overall tale is one of the tasks of the critics, and I am compelled to say once again that our critics are a fairly lackluster bunch. I'm always struck by that when I compare articles and speeches done by this one or that one to what comes tumbling easily and brilliantly out of the mouth of Eleanor Traylor. Do watch for her work. If there is anyone who can throw open the path and light the way, it's that sister.

What I strive to do in writing, and in general—to get back to the point I was making in direct response to your question—is to examine philosophical, historical, political, metaphysical truths, or rather assumptions. I try to trace them through various contexts to see if they work. They may be traps. They may inhibit growth. Take the Golden Rule, for example. I try to live that, and I certainly expect it of some particular others. But I'll be damned if I want most folks out there to do unto me what they do unto themselves. There are a whole lot of unevolved, self-destructive wretches out there walking around on the loose. It would seem that one out of every ten people has come to earth for the "pacific" purpose, as grandma would say, of giving the other nine a natural fit. So, hopefully, we will not legislate the Golden Rule into law.

The trick, I suspect, at this point in time in human history as we approach the period of absolute devastation and total renewal, is to maintain a loose grip, a flexible grasp on those assumptions we hold to be true, valid, real. They may not be. The world Einstein conjured or that the Fundamentalists conjure or your friendly neighborhood mystic or poet conjures may be a barrier to a genuine understanding of the real world. I once wrote a story about just that—a piece of it is in the novel, *The Salt Eaters*. A sister with a problem to solve is dawdling in the woods, keeping herself company with a small holding stone, fingering it like worry beads. It falls into a pool; she tries to retrieve it—clutching at water, clutching at water. Better to have pitched it in and stood back to read the ripples—the effects of her act. The universe is elegantly simple in times of lucidity, but we clutter up our lives with such senseless structures in an effort to make scientific thought work, to make logic seem logical and valuable. We blind ourselves and bind ourselves with a lot of nonsense in our scramble away from simple realities like the fact that everything is one in this place, on this planet. We and everything here are extensions of the same consciousness, and we are co-creators of that mind, will, thought.

C.T.:   How have your creative interests evolved in terms of your writing?

BAMBARA:   I don't know how to chart the evolution of my creative interest. Suffice to say that the lens has widened, the scope broadened, and the demands on myself have increased. How do we insure space for our children was a concern out of which the stories in the first collection, *Gorilla, My Love,* grew. When my agent in those days, Hattie Gossett, nudged me and said I ought to put together some of the old stories for a collection, I thought, aha, I'll get the old kid stuff out and see if I can't clear some space to get into something else. Most of those stories are what I would call on-the-block, in-the-neighborhood, back-glance pieces, for the most part.

How are we faring now that the energy is shifting? How do we sustain ourselves between the sixties and the eighties? Out of that concern some of the stories in the second collection, *The Seabirds Are Still Alive,* sprang. Stories like "Broken-Field Running" and "Am I Spoiling You," also known as "The Apprentice" in other anthologies, speak directly to that issue. They are both on-the-block and larger-world-of-struggle pieces, very contemporary, and much less back-glance.

How do we rescue the planet from the psychopaths? Do we have a future as sane, whole, governing people? Do we realize we are a people at the crossroads? *The Salt Eaters* is a thrown-open sort of book generated by those questions. It's on-the-block, but the borders of the town of Claybourne, Georgia where the story is set, do not contain or hem in the story. It gets downright cosmic, in fact, in the attempt to sound the alarm about the ineptness and arrogance of the nuclear industry and call attention to the radical shifts in the power configurations of the globe and to the massive transformations due this planet in this last quarter of the twentieth century.

What seems to inform the works I'm up to my eyebrows in

now—a script (whose not-so-hot working title is "Ladies-in-Waiting") about a group of women of color in 1979, 1968, 1942, 1933, getting ready to rescue or ransom their husbands, lovers, fathers, brothers from various hostage-keeping institutions; and a new collection of short stories about "families" of blood, of struggle, traveling troupes, etc.—are questions like: what alliances make sense in this last quarter? Where are the links of resistance to be forged, the links of vulnerability to be strengthened? Once again, I'm exploring ways to link up our warriors and our medicine people, hoping some readers will fling the book down, sneer at my ineptitude, and go on out there and show how it's supposed to be done. Too, I'm staying with a group of women from my novel, The Seven Sisters—a group of performing artists from the African-American, Asian-American, Chicano, "Puertoriquena," and Native American communities—also in hopes that sisters of the yam, the rice, the corn, the plantain, might find the work to be too thin a soup and get on out there and cook it right.

What is noticeable to me about my current writing is the stretch out toward the future. I'm not interested in reworking memories and playing with flashbacks. I'm trying to press the English language, particularly verb tenses and modes, to accommodate flash-forwards and potential happenings. I get more and more impatient, though, with verbal language, print conventions, literary protocol and the like; I'm much more interested in filmmaking. Quite frankly, I've always considered myself a film person. I am a fanatic movie watcher, and my favorite place to be these days is in a screening room, or better yet, in the editing room with those little Mickey Mouse gloves on. There's not too much more I want to experiment with in terms of writing. It gives me pleasure, insight, keeps me centered, sane. But, oh, to get my hands on some movie equipment.

An awful lot of my stories, particularly the first-person riffs and bebop pieces, were written, I suspect, with performance in mind. I still recall the old days, back in the fifties, looking for some damn thing to use in auditions. There's just so much you can do with Sojourners' "Ain't I a Woman" and trying to recast Medea as a New Orleans swamp hag. It does my heart good to have Ruby Dee swoop down on me—which she manages to do somehow, that Amazon of small proportions—for writing things like "Witchbird," an eminently performable story about a mature woman—as they say in the fashion ads—tired of being cast as mammy or earth mother of us all. I've started a lot of plays, mainly because I can't bear the idea of sisters like Rosalind Cash, Gloria Foster, Barbara O. Jones—the list goes on—saddled with crap or given no scripts at all. But finally, I think I will be moving into film production because I want to do it right; I want to script *Marie Laveau* for Barbara O. Jones and do *Harper's Ferry* with the correct cast of characters—Harriet Tubman, Mary Ellen or Mammy Pleasants, Frederick Douglass, the Virginia brothers and sisters waiting to be armed. Now can't you just see Verta Mae and Maya Angelou and William Marshall and Al Freeman, Jr., in a movie such as that?

My interests have evolved, but my typing hasn't gotten any better. I no longer have the patience to sit it out in the solitude of my backroom, all by my lonesome self, knocking out books. I'm much more at home with a crew swapping insights, brilliances, pooling resources, information. My main interest of the moment, then, is to make films.

C.T.:   Let's look at this excerpt from *The New York Times* review on your *Gorilla, My Love:*

> Toni Cade Bambara's *Gorilla, My Love* is one of a few books published recently by black writers that fulfills the requirements of the Yeats quotation, "Only that which does not teach, which does not cry out, which does not condescend, which does not explain, is irresistible." I am tired of being shouted at, patronized, bullied, and antagonized by black writers. If I've bought their books, it means I intend to give them my attention; if I've spent $6.95 to "hear" what they have to say, I dislike being told I'm an insensitive, arrogant honky who won't listen. Toni Cade Bambara tells me more about being black through her quiet, proud, silly, tender, hip, acute, loving stories than any amount of literary polemicizing could hope to do. She writes about love: a love for one's family, one's friends, one's race, one's neighborhood, and it is the sort of love that comes with maturity and inner peace.
>
> C.D.B. Bryan
> *The New York Times Book Review,*
> October 15, 1972, p. 31.

BAMBARA:   I recall that the comment about being antagonized by black writers struck me as funny. There were other white reviewers who went off their nut because I didn't get on their case, didn't seem to be paying them due attention. What the hell? The feedback, though, that has mattered is that which comes through letters or in reviews in periodicals like *Freedom Ways* and *First World* and that wonderful review—my God, it was so much better written and thought out than my book—Michele Russell did of *Seabirds* in *The New American Movement*. Children still write and call about the Doubleday book, *Tales and Short Stories for Black Folks*, which convinced me that they are good readers and not the remedial compensatory-education, basket-case students their teachers swear they are. And every once in a while, some mama will put her hands on my shoulders, the way Alice Childress did some ten years ago—and the grip still resonates—and said, "Daughter, what you tried to do with *The Black Woman* was mighty fine. Try it again."

I'm very fortunate in that my readership is not anonymous and the feedback is personal. I meet readers on the bus, in the laundromat, at conferences, in the joint, damn near everywhere. I get letters, calls, reviews here and there, and even appear in an occasional CLA [College Language Association] or MLA [Modern Language Association] paper. It keeps me going. I've been told, of course, everything from A to Z—that all my political polemicizing is destroying whatever gift for storytelling and conjuring characters I have, or that my work is too soft, too much about ordinary people and that I ought to tackle "big" figures and "big" revolutionary events, or that it's a pleasure to read about my men and women, who don't seem to be all up in each other's face, or that I am not fearless enough, angry enough about sexist behavior in the community. Of course, everyone has a story that I should write for them. I appreciate all the feedback. Keeps me going. So finally, primarily and ultimately, I'm not at all concerned about whether white reviewers are comfortable or ill at ease with my work. I've been told this is a foolish attitude on my part. But while I may not be very shrewd about my, ah, "lit-tur-rary car-rear," I am quite clear and serious about my work in the world. It's a very big place, the world. There are actually readers out there who do not take their cue from *The New York Times*; and, of course, there are millions right here in our community who don't read books at all. That's okay. I plod ahead. I do my work. I try to stay centered and not get poisoned, or intoxicated, as they say, with whatever success I've had.

    C.T.:  Who has influenced your writing?

BAMBARA:   My mama. She did *The New York Times* and *The London Times* crossword puzzles. She read books. She built bookcases. She'd wanted to be a journalist. She gave me permission to wonder, to dawdle, to daydream. My most indelible memory of 1948 is my mother coming upon me in the middle of the kitchen floor with my head in the clouds and my pencil on the paper and her mopping around me. My mama had been in Harlem during the renaissance. She used to hang out at the Dark Tower, at the Renny, go to hear Countee Cullen, see Langston Hughes over near Mt. Morris Park. She thought it was wonderful that I could write things that almost made some kind of sense. She used to walk me over to Seventh Avenue and 125th Street and point out the shop where J. A. Rogers, the historian, was knocking out books. She used to walk me over to the Speaker's Corner to listen to the folks. Of course, if they were talking "religious stuff," she'd keep on going to wherever we were going; but if they were talking union or talking race, we'd hang tough on the corner.

I wasn't raised in the church. I learned the power of the word from the speakers on Speaker's Corner—trade unionists, Temple People as we called Muslims then, Father Divinists, Pan-Africanists, Abyssinians as we called Rastas then, Communists, Ida B. Wells folks. We used to listen to "Wings Over Jordan" on the radio; and I did go to this or that Sunday school over the years, moving from borough to country to city, but the sermons I heard on Speaker's Corner as a kid hanging on my mama's arm or as a kid on my own and then as an adult had tremendous impact on me. It was those marvelously gifted, extravagantly verbal speakers that prepared me later for the likes of Charlie Cobb, Sr., Harold Thurman, Revun Doughtery, and the mighty, mighty voice of Bernice Reagon.

My daddy used to take me to the Apollo Theater, which had the best audience in the world with the possible exception of folks who gather at Henry Street for Woodie King's New Federal Theater plays. There, in the Apollo, I learned that if you are going to call yourself some kind of communicator, you'd better be good because the standards of our community are high. I used to hang out a bit with my brother and my father at the Peace Barber Shop up in Divine territory* just north of where we lived, and there I learned what

---

* An area in Harlem around Father Divine's church.

it meant to be a good storyteller. Of course, the joints I used to hang around when I was supposed to be walking a neighbor's dog or going to the library taught me more about the oral tradition and our high standards governing the rap, than books.

The musicians of the forties and fifties, I suspect, determined my voice and pace and pitch. I grew up around boys who carried horn cases and girls who couldn't wait for their legs to grow and reach the piano pedals. I grew up in New York City, bebop heaven—and it's still music that keeps that place afloat. I learned more from Bud Powell, Dizzy, Y'Bird, Miss Sassy Vaughn about what can be communicated, can be taught through structure, tone, metronomic sense, and just sheer holy boldness than from any teacher of language arts, or from any book for that matter. For the most part, the voice of my work is bop. To be sure, pieces like "The Survivor" [*Gorilla*] and others that don't come to mind quickly because I can never think of titles, show I can switch codes and change instruments; and since moving South, I've expanded my repertoire to include a bit of the gospel idiom. Certainly, "The Organizer's Wife" [*Sea Birds*] and sections of *The Salt Eaters* are closer to gospel than to jazz. The title story of the last collection, "The Seabirds Are Still Alive," would not have worked in bop, as it is set in Southeast Asia with a cast of characters that are Asian, European, South American, Euro-American, and a narrator who must remain as close as possible to a camera lens and stay out of the mix.

C.T.:    Who have been your mentors?

BAMBARA:    There have been a great many inspirational influences, and they continue to be so. I'm still in first gear. Addison Gayle, for example, a friend and colleague back in the early sixties, urged me to assemble a book on the black woman rather than run off at the mouth about it. It was Addison who got me the contract to do the second book, *Tales and Short Stories for Black Folks.* I can't remember who clubbed me over the head to start doing reviews for Dan Watts's *Liberator,* but that experience certainly impacted on what and how and why I write; and the support I get now from my editor and friend, Toni Morrison—well, I just can't say what that does for me. She'll feed me back some passage I've written and say, "Hmm, that's good, girl." That gives me a bead on where I am and keeps me going.

I suspect the greatest influence now, what determines the shape and content of my work, is the community of writers. While black critics are woefully lagging behind, it seems to me, not adequately observing trends, interpreting, arguing the value of products for both practitioner and audience, there is, nonetheless, a circle, if you will—not to be confused with clique, coterie, or even school of writing. But writers have gotten their wagons in a circle, which gives us each something to lean against, push off against. It's the presence on the scene of Gwen Brooks, Ron Milner, Alice Walker, and Lorenzo Thomas that helps me edit, for instance, that helps me catch myself when I blunder in the elements of the craft—a slip of voice or mask, a violation of spatial arrangement, a mangling of theme, a disconnectedness to traditions. I'm influenced by Ishmael Reed, Quincey Troupe, Janet Tolliver, Lucille Clifton, Ianthe Thomas, Camille Yarborough, Jayne Cortez, etc., in the sense that they represent a range and thus give me the boldness to go headon with my bad self. The found voice of writers from other communities—Leslie Silko, Simon Ortiz, Rudy Ananya, Sean Wong, Wendy Rose, Lawson Inada, Janice Mirikitani, Charat Chandra, etc.—also influences my reach, my confidence to plumb our traditions, do more than just scan our terrain but stretch out there.

It's a dismally lonely business, writing. It has never given me a bad time in and of itself. I love the work; but to keep at it, I need to slap five every now and again with Pearl Lomax, Nikki Grimes, Victor Cruz, Toni Morrison, or Verta Mae, whether they're in slapping distance or not. It's not well enough appreciated, I think, what the presence or absence of certain spirits in the circle mean to keep one energized and awake. I'm always stunned, appalled, by reviewers and interviewers who don't realize this is not a popularity contest or a tournament. Not long ago, some crazy TV person was running off at the mouth about how wonderful it was to read my work as compared to this writer, that writer, as though I'd be overjoyed to hear my colleagues "murder-mouthed." It took me three beats to plant my hands safely in my pocket before taking off on the assumption, not to mention his head. That we keep each other's writing alive is the point I'm trying to make. The literature of this crucial time is a mixed chorus.

C.T.:  Would you describe your writing process?

BAMBARA:  There's no particular routine to my writing, nor have any two stories come to me the same way. I'm usually working on

five or six things at a time; that is, I scribble a lot in bits and pieces
and generally pin them together with a working title. The actual sit-
down work is still weird to me. I babble along, heading I think in
one direction, only to discover myself tugged in another, or sometimes I'm absolutely snatched into an alley. I write in longhand or
what kin and friends call deranged hieroglyphics. I begin on long,
yellow paper with a juicy ballpoint if it's one of those 6/8 bop
pieces. For slow, steady, watch-the-voice-kid, don't-let-the-mask-
slip-type pieces, I prefer short, fat-lined white paper and an ink pen.
I usually work it over and beat it up and sling it around the room a
lot before I get to the typing stage. I hate to type—hate, hate—so
things get cut mercilessly at that stage. I stick the thing in a drawer
or pin it on a board for a while, maybe read it to someone or a
group, get some feedback, mull it over, and put it aside. Then, when
an editor calls me to say, "Got anything?" or I find the desk clut-
tered, or some reader sends a letter asking, "You still breathing?" or
I need some dough, I'll very studiously sit down, edit, type, and send
the damn thing out before it drives me crazy.

I lose a lot of stuff; that is, there are gobs of scripts and stories that
have gotten dumped in the garbage when I've moved, and I move a
lot. My friend, Jan, was narrating a story I did years ago and someone asked, "Where can I find it?" Damned if I know. It was typed
beautifully, too, but it was twenty-four pages long. Who can afford
to print it? It'll either turn up or not. Nothing is ever lost, it seems to
me. Besides, I can't keep up with half the stuff in my head. That's
why I love to be in workshops. There are frequently writers who get
stumped, who dry up and haven't a clue. Then, here I come talking
about this idea and that scenario—so things aren't really lost.

The writing of *The Salt Eaters* was bizarre. I'll spare you the saga
of the starts and fits and stutterings for the length of a year. I began
with such a simple story line—to investigate possible ways to bring
our technicians of the sacred and our guerillas together. A Mardi
Gras society elects to reenact an old slave insurrection in a town
torn by wildcat strikes, social service cutbacks, etc. All hell breaks
loose. I'm sliding along the paper, writing about some old Willie
Bobo on the box and, next thing I know, my characters are talking
in tongues; the street signs are changing on me. The terrain shifts,
and I'm in Brazil somewhere speaking Portuguese. I should mention
that I've not been to Brazil yet, and I do not speak Portuguese. I

didn't panic. It was no news to me that stuff comes from out there somewhere. I dashed off about thirty pages of this stuff, then hit the library to check it out. I had to put the novel aside twice; but finally, one day I'm walking out in the woods that some folks here call a front yard, and I slumped down next to my favorite tree and just said, "Okay, I'm stepping aside, y'all. I'm getting out of the way. What is the story I'm supposed to be telling? Tell me." Then I wrote *The Salt Eaters*. It was a trip to find the narrator's stance. I didn't want merely a witness or a camera eye. Omniscient author never has attracted me; he or she presumes too much. First person was out because I'm interested in a group of people. Narrator as part-time participant was rejected, too. Finally, I found a place to sit, to stand, and a way to be—the narrator as medium through whom the people unfold the stories, and the town telling as much of its story as can be told in the space of one book.

This business of narrating is a serious matter. Oftentimes I've been asked, "Where's your narrator?" or told, "Your narrator is alway so unobtrusive unless the story is first person." Most of the time it seems that way because the narrator speaks the same code and genuinely cares for the people, so there's no distance. That suits my temperament. I am not comfortable conjuring up the folks and then shoving them around like pawns. I conjured them up in order to listen to them. I brought Virginia out, for example, the sister in "The Organizer's Wife," because I wanted to know what those quiet-type sisters sound like on the inside. It was always the quiet, country students that slipped my grasp in the classroom. When I get back to teaching, I want to be able to service them better than I have, so I have to get the narrator out of the way. One way to do that is to have the narrator be a friend, be trustworthy.

The work in *The Salt Eaters* was far more difficult. The narrator had to be nimble, had to lend herself to different voices and codes in order to let the other characters through. There are only two sections in the whole book where something is being said, viewed, pondered, that is not in some particular character's terms: once, when we get the history of the Southwest Community Infirmary and the tree the elders planted as a marker in case the building was destroyed—originally, that section was narrated by the tree; in rewriting I had one of the loas sing it . . . either was a bit much, given all the other goings-on in the book; and then, in the cafe during a storm when the future of Claybourne is glimpsed—originally, the rain narrated that section, but that also got to be a bit much.

In my current work I'm far more disciplined and orderly. I've mapped out a collection of stories. Some are from the point of view of young men, some from elders; some are set in the States, others in the Caribbean. One is narrated by Pan—every time I see Nick Ashford, I want to do a movie about Pan and rescue that bro', Pan I mean, from the bad press the early Christian church gave him—another by an angel. I've gotten more regular of late in my habits because my daughter asked me when, if ever, I'm going back to work. I discovered that I'd rather hang around the house so I must look like I'm working, you see.

C.T.:    The name Hazel recurs in your work. Is there any particular reason for that? Also, the image of a gorilla is very curious.

BAMBARA:    The first time I heard those sounds, "hay zil," my mother was stretching out on the couch, putting witch hazel pads on her eyes, and I thought, "Hmmm, witch hazel." I was fond of witches, still am, the groovy kind. I once had a belt made out of shellacked hazel nuts. But the combination—witch hazel—I was off and running. It's a powerful word, "hazel," a seven, and the glyph we call "zee" is ancient and powerful. The critic—I should say aesthetic theorist or something fancy to suit her style—Eleanor Traylor, calls me "Miss Hazel" and maintains that the Miss Hazel we meet in the story "My Man Bovanne" is the central consciousness in the whole Bambara canon. Ahem!

As for gorilla—the term has always been one of endearment. It comes up in "Raymond's Run," [*Gorilla, My Love*] and in "Medley" [*Sea Birds*] in different ways. In "Medley" it signals macho, but the charge is made with affection. While I was typing up "Raymond's Run" to send out years ago, I noticed I had the boy shaking the fence like a gorilla; and I thought, "Oh, my God, Cade! What the hell are you doing? How pro-racist!" I kept juggling that passage around. I felt uncomfortable with it but ran with it anyway. People get on my case about it—"What kind of thing is that to say about a young Blood?"—shades of King Kong and the nigger-as-ape and all. What kind of thing, indeed? They're right. I was wrong. I've some nerve expecting my personal idiolects to cancel out, supersede, or override the whole network of racist name-calling triggered by that term.

C.T.:   What impact has the women's movement had on black women?

BAMBARA:   What has changed about the women's movement is the way we perceive it, the way black women define the term, the phenomena and our participation in it. White bourgeois feminist organizations captured the arena, media attention, and the country's imagination. In the past we were trained to equate the whole phenomena with the agenda, the concerns, the analysis of just those visible and audible organizations. Black women and other women of color have come around to recognizing that the movement is much more than a few organizations. The movement is exactly what the word suggests, a motion of the mind.

Everybody has contributed to the shifts in mental attitude and behavior, certainly everybody has been affected by those shifts—men, women, children, here and abroad. We're more inclined now, women of color, to speak of black midwives and the medicine women of the various communities when we talk of health care rather than assume we have to set up women's health collectives on the same order as non–colored women have. In organizing, collectivizing, researching, strategizing, we're much less antsy than we were a decade ago. We are more inclined to trust our own traditions, whatever name we gave and now give those impulses, those groups, those agendas, and are less inclined to think we have to sound like, build like, non–colored groups that identify themselves as feminist or as women's rights groups, or so it seems to me. There's still much work to be done in terms of building protective leagues in our communities—organizations that speak to the physical/psychological/spiritual/economic/political/creative safety and development of our sisters. Also, bridges need to be built among sisters of the African diaspora and among sisters of color. I'm not adamantly opposed to black-white coalitions; there are some that speak to our interests, but I personally am not prepared to invest any energy in that kind of work. There are too many other alliances both within the black community and across colored communities, both at home and abroad, that strike me as far more crucial.

C.T.:   On *For Colored Girls* and *Black Macho* . . .

BAMBARA:   Before getting to critical responses and battles, I still am interested in knowing what on earth Wallace's editor at Dial Press thought he or she was doing? There is a wonderful book locked up in *Black Macho*—the story of a young woman who begins to view the women of her family in a new way, who comes down from Sugar Hill in time to catch the tail end of the sixties, who has experienced life in such a, oh, I dunno what kind of way, as to state as she does that black women have never listened to each other—oh, I feel bad for her—who sees shortcomings in the black movement and attempts to find a home in the feminist movement. There's a fine book there. It got buried under the one we got. I, for one, however, am pleased with the one we got for all its inaccuracies and shortcomings. It has broken open a question too many of us would like to ignore, would like to leave festering; that is, the power perversities and degrading lunacies we get caught up in, in playing out the man-woman comic opera. The book is a challenge to take a hard look at the cost of machismo for the total community. It is also a challenge to sisters who did not fall back in the sixties, who did not think "prone" was/is our position, but who kept on keeping on—to set the record straight.

I've read reviews of *Black Macho* and Shange's *For Colored Girls*, heard each and both discussed on campuses, in prisons, in beauty parlors, in the food co-op, at conferences, on buses, you name it. I've heard one or both called "dirty feminists" and heard feminism equated with ball-busting anger, with mental derangement, with treason. I've also heard equally passionate discussions of each or both together that have led to intense inquiries into the dynamics of sexism, misogyny and gynophobia, and the theory and practice of systematically or individually underdeveloping women based on the premise that women are inferior, are not worthy of equity and respect, are dangerous. I've been part of discussions about either or both that have led many sisters and brothers to the conclusion that it is not enough to take a stand against sexism; we must push each other to take a stand for feminism, for systematically and individually encouraging and equipping our women to develop power in all realms.

Of course, if Faint Heart can reduce Shange and Wallace—I hate lumping them together; I see so little resemblance—to a stereotype—evil ole black bitches—why then Faint Heart is exempt from having to deal with the alarm one's sounding, with the complexity one's depicting, with the challenge, the demand to change. Faint Heart attempts to stereotype for the same reason any other faint hearts stereotype—it relieves one from the burden of thinking, of wrestling with the vibrancy of real, live women, real live observers, who have put their fingers on real, live problems. The anger, dismay, disappointment, or just sheer bewilderment that many women experience as a way of life in regard to the man-woman setup is something we're all going to have to get used to airing. Women are not going to shut up. We care too much, I think, about the development of ourselves and our brothers, fathers, lovers, sons, to negotiate a bogus peace.

I was asked to contribute a piece to *The Black Scholar,* to respond to an article Robert Staples wrote in response to so-called angry black feminist writers. I declined. It didn't feel right. After I read the Staples piece, I wept for the brother, ya know? I mean, damn, where's he been? I read the other pieces. Sarah Fabio, as usual, knocked me out. Finally, I thought to myself, why go to sisters to comment every time some brother wants to speak his part on the issue? Let Kalamu Yaa Salaam answer Staples. Turn an issue of *Black Scholar* over to Peter Harris or Haki or some of the other brothers around the country trying to put a brotherhood/manhood conference together. Brothers ought to take responsibility for enlightening brothers. At this point in time I'm not even sure there's a damn thing sisters can tell brothers, ya know what I mean?

It's getting a little crazy. Brothers snarling at *Sula* 'cause Sula takes all the male prerogatives, the bold-ass bitch. If a sister had written *Jane Pittman,* there would have been a furor about that passage where the sister stands there, after what's-her-name got raped, sputtering at the men: "Dammit, would you men for once . . . can't you just . . . don't just stand there like asinine fools . . . for crying out loud . . . can't men do a goddam thing . . . go get the lantern." If a sister had written half the works of Ousmane Sembene, there'd be back-and-forth debates raging about reverse sexism: how come the heroics are always done by the women? How come the women in *God's Bits of Wood* outdo the men in courage? I'm telling you, any woman who even stumbles backwards into sexual politics is going to draw fire, at this moment in time anyway.

Whatever the case, I am happy for Ntozake. She has spirit and flair and lyricism, and I wish her well. I hope she has good people around her who will keep her on her course, and I hope we don't drive her into a ditch or over the edge. *Black Macho* is the only work

I know by Wallace. I think it has accomplished good things for us. I wish her well, and I hope she'll be a lot more wary and shrewd when next she comes out with a book and realize that certain folks will attempt to throw her to the wolves.

I suspect I am getting old. A friend read my review of *Black Macho* in *The Washington Post* and jumped all in my chest: "You would've crucified her five years ago. You would have torn that book to shreds ten years ago. You would have blah, blah ..." I dunno. A couple of writers who recently joined the Pamajo Writers Workshop were saying how refreshing it was to come to our gathering where we are not tied up in knots every second arguing the ideological correctness of this or that comma. I knew what they meant. People have to have *permission* to write, and they have to be given space to breath and stumble. They have to be given time to develop and to reveal what they can do. I'm still waiting for another Gayl Jones novel or two so I can gauge whether I've been reading the first two correctly. There's a dynamite sister in the Pamajo Workshop, Joyce Winters, and I can't wait to read what she's going to be doing five, ten years from now. I'm not for knocking folks out of the circle just because they make some of us uncomfortable. There are no soloists after all; this is group improvisation. The literature of this moment is made up of a whole lot of voices. I'm very glad Shange's around, and I'll be glad when the smoke clears and we can step into *Black Macho* and excavate those shards that can help us reconstruct—do some serious changes in mind sets and actions. The truth of it is, a whole lot of organizations back then in the sixties floundered, fell apart, and wasted a lot of resources in the process, due in large measure to male ego, male whim and macho theatre. That story needs to be told. Had Wallace been a part of the black movement, I do not doubt that she would have had the fearlessness and the data to do it. It needs getting said. We can't keep wasting each other. There's a war going on.

C.T.: What advice can you share with new writers?

BAMBARA: Well, there's lots of advice I need to give myself and have been trying to get from others, so I'll lay it all out.

Writers ought to form workshops, collectives, unions, guilds, for several reasons. One, it is not fun to be so frequently alone. Two, there are a helluva lot of things writers need to know about markets, copyright laws, marketing, managing money, taxes, the craft itself, etc., that can more easily be mastered if people pool their resources. Three, writers get screwed right and left in the marketplace because we are individually represented, but collectives can have as much clout with city, state, and federal arts councils as dance companies and symphonies.

If you live in the Southeast you ought to join SCAAW, the Southern Collective of African American Writers, a regional service organization that conducts an annual conference, publishes a monthly newsletter, holds regular readings in the Atlanta area, hosts receptions for visiting writers, and conducts workshops to maximize the effectiveness of writers, editors, publishers, typesetters, and anyone else connected with books and journals. The yearly dues is five dollars. Send same to SCAAW, The Neighborhood Art Center, 252 Georgia Avenue, S.W., Atlanta, Georgia 30313. If you live in a region without a collective, organize one and then contact Haki* at the Institute of Positive Education in Chicago [7524 So. Cottage Grove Ave., Chicago, Illinois 60619], and let's all see about forming a national organization, finally.

Get businesslike about the business of writing. Not only can you get ripped off, you can get lost. Just as musicians need to take a few law courses—not to mention karate and target practice, given the filthy nature of the recording industry—so, too, writers need to deglamorize publishing and study marketing, distributing, printing—the entire process including bookbinding.

Read a lot and hit the streets. A writer who doesn't keep up with what's out there ain't gonna be out there.

Basically, that's the advice I recite to myself at least once a month. I forced myself to organize a workshop although I hate routine in my life, and I stick closely with the development of SCAAW although it means I can't always take a gig out of the city, because I know that I will try to get it together for younger writers even if I don't for myself.

* Haki Madhubuti (or Don Lee).

# · GWENDOLYN BROOKS ·

*G*wendolyn Brooks was the first black American woman to receive the Pulitzer Prize in poetry in 1950 for Annie Allen. *She was born in 1917 in Topeka, Kansas, and grew up in Chicago. Brooks graduated from Wilson Junior College in 1936, married Henry L. Blakeley in 1939, and together they raised two children.*

*Brooks's reputation is based on technical skill and authentic portraiture of black people. In fact, critics frequently labeled her early work "intellectual and sophisticated." This includes* A Street in Bronzeville *(1945),* Annie Allen *(1949),* Maud Martha, a novel *(1953),* The Bean Eaters *(1960), and* Selected Poems *(1962). In many respects the critics were correct. Some of the poems in these collections are very complex, and demand close textual readings in order to appreciate Brooks's skillful execution of complicated techniques. Despite these "academic" qualities, Brooks always focused on the plight of those who lived around her.*

*After 1967 Brooks's work achieved a new tone and vision. These include* In the Mecca *(1968),* Riot *(1969),* Aloneness *(1971),* Family Pictures *(1971),* Report from Part I, an autobiography *(1972),* The Tiger Who Wore White Gloves *(1974),* Beckonings *(1975), and* Primer for Blacks *(1980).* Aloneness *and* Tiger *are verses for children. These works were specifically written for all black people; in all of them, her techniques and the expression of her themes are more direct. In fact, her messages are often blatantly clear, and she has been known to test their relevance as well as her skill at clear communication by giving readings in taverns and other public places.*

*Gwendolyn Brooks lives in Chicago and spends most of her time writing poetry, lecturing in colleges and encouraging young poets.*

◆  ◆  ◆

CLAUDIA TATE:   You place your work into two distinct categories, pre-1967 and post-1967. Would you reconstruct the events of
1967, the year of transition?

GWENDOLYN BROOKS:   In 1967 I met some "new black people"
who seemed very different from youngsters I had been encountering
in my travels to various college campuses. I'd been meeting some
rather sleepy, unaware young people. I'm sorry to say many young
people are now returning to that old sleepiness but with a difference.
I have more hope for them now than I used to have because I cannot
see us going back to the temper of the fifties. After what happened
in the late sixties, I just can't see us crawling. But I'm getting ahead
of myself. I met some of these young people at a black writers' conference at Fisk University in 1967. They seemed proud and so committed to their own people. I was fascinated by them. I returned to
Chicago, still going over what they had said to me. The poets among
them felt that black poets should write as blacks, about blacks, and
address themselves *to* blacks. I had never thought deliberately in
such terms. Now if you look at some of my older works, you'll see
that they seem to suggest I might have had that model in mind. But I
wasn't writing consciously with the idea that blacks *must address*
blacks, *must write* about blacks. Much of that early work was addressed to blacks, but it happened without my conscious intention.

When I got home I had a telegram on my dining room table from
Oscar Brown, Jr., asking me to attend a preview of a musical he had
developed out of the talents of the Blackstone Rangers. I went to the
preview, and I was electrified. I praised the show, and asked Oscar if
there were not some writers among the dancers and singers. Oscar
told me there were some youngsters in the group who wanted to
show me their writing. I decided to start a workshop for some of the
Rangers. Haki Madhubuti (who was then Don L. Lee) came to this
workshop, also Mike Cook, Johari Amini Konjufu (formerly Jewel
Latimore). Walter Bradford, now a highly respected Chicago-based
writer, helped me organize the Rangers. He had been working
among them as a teen organizer. Walter was not a teen himself; he
was in his late twenties at that time. So these "Little Rangers" would
just sit there and look at me. I'll never forget that first meeting. They
didn't know what in the world I was "about." And why should they?

But we worked. The Rangers drifted away after awhile, but I didn't want to lose all contact with them. I asked Walter to start a Ranger workshop of his own—and I financed it. I bought books, dictionaries, various magazines for them. I paid him for a year to run the workshop, and it was quite successful.

In the meantime, a second group of young people started to meet here in my home in a workshop environment, and they were the ones who changed my whole life. They would talk about all kinds of things happening right here in Chicago. Things I knew little or nothing about: Haki introduced me to books like *The Rich and the Super Rich* [by Ferdinand Lundberg], which taught me a lot about what's going on in this society, about suppression and oppression. Haki, in fact, has had a great influence on my thinking. As a group we "workshop" people did many exciting things. We would go out and recite our poems in Malcolm X Park. In the late sixties black people put up a sign and renamed Washington Park to honor Malcolm. It was *our* park, not "Washington" park. We would go to a tavern and just start reciting our poetry. Haki usually led us in, and he would say, "Look, folks, we're gonna lay some poetry on you." Then he would start reciting his poems—which were relevant. Relevant poetry was the only kind you could take into that kind of situation. Those people weren't there to listen to "Poetry," spelled with a capital P. The kind of poem I could recite in that atmosphere would be my short poem, "We Real Cool." Later on, once the atmosphere had been set by a couple of the others, who had brought tight, direct, bouncy poems, the audience would be "softened" and *ready* to listen to something of my own with more length—something like "The Life of Lincoln West."

As I said, I'm trying to create new forms, trying to do something different. I'm trying to write the kind of poem that could be presented in a tavern atmosphere—on a street corner. I always like to use the tavern as my recitation's background symbol. I also visit prisons. I go to any prison in my reciting area that invites me. The inmates are so happy to have you pay attention to them. It's really rewarding to work with them. Many inmates send me their work. And awhile back I ran a writing contest at Greenhaven Correctional Facility in Stormville, New York. It was effective. The inmates enjoyed it. *They* were the judges.

c.t.:    Your earlier works, *A Street in Bronzeville* and *Annie Allen,* don't seem to focus directly on heightened political awareness. Do your more recent work tend to deal more directly with this concern?

BROOKS:   Well, let me just run down the table of contents of *A Street in Bronzeville*: "of De Witt Williams on his way to Lincoln Cemetery," "The Sundays of Satin-Legs Smith". . . .

Many of the poems, in my new and old books, are "politically aware"; I suggest you reread them. You know, when you say "political," you really have to be exhaustive. You aren't always to think of Andy Young and his comments on Africa, for example. I try to picture in "The Sundays of Satin-Legs Smith" a young man who didn't even know he was a tool of the establishment, who didn't know his life was being run for him from birth straight to death, and even before birth. As I say in that poem: "Here are hats/Like bright umbrellas; and hysterical ties/Like narrow banners for some gathering war." Now this book was published in '45 and even then I could sense, although not brilliantly, not in great detail, that what was happening to us was going to make us erupt at some later time.

C.T.:   I'm thinking of the blatant, assertive, militant posture we find in the "new black poetry" of the early seventies. Do any of your early works assume this posture, this tone?

BROOKS:   Yes, ma'am. I'm fighting for myself a little bit here, but not overly so, because I certainly wrote no poem that sounds like Haki's "Don't Cry, Scream" or anything like Nikki's "The True Import of Present Dialogue, Black v. Negro," which begins: "Nigger/ Can you kill/ Can you kill?" But I'm fighting for myself a little bit here because I believe it takes a little patience to sit down and find out that in 1945 I was saying what many of the young folks said in the sixties. But it's crowded back into language like this:

> The pasts of his ancestors lean against
> Him. Crowd him. Fog out his identity.
> Hundreds of hungers mingle with his own,
> Hundreds of voices advise so dexterously
> He quite considers his reactions his,
> Judges he walks most powerfully alone,
> That everything is—simply what it is.

Or a little earlier in the same poem:

> Since a man must bring
> To music what his mother spanked him for

*When he was two: bits of forgotten hate,*
*Devotion: whether or not his mattress hurts:*
*The little dream his father humored: the thing*
*His sister did for money: what he ate*
*For breakfast—and for dinner twenty years*
*Ago last autumn: all his skipped desserts.*
                    *—"The Sundays of Satin-Legs Smith"*

In *Annie Allen* I wrote:

*Let us combine. There are no magics or elves*
*Or timely godmothers to guide us. We are lost, must*
*Wizard a track through our own screaming weed.*
                                        *—"XV"*

Granted, that kind of verse is not what you'd take into a tavern.

The poets of the sixties were direct. There's no doubt about it. I am the champion of those poems. I take them with me; I read them right along with my own poetry.

My works express rage and focus on *rage.* That would be true of a poem like "Negro Hero" [*A Street in Bronzeville*] and "A Bronzeville Mother Loiters in Mississippi, Meanwhile a Mississippi Mother Burns Bacon." The latter poem is from *The Bean Eaters,* which was published in '60. That book was a turning point, "politically," if you want to use that much-maligned word. So much so, in fact, that *The Bean Eaters* had a hard time getting reviewed. When it was reviewed, it got one excellent review from Robert Glauber, who used to be an editor of the *Beloit Poetry Journal.* But Frederick Bock, who was a reviewer for *Poetry Magazine,* gave us to understand that he was very upset by what he thought was a revolutionary tendency in my work. I don't even remember if he used the word "revolutionary" because after all, it was 1960. He did say he thought I was bitter. He didn't like "Bronzeville Mother," or "The Lovers of the Poor." In fact, a lot of suburban white women hate "The Lovers of the Poor" to this day.

A lot of women are now observing that a good many of my poems are about women. I don't know whether you want to include woman rage in this discussion or not. But I hope you sense some real rage in "The Ballad of Pearl May Lee" [*A Street in Bronzeville*]. The speaker is a very enraged person. I know because I consulted myself on how I have felt. For instance, why in the world has it been that our men have preferred either white or that pigmentation which is as close to white as possible? That's *all* political.

C.T.:  Does your post-1967 poetry suggest a black standard of beauty?

BROOKS:  Do you remember "at the hairdresser's" from *A Street in Bronzeville*?

### at the hairdresser's

*Gimme an upsweep, Minnie,*
*With humpteen baby curls.*
*'Bout time I got some glamour.*
*I'll show them girls.*

*Think they so fly a-struttin'*
*With they wool a-blowin' 'round.*
*Wait'll they see my upsweep.*
*That'll jop 'em back on the ground.*

*Got Madam C. J. Walker's first.*
*Got Poro Grower next.*
*Ain't none of 'em worked with me, Min.*
*But I ain't vexed.*

*Long hair's out of style anyhow, ain't it?*
*Now it's tie it up high with curls.*
*So gimme an upsweep, Minnie.*
*I'll show them girls.*

Well, I read it along with a recent poem called "To Those of My Sisters Who Kept Their Naturals"—with the subtitle "Never To Look a Hot Comb in the Teeth"—which is in *Primer for Blacks*. This is what I'm fighting for now in my work, for an *expression* relevant to all manner of blacks, poems I could take into a tavern, into the street, into the halls of a housing project. I don't want to say these poems have to be simple, but I want to *clarify* my language. I want these poems to be free. I want them to be direct without sacrificing the kinds of music, the picturemaking I've always been interested in. I'm not afraid of having a few remaining subtleties.

C.T.:    Is there a liability in promoting the practice of segregated literary criticism? Should black writers heed criticism by black critics only?

BROOKS:    How are you going to force white critics to learn enough about us? Most of them have *no* interest in us or in our work. So how are you going to make them sensitive?

C.T.:    I agree. But were these critics interested in any way in the works of white women before they were forced to clean up their sexist responses?

BROOKS:    I don't think white male critics have a great deal of interest in white women writers either. I believe whites are going to say what they choose to say about us, whether it's right or wrong, or just say *nothing,* which is another very effective way of dealing with us, so far as they are concerned. We should ignore them. I can no longer decree that we must send our books to black publishers; I would like to say that. I have no intention of ever giving my books to another white publisher. But I do know black publishers are having a lot of trouble. Many of them have disappeared from the scene. So I feel a little uneasy about saying to somebody, "Don't send your work to anyone but a black publisher." What are you going to do, send everything to Third World Press? I do believe we blacks should create more black publishing companies.

We must place an emphasis on ourselves and publish as best we can and not allow white critics to influence what we do. And if you think this is an idle statement, I know of black writers who are writing in such a way—*they think*—as to be "accepted" by the white literary world "runners." They twist their language and put in a few big-sounding words here and there, and try to obscure their meaning, thinking this will make the white literary establishment love them.

C.T.:    Does it work?

BROOKS:    It does to a certain extent. Of course, this kind of literary "hair-straightening" is always contemptuously understood.

C.T.:    Let's talk a little about the "black aesthetic."

BROOKS:    I'm so sick and tired of hearing about the "black aesthetic." I thought that expression had been dispensed with, that it was one of our losses following the sixties. And I was glad of that loss. What does it mean to you?

C.T.:    The book *The Black Aesthetic* [by Addison Gayle, Jr.] suggests a prescribed method of writing for black authors involving positive race images and heightened political consciousness.

BROOKS:   But we have been talking about this all along. An announcement that we are going to deal with "the black aesthetic" seems to me to be a waste of time. I've been talking about blackness and black people all along. But if you *need* a reply to the question, you can say I do believe in blacks writing about black life. There are many aspects of black life we need to go into further. For instance, the whole church area needs more attention. I'm not just talking about sisters in their wide hats, shouting. There's a whole lot going on in the church, and somebody ought to tackle it.

C.T.:   You said earlier that people are always accusing you of not being religious.

BROOKS:   My poem "the funeral" [*A Street in Bronzeville*] doesn't suggest everything's going to turn out all right in the end. I hope you hear how this poem cries out for our doing something about our plight *right now,* and not depending on acquiring God or whatever. My poem "the preacher" has, in fact, been accused of being sacrilegious because I suggested that God Himself might be lonely and tired of looking only down instead of across or up. The popular protest is that anything God does is right! He could never be so vulnerable as to be lonely and need someone to slap Him on the shoulder, tweak His ear, or buy Him a beer. I can't think of anything I've written that speaks sweetly of religion.

My mother was "religious." Both my parents believed in doing "right." My mother, who died at the age of ninety, subscribed to dignity, decency, and duty. And she brought up her two children to subscribe to those ideals. We were taught to be kind to people. The word "kind" best describes my father. He was kind, and he believed people ought to be kind to each other. His religion was kindness. My father, as an adult, did not go to church, but he was kinder than swarms of church-goers. So I grew up thinking you're supposed to be nice. You're supposed to be good. I grew up thinking you're supposed to treat people right.

C.T.:   George Kent said in *Blackness and The Adventure of Western Culture* that your poetry is form-conscious and intellectual, that you write from the heart and personal experience. Is his assessment accurate?

BROOKS:   He was a great friend of mine. He was always talking to me about my use of form, and telling me that he considered my work to be intellectual. As a matter of fact, I do not. I don't want people running around saying Gwen Brooks's work is intellectual. That makes people think instantly about obscurity. It shouldn't have to mean that, but it often seems to. I do write from the heart, from personal experience and from the experiences of other people whom I have observed. Very early in life I became fascinated with the wonders language can achieve. And I began playing with words. That word-play is what I have been known for chiefly.

You know, I would like to have nothing to do with critics. I would like to forget them. I would like to forget biographers. And I did adore George Kent! But we must have our black critics because if we don't black writers will vanish.

C.T.:    You've insisted you are a black poet and not a poet who just happens to be black.

BROOKS:    The cultural experience of being Afro-American is integrally important to my work, but I call myself an African. This identity change was probably situated, at least officially, in 1967 because before then I called myself a Negro.

C.T.:    Do you think there's been a shift in focus in the recent writings by black women, a shift from confrontation with social forces to intimate male-female encounters?

BROOKS:    There's a lot going on in this man-woman thing that bothers me. I'm always saying, yes, black women have got some problems with black men and vice versa, but these are family matters. They must be worked out within the family. At no time must we allow whites, males or females, to convince us that we should split. I know there's a lot of splitting going on now. And I hope it's going to stop. I don't know what's going to stop it. Maybe some poets writing some good poems can help! It's another divisive tactic dragging us from each other, and it's going to lead to a lot more racial grief. The women are not going to be winners on account of leaving their black men and going to white men, to themselves, or to nobody.

C.T.:    Does your work attempt to record, to put in order black female experience.?

BROOKS:    I think so. But I don't believe in sitting down and saying, "I'm going to use this poem as a vehicle through which life can achieve some order for black women." I get an idea. I see something happening out in the street, or somebody tells me something. Or I go into my interior and pull out something and try to put it on paper. I take a lot of notes. I start revising after the first drafts. They often sound very silly as you can see if you were to look at the stages my poems go through. Perhaps after this process, the poem will turn out to be a vehicle by which means life has reached some order, or perhaps it suggests there can be an arrival at some kind or degree of order. Maybe not. It's not mechanical.

C.T.:  What about your works in progress?

BROOKS:  I'm writing the second volume of my autobiography, plus a book of poems. I want to read this poem; it's the title poem of *Primer for Blacks*, a recent book of mine. I write my poems on scraps of paper because I want to carry them in my address book. I'm likely to read them at a moment's notice.

# · ALEXIS DEVEAUX ·

*A*lexis DeVeaux was born in 1948 in New York City. She received her B.A. from Empire State College of the State University of New York, and has had a variety of employment experiences, including being an instructor in English and creative writing, and a community worker. She is a prolific freelance writer, contributing poems and short stories to numerous national periodicals and small press publications, and is currently a contributing editor of Essence magazine.

DeVeaux's publications include a children's story, Na-Ni *(1973)*, which received an Art Books for Children Award from Brooklyn Museum in 1974 and 1975; Spirits in the Street *(1973), a mixture of narrative, lyric, and dialogue interspersed with DeVeaux's own surrealistic drawings, and unified around the theme of preserving spiritual vitality in a ghetto environment; and stories included in the anthology* Midnight Birds, *edited by Mary Helen Washington (1980). Her most recent work,* Don't Explain: A Song of Billie Holiday *(1980), is a biographical study of the singer. DeVeaux is also a playwright of growing repute. Among her plays are the one-act* Circles, *which was produced in New York City in 1973, and* The Tapestry, *a full-length drama which appeared on the PBS (Public Broadcasting System) in New York City in March 1976.*

Deveaux's work is characterized by its focus on the psychological inner space in intimate relationships, whether these be lesbian affairs, conflicting forces in a love triangle, or the struggle between a daughter and her parent. Regardless of DeVeaux's specific subjects, her constant concern is love—a love that is always complex and that involves painful reconciliation as the prerequisite for personal growth.

◆   ◆   ◆

CLAUDIA TATE:   What was your family's response to a daughter who says she wants to be a writer?

ALEXIS DEVEAUX:   Well, I think at the time I decided to be a writer, which was in the early sixties, my family had no idea of what that would mean in terms of my surviving and continuing in the manner in which they had prepared me. My mother had prepared me for a certain kind of lifestyle: you grow up, you get a decent job, hopefully you get married and have children. You do something that appears normal to prepare your place in the community. Deciding to live my life as a writer, as a woman who wants to write, was totally out of the framework for my folks. There was always some kidding as to whether I could honestly live and eat, or was I going to starve. I think the image of blacks as writers, as artists, as creators, has somehow abated in recent years after the whole surge of the sixties. But I also think that there is still an underlying lack of understanding about this kind of creativity, why it's necessary, and why it's very important to further the image of the woman-as-artist.

My mother brought me up. I think that she saw my being an artist as "different." And if I were different, I was therefore uncontrollable. And if I were uncontrollable, did that mean I was setting myself up to be endangered in terms of the larger white society? If I were different, would I have a place in the black community? And how would she respond to me herself? This difference kept coming up a lot.

C.T.:   Do you think writers are different from other kinds of folks?

DEVEAUX:   There's the essential difference of the responsibility of seeing. We who see ourselves as writers and artists are given that position, so we have no choice but to live it out, just as some of us are given the position of being ministers and laborers, butchers and bakers. Writers are given the responsibility of sight. I think that the whole burden, responsibility and beauty of the gift forces us to construct our lives differently so that we are able to become vehicles to transcend, to encompass and articulate not only our own experience but the experiences of others. For me it's being in a position to interpret my life, so that in some degree I can interpret the lives of those around me: those who came before me, and if possible lay down some kind of framework for those who come after me. So, I do think writers have an essential responsibility that's different. But I'm not saying that the responsibility of the baker is not valid; it's just different.

C.T.:  For whom do you write?

DEVEAUX:  In large measure my first duty is to write so that other black people have an understanding of what I'm trying to say about my black life and possibly what I'm saying about their black lives. And then I try to write for myself in order to try to understand or objectify my own experience, to somehow remove it from me, to look at it so that I can see the meaning. And then I want to talk specifically and with greater urgency to and about black women, as my own relationships to black women crystallize, and as it becomes clearer to me what my needs are with respect to our history as black women. In all of the work I've done, there is a certain and deliberate care I've taken with laying out the image of the black woman as I have seen or experienced her, which indicates that there is a clear and conscious desire to address myself to her.

C.T.:  Do you write from autobiographical situations?

DEVEAUX:  Certainly, I am in all of my characters to some degree because I have used them as vehicles to understand certain kinds of emotions or situations that I, as a black woman, have found myself in or they, as black women, find themselves in. But lately I have found myself reaching further out away from myself. For example, my book on Billie Holiday was a real effort to reach out. The collection of short stories I'm doing is an effort to reach out, a moving away from myself as the essential source of information and looking out to the lives of other black women as sources of information. My full-length play *When the Negro Was in Vogue* is outside my immediate experience. It's about a black woman who finds herself confronted with a daughter whom she had denied in order to live a life of respectability. The whole conflict of the play is whether or not she will come to grips with her past which is represented by the lost child. Again it's an exploration of the relationships among black people, especially among black women.

C.T.:  How have your lesbian pieces been received?

DEVEAUX:  I sometimes have trouble placing my work in black publications, especially black journals. Again there is that essential conflict in the black community, which is reflected in the black liter-

ary establishment, as to whether these are valid and legitimate experiences, images that black writers should deal with, and whether or
not it undermines the whole concept of the black family or the black
community or the black male-female relationship. Of course, I don't
see it that way. I see whatever experiences we have as valid. It's just
like in the sixties when we used to be hung up on who was blacker
than who. If you grew up in the suburbs and your family was considered middle-class, then you weren't as black as the kid who grew
up on 116th Street [New York City]. Division across such superficial
lines is detrimental. So what has happened is that I have gotten a lot
more "page play" in the media and in situations where this is not "a
problem," where relationships between women are not seen as a
questionable image—as if black people don't have homosexual experiences, as if Africans on the continent don't have homosexual experiences.

C.T.:   Do you find that you are concerned with finding different
ways of presenting emotions in dramatizing lesbian relationships as
opposed to heterosexual ones?

DEVEAUX:   I love to talk about love. I think that love doesn't distinguish itself as homosexual or heterosexual. So that when I talk
about the two women in "The Sisters" and the love they have for
each other, I am not saying I'm going to talk about this homosexual
love or this heterosexual love. I am saying that I want to take a look
at this relationship and look at what the primary problem is between
the two people and highlight it because that's where the story is.
What I try to explore is how the love comes to itself, rather than
the gender or the name—that is, mother, father, sister, etc.—of the
love.

When Selina says to Ntabuu: "Why do you have to have this
kid?" Ntabuu's reasoning is: "If we could do it, we'd do it, but since
we can't let's be realistic. We need to pass on our image to somebody. We need an heir. And let's understand that. We have a duty to
pass this on: it cannot die with us . . ." This is what I have to say
more than that *this* is "lesbianism" (and therefore negative) and *this*
is "heterosexuality" (and therefore positive). My concern is: what is
the duty of the love? And the duty is to pass it on. A man wants to
pass his name on, who he is, his property. A woman can also want to
pass on who she is, her name, wealth, her property. As black people,
in literature and in life, we have to pass our experience on. We don't

have the luxury of forgetting it and starting all over again. It's too easy to have something new all the time. And it's too dangerous to let someone else have the responsibility for passing it on.

C.T.:   What determines your interest as a writer?

DEVEAUX:   The black woman as a fictional character in different dramatic and fictional settings, to see her as a role model in places where she might not normally be, but where she is being found more and more and in greater numbers. To look at what kind of pressures and situations she finds herself in and how she resolves emerging conflicts. To look at what it means for a black woman to say she loves someone and to see how she interprets, manifests, and constructs that love vis-à-vis her lover and her society.

Music is also a great influence on my work. Each piece has a different rhythm. In "The Sisters" I hear the blues of Taj Mahal and Big Mama Thornton. "Spirits in the Street" is much more like the popular music of the sixties. "Egypt Brownstone" is like jazz, each instrument/character playing variations on the melody so that the story is told not as a linear experience but as a holistic one.

C.T.:   Do you have a way of evoking the muses?

DEVEAUX:   Five years ago I used to get up and go to my desk with sleep in my eyes and just write from sleep. But I now find that it is far more important to get up and go outside, walk around, feel some air, run, ride my bike, essentially get my body moving. Then my mind wakes up immediately. I come home and I shower. The house has to be clean and in order because I have to be able to sift through the creative disorder in my mind. The mental disorder that I'm exploring has to bounce off the walls. It has to go in and out of different rooms. If the room is not in order, then I can't distinguish which is which, and that really drives me crazy. I can work for two or three hours or five or six hours, depending on how moved I am. Sometimes it can be a very shattering experience to get it all out coherently.

I keep a journal. If I'm going to write a story, I usually know what the whole story is about before I start. I try to write a sentence—this story is about . . . and then I go from there. I don't plot out my stories; I barely plot out my plays. By the time I have that one sentence I have thought about the story for a long time, and I've felt it. So that when I write it, I know basically what it feels like from one section to another.

C.T.:    Do you discern differences in how men and women portray emotions in their work?

DEVEAUX:    Women, I think, are less afraid to have the psychic experience in writing. Men are more afraid because of the way they are taught to experience themselves and because they have such a heavy burden to live up to in terms of what they think manhood is. I think that women have far more room to explore womanhood than men do to explore manhood.

Women have a certain sense of primary things like blood, which is life. I think it's because women are connected to such primal things that we have not necessarily a greater facility but a broader vehicle for exploring our experience. We're dealing with the nuances in emotions, the very fine and subtle points of experiences and relationships, the planes and the levels of "sight" that we have about them. We have common sense and intuition which have a bearing on our analyis and communication. For example, I heard my mother talk about the sixth sense all the time. I never heard my father talk about anything like that even though he was very much a part of street activity and had to rely on his wits a lot to get around. But I never heard him articulate what that wit meant or categorize it in any way. And with the sixth sense we're already talking about psychic experience.

Men also seem somewhat more conservative in their treatment of "taboo themes." Women tend to explore subjects that are not "taken seriously" by [black] male writers or that are far less concerned with bravado and being number one and some other mythologies created by the male experience. Perhaps with the exception of writers like Wes Brown and James Baldwin, black male writers are less inclined to want to explore new themes, new images of themselves. This puts them in a frail and sensitive position oftentimes.

C.T.:    In this regard black women writers seem to be an innovative force in literature.

DEVEAUX:    There is a great exploration of the self in women's work. It's the self in relationships with an intimate other, with the community, the nation and the world. Self is universal in this context because it has an understanding of the one as the beginning one and then moves beyond that. Male writers don't seem to have this concept in their work yet. And they could very well learn from us to incorporate it: an understanding of the one, both how divine and how low one is. I see a greater and greater commitment among black women writers to understand self, multiplied in terms of the community, the community multiplied in terms of the nation, and the nation multiplied in terms of the world. You have to understand what your place as an individual is and the place of the person who is close to you. You have to understand the space between you before you can understand more complex or larger groups. Thus, the exploration of this space is a main focal point in our work.

C.T.:   You've been writing for publication for about ten years, although you've been writing for yourself since you were very young. Can you see any evolution in your writing in terms of themes and the media you select to portray your ideas? Do you see where you're headed?

DEVEAUX:   I'm trying to explore with greater concentration the black woman and her love, whatever that breaks down to be. It might be her music is her love as in the case of Billie Holiday, or another woman as in the case of "The Sisters," or a father as in the case of "Egypt Brownstone." Whatever it is, I'm interested in presenting woman in relation to her eros, her sexuality. Where is she in relation to that? Is it a place of beauty for her, a place of harmony, conflict, change, antagonism? What does it have to do with her sense of herself as a political person? Where is she going? That's where I'm going in my writing. And I don't think I'm there yet by any means. I know I'm *going* there. I can look at my past work and see a pattern, and it's not happening by my own design.

C.T.:   Have you gotten much critical response to your work?

DEVEAUX:   I have had response in terms of reviews of my plays and my books. "The Riddles of Egypt Brownstone" was included in Mary Helen Washington's second collection of short stories, *Midnight Birds.* So I think there's been a cross section in terms of response.

People who allow themselves to understand that I'm involved in experimentation, in exploring black women and their sexuality, are far more open to examining the nooks and crannies of that experience as portrayed in my work. And the fact that people are seeing this has been very encouraging. I think the fiction has been better received than one or two of the theater pieces I've done. I did a play which was performed by the Negro Ensemble Company. It was called "The Season to Unravel," and it was about a black woman who tried to explore her relationship to herself as a sexual person and how that affected her relationship to her father who was dead. Clive Barnes reviewed it for the [New York] Post and Mel Gussow for the [New York] Times. They are two white male theater critics with particular ideas about what theater is supposed to be, whether it is black or white. And they expect a certain kind of theater, especially if it's black: it's got to be a "darky" musical or a kitchen drama, and it can't be experimental, and certainly it can't talk about themes they don't expect black people to address. Because those two reviewers didn't have any vehicle for allowing the material to express itself, however raw it was—and I'm not saying it was a perfect piece; it was quite raw—because of their inability to handle such ideas coming from a black woman writer, essentially what they did was they chewed the play up in their reviews. They had certain prescribed expectations. They didn't seem to be aware that I didn't have to follow the prescription.

C.T.:   Do you find the presence of African racial memory in the writings of black Americans?

DEVEAUX:   Yes, of course. All through it. It's in the language. I try to listen to language. I'm very interested in how words work. I try to write each piece in the language of the piece, so that I'm not using the same language from piece to piece. I may be using ten or twenty languages. That multiplicity of language and the use of words is African in tradition. And black writers have definitely taken that up and taken it in. It's like speaking in tongues. It may sound like gibberish to somebody, but you know it's a tongue of some kind. Black people have this. We have the ability as a race to speak in tongues, to dream in tongues, to love in tongues. We have that. We do it. That's what excites me in terms of how we communicate. It's not just that we are naturally poetic or all the things we said we were in the sixties. It goes further back than that. I'm interested in how we construct sentences; I'm not just talking about Black English, which is a valid tongue for us, but I'm interested in how we say things, where we put verbs, where we put pronouns, and why, for example, our language is different in the Caribbean.

C.T.:   Has the women's movement fostered greater development among black women writers?

DEVEAUX:   Yes, but we've been writing all along, taking this all the way back to Phillis Wheatley. There's always been this line of black women writers. What the women's movement has done is to raise some very key issues about our visibility, our image, and our role models. It has given us greater voice and weight. It has also allowed us to have some comradeship, because we as women, as black women, are in the revolution, too. Black women are involved in the revolution on many fronts. We fight the central oppression of all people of color as well as the oppression of women by men. The women's movement has opened up an area for us to have a more visible collective space, but actually we have been there all the time.

c.t.:   Do you think that *Black Macho* and *For Colored Girls* have widened this space because they have had large commercial appeal?

DEVEAUX:   They have very definitely stimulated communication among black women and between black women and men. And they have forced us to confront some of the personal and sexual myths black people have created and accepted about each other for years. These two works, especially *For Colored Girls,* have been the impetus for a long overdue, collective conversation, which means there's going to be conflict and pain if there's going to be any real significant change. But it's a strange, festering time we're living in, and we should be careful not to swallow everything we're fed—like Michele Wallace's book, *Black Macho.* While it raises some interesting questions, the scholarship is flawed and her conclusions are curious ones, to say the least.

*For Colored Girls* did show us just how male-identified black women really are. We identify very heavily with men: our brothers, fathers, lovers, sons, heroes, etc.; and though we have relationships with women as friends, mothers, lovers, daughters, sisters, aunts, we somehow have looked on these relationships as being less legitimate. We do not yet love ourselves as women. We've been taught to love everyone else; we've been taught, in fact, that it's *shameful* to love ourselves. We are supposed to be self-sacrificing and think of ourselves as unworthy, ugly people. This has crippled us in so many ways that we have to do some deep healing in order to bring back self-love. I'm not saying that we should live our lives totally without men; I'm not suggesting that at all. Some of us should because some of us can't live with men. Some people just shouldn't live with other people; those are personal problems, and I'm not talking about that.

I'm saying that on the broadest scale we have to do some very deep healing in order to understand what has been done to us and what we have done to ourselves as women.

The black sexist debate is real. Black men can be very sexist. Their sexism arises out of the burden of being male and the whole myth of black male sexuality. Of course, there are always individuals who don't fit the pattern. I have had the good fortune of having met some men who have taught me a great deal, who have been very sensitive men. And so I cannot make a blanket statement; all black men ain't "shit." But black women and this society, in collusion, have bred a very superficial macho man who is not really like that, but who projects that image for us and for himself. There is such a wide space between him and his image that it's frightening for him; and whenever we begin to analyze it, it becomes even more frightening for him. Because if we're talking about him, making him self-conscious and defensive, he has to do something: either he has to grow a harder shell or he has to break the shell down. Either way, it's painful. As black women, we need to look at sexism and acknowledge its existence, but more importantly, we must address it. And we have to admit that we have bred this situation.

These problems exist throughout society, but when they involve an oppressed group, they will always be intensified, magnified. Therefore, we have to look at ourselves in terms of this oppression. Sometimes we forget that we're in an oppressed situation, that the psychic oppression of our people continues to damage generations. How long have we been psychically oppressed? A long time to say that we have not won the stuggle. We have to look at this psychic oppression in order to see how long this mythology about us has been building.

We're going to have to return to very fundamental beliefs and healing practices. How we treat the elders of the community, for example. How everyone in the community can have a place. We will have to go back to the community because it is essentially all we'll have to deal with as we move through the eighties into the twenty-first century. We've had these beliefs and healing practices all along, and we've dealt with them; that's why we're still here. Had we not had them, a sense of race consciousness and racial memory, we would have been extinct by now. After all, it has been a four-hundred-year war.

Keeping these traditions alive is the duty of writers, the responsibility of our sight: to be able to see the past, the present and the future; to make the connection and preserve what is viable in terms of
what has worth and what makes the proper mélange, so we can say
what our possibilities are. We must look at us in a new light. This is
part of the writer's calling: to look at our potentialities; to determine
positive, productive levels we can operate on. Are we always going
to be operating on the level of struggle, or can we begin to set our
sight on the level of potentiality?

This is what I was trying to say in "The Sisters." First, we have to
look at all the elements that comprise us now and, second, we have
to think about the future. What are we going to leave other people?
Is that what you're going to leave—a car, two color TVs? Is that
going to be the nature of your legacy? We have to say something
about us that's different from the ways that white people speak of us.
White people leave their kids practical, viable ways to survive. We
have to begin to look at what the real legacy of our people is, how it
has helped us to survive, and what we must do to insure that survival through time.

# · NIKKI GIOVANNI ·

*N*ikki Giovanni began her literary career as a poet in the late sixties during the so-called "Black Revolution," and much of her verse at that time encouraged social and political activism among Black Americans. Her later work also addresses contemporary issues, but the focus falls instead on human relationships rendered from the vantage point of a mother, a lover, and a woman. Giovanni's language remains startling, energetic, enraged, and loving.

She was born in 1943 in Knoxville, Tennessee and was named after her mother, Yolande Cornelia Giovanni. She graduated with honors from Fisk University in Nashville, Tennessee in 1967 and later attended the University of Pennsylvania and Columbia University. She has held academic appointments at Queens College of the City University of New York and at Livingston College of Rutgers University in New Brunswick, New Jersey. Giovanni's literary activities and uncompromising outspokenness have consistently put her in the academic spotlight.

Giovanni has published prolifically. Her books include: Black Judgment (1968); Black Feeling, Black Talk (1970); Re: Creation (1970); Spin A Soft Black Song: Poems for Children (1971); My House (1972); Ego Tripping and Other Poems for Young Readers (1973); The Women and the Men (1975); Cotton Candy on a Rainy Day (1978); and Vacation Time; Poems for Children (1980). Her collection of essays, Gemini: An Extended Autobiographical Statement: My First Twenty-five Years of Being a Black Poet (1971) received considerable critical acclaim. She has also published two literary dialogues with prominent writers: A Dialogue: James Baldwin and Nikki Giovanni (1972) and A Poetic Equation: Conversation Between Nikki Giovanni and Margaret Walker (1974). A prominent figure in

*the tradition of black oral poetry, she has several recordings of verse to
her credit.*

*Giovanni currently writes full-time, is a frequent contributor to na-
tional magazines and scholarly journals, and is also a popular lecturer.*

◆  ◆  ◆

CLAUDIA TATE:    The black revolutionary fervor of the sixties
seems to be gone. We no longer even hear the rhetoric. Does this
suggest that the revolution is over?

NIKKI GIOVANNI:    I bought three new windows for my mother's
basement. Have you ever bought windows for your mother's basement? It's revolutionary! It really is.

I have a problem I think I should share with you. For the most
part this question is boring. We're looking at a phenomenon as if it
were finished. Everyone says, "Well, what happened to the revolution?" If you want to deal with states [dialectical transitions] you
have to deal with Marx. But I'm not into that. From where I am, I
see a continuous black revolution going on for the last four hundred
years in America. There has been a continuous revolution of black
people for the last two thousand years. And it's not letting up.

When you look at the decade from 1954 to 1964, you're forced to
say black Americans won their objectives. We didn't like the segregated buses. We didn't like the segregated schools. We didn't like
the way we were treated in stores. We didn't like the housing patterns. We didn't like the number of doctors or lawyers we had. We
didn't like our lack of professionals. We won. But looking at the late
seventies, there's no way you can consider the Bakke decision to be
favorable. It was 5–4. It was really a bad decision. Close cases make
bad law. There's no question Bakke should have come in 9–0 either
way, if it's going to be definitive. Then you would have had a law.
You don't have a law now.

I'm looking for a riot. I'm living in a city that kills cops like people kill flies. Cincinnati, Ohio is leading the nation in the number of
policemen killed. We're number one. The black community seems
to be saying, "Well, you can play Nazi, but we ain't playing Jew."
And black folks have been shooting back. We're saying, "Wait a
minute. Who do you think you're playing with?" Nobody's going

back to 1954. No matter what the rollback is. It's not even going back to '64. No matter what "let's take the breather" is.

When people start to say "What happened to the sixties," we've got to remember, "Hey, this is the eighties and what are we going to do now?" Where are we going because it's going to continue. My generation didn't start the bus boycotts. But we decided where they should go. Now it's time again to decide on a direction. We weren't the first generation to say "This ain't right." But we were the first to know we had to fight in terms of our bodies. We recognized we were going to have to go to jail, and we were going to have to get killed. And all of that is really sad. We were going to get beaten; our houses were going to get bombed. But we went on the line. I mean bodies, a lot of bodies. I'm not the first poet, neither is Carolyn Rogers nor Gwen Brooks, to say, "Hey, this is intolerable." Neither was Langston Hughes, nor Claude McKay. We're talking about a struggle for freedom that keeps going on and on. People are tending to approach the whole problem like, "Oh! Wow! It's all over. It's been done." This is not a movie!

Sure the militant posture has left contemporary writing. First of all it was boring. That's a very serious word for me; I use it a lot, I realize, but what do you want? You want me to rewrite "Nigger can you kill/Can you kill/Nigger can you kill?" I wrote it. It's not just that it's written, but I wrote it. And I wasn't even the first person to write it. Nor will I be the last. But I did it *my* time. Now it's time for me to do something else.

C.T.:   Your earlier works, *Black Feeling, Black Talk, Black Judgment* and *Re: Creation,* seem very extroverted, militant, arrogant. The later work, *The Women and the Men* and *Cotton Candy on a Rainy Day,* seem very introverted, private, lonely, withdrawn. Does this shift in perspective, tone, and thematic focus reflect a conscious transition?

GIOVANNI:   I'll tell you what's wrong with that question. The assumption inherent in that question is that the self is not a part of the body politic. There's no separation.

I'm not a critic of my own work. It's not what I'm supposed to be about. I think literary analysis gives academics something to do. Books are generally amusement parks for readers. They will ultimately make a decision about which book to ride. But as for critics, they have to write a book as interesting as the one they're criticizing or the criticism is without validity. If they succeed, then the book they're writing about is only their subject; it is not in itself necessary. The critics could have written about anything. And after all, they've got to have something to do. It's Friday and it's raining, so they write a critique of Nikki Giovanni. It's not serious. And I'm not denigrating myself; it's just that it's no more serious than that.

c.t.:    Is there a black aesthetic? If so, can you define it?

GIOVANNI:    It's not that I can't define the term, but I am not interested in defining it. I don't trust people who do. Melvin Tolson said you only define a culture in its decline; you never define a culture in its ascendancy. There's no question about that. You only define anything when it's on its way down. How high did it go? As long as it's traveling, you're only guessing. So too with the black aesthetic.

As the black-aesthetic criticism went, you were told that if you were a black writer or a black critic, you were told *this* is what you should do. That kind of prescription cuts off the question by defining parameters. I object to prescriptions of all kinds. In this case the prescription was a capsulized militant stance. What are we going to do with a stance? Literature is only as useful as it reflects reality. I talk about this in *Gemini*; I also say it's very difficult to gauge what we have done as a people when we have been systematically subjected to the whims of other people.

c.t.:    One essay in *Gemini* discusses the effects of slavery on Phillis Wheatley's life and work.

GIOVANNI:    You talk to Margaret Walker about Phillis because I would like to be very clear about her. There is nothing wrong with the poems she wrote. And I dare say, from what I see of history, there was no particular reason why Phillis Wheatley didn't mean exactly what she said. There is no reason for me to reject what Phillis Wheatley had to say about her experience. And I don't. People get upset because she talks about Africa in terms of how delighted she was to discover Christianity. Well, from what little I know, she might have been damned delighted. Life for an African woman can be very difficult even today, and she was writing in the eighteenth century. We can't talk about freedom for the African woman *now*. That's a battle yet to be fought.

I just want to be clear on Phillis because I think she gets a bad rap. People haven't read her and don't know a damn thing about her and don't want to empathize with her life. I think she had a difficult life. If she could say she was delighted to be on these shores, then we have to look at that.

Critics should do one thing and that is understand the work. It doesn't make any difference whether they are white or black, they should try to understand the work. I've been so consistent on this point that I would just like to point out my consistency. (People never read what I say, and I don't know where they get what they come up with.) I can both read and appreciate literature, as I was taught to do. I can do this with Shakespeare, though I am not a great lover of Shakespeare. Therefore, it is incomprehensible to me that Robert Bone, a white critic, can't read and appreciate Nikki Giovanni, a black poet. I think I'm probably brighter and more sensitive than he is, and I'm saying Bone because he's the first white critic who comes to mind. I have not created a totally unique, incomprehensible feat. I can understand Milton and T.S. Eliot, so the critic can understand me. That's the critic's job.

We have made literature in the Western world a big bugaboo. I remember when I was in a humanities class, we read Theodore Dreiser's *Sister Carrie* because it was short enough to be put into a six-week course. But if you're going to read Dreiser, there's only *An American Tragedy.* He *didn't* write anything else! If you're going to read Tom Wolfe, you're going to read *Look Homeward, Angel.* That's what you're going to have to do. If you're going to read Thomas Mann, you're going to read *The Magic Mountain.* But we generally don't read a writer's best work. So people end up not liking literature. And they are discouraged, absolutely discouraged from reading literature because we've given them the worst but what was most convenient. What we've been taught for the last five generations of public education is expediency. And that's what we are dealing with right now. Kids say, "If I'm going to read shit why should I read?" That's exactly what it comes down to. Why should I read the worst of some author? Because it's safer; it's sanitized, and he or she didn't use bad words. And all of us let this happen, because we have our jobs or whatever.

Poetry is the most mistaught subject in any school because we teach poetry by form and not by content. I remember reading Edna St. Vincent Millay—and nobody was reading Millay, you know, except me and the teacher. I really liked "I Burned My Candle at Both

Ends," and I wanted to discuss the poem in class. But I was told, "We don't discuss that." It had nothing to do with the fact of how one can read Edna St. Vincent Millay and not read that poem. But we did! Another time I was reading *The Well of Loneliness* [by Radclyffe Hall] and I wanted to do a book review on it. Miss Delaney said, "My dear, we don't review books like that." What the hell! If you can't review what you want, if schools aren't interested in teaching literature on the level of serious reading, how are we going to get a critic?

I read an article called "The Great Literary Hoax" in *Atlantic* magazine. The guy says every book that comes out is treated as a literary event. Of course, they mostly aren't. If you look at the Nobel list and the Pulitzer list, you'll be lucky if you find two books worth reading. I'm serious! You're a Ph.D. and I would bet that you haven't read ten books on both lists. Nobody does. You know why? Because they're shit. These books get awards because they're safe. But they're shit. The National Book Award list isn't a whole lot better, but at least I was able to read ten or so books on that list. I can't say that for the Pulitzer Prize list. These lists don't reflect our best literature. They don't support excellence in any way, shape, or form. Mediocrity is safe.

If there were just one critic, and it doesn't matter what color, race, none of that, who looked at literature and decided he or she was going to write a book saying what was really great for whatever reason, it would never see the light of day. The critic controls nothing. He or she has to submit their book to a publisher. For example, you have to submit your book to an editor who will probably be Jewish and won't like the fact that you're black. If you were white, you would have to submit it to an editor who probably won't like the fact that you're a woman. Even if you were a white man, you would have to submit it to an editor who probably can't read. Winning is very hard. And I'm just being serious. I'm not saying give up because I'm not a give-up. Something's got to change. Sure, people say what's the point in trying. But of course, there's a point in trying. At some point those of us who are about what is called "truth" have to be as willing to fight for our reality as those who are fighting against us. I could grow up in America and think the Civil War was an awful thing, and I grew up black in Tennessee. And it might be a long time before I'd realize, hey, you motherf---ers are *crazy*! This is *me* you're talking about. I know we're talking about a lot of different things here; it's all got to be connected. Otherwise I could answer yes or no.

Writers have to fight. Nobody's going to tell you that you're going to have to change three words in your book. It doesn't come down like that. People think, "Oh, they're going to mess with my work." They're not. It never happens like that. It's just going to be that you get no response. We who are interested have to be as willing to fight as those who fight against us. "Life is not a problem," as I said in *Cotton Candy* [*on a Rainy Day*]. "It is a process," and we have to make choices. We frequently act like life is a drama, think there's a problem to be resolved with a climax. So we're always dissatisfied because there are no answers.

C.T.:   Is there validity to *For Colored Girls Who Have Considered Suicide When the Rainbow Is Enuf* and *Black Macho and the Myth of the Superwoman,* and the subsequent criticism these works incite?

GIOVANNI:   Evidently there is validity or it wouldn't fly. You're essentially asking does it have a motor? It's got to have a motor or it wouldn't fly. Otherwise it'd just sit out on the runway. I have problems with this man-woman thing because I'm stuck on a word. The word's "boring."

I can't think of anything that could interest me less. I've turned down a lot of contracts on this topic. The man-woman thing is a boring subject. It's essentially a dead end. It's going to come down to one of two things: either you're going to take off your clothes or you're not. Men and women do that. Show me a man and a woman and that's what's going to happen. You show me a man without a woman and something else will happen. Show me a woman without a man and something else will happen. But as long as there are men and women, there's no race; there's no color; there's no age. As long as they're men and women, they're going to do what men and women have been doing for the last two million years. This man-woman thing is not even a case of making a mountain out of a mole hill. We don't even have a mole hill yet! It's sort of like cotton candy. We're just spinning around.

I remember in Harlem there used to be these "Save Our Men Meetings" and I was invited to one. I try to get along with people. I'm not as difficult to get along with as people think. I went to the Save Our Men Meeting, and I said, "What are we talking about?

Which men do you own? Save my car, yeah. I've got a Peugeot out there on the street, and I'd like to save it. I'd like to save my record collection because I really like it. But I don't *have* a man." I have a *relationship* with a man, and he has a *relationship* with me. Certain things are going to happen to make it either a good or a bad relationship. If it's a good relationship, everybody's happy. If it's a bad one, there's going to be a change.

I'm not inextricably tied to black men. Black women who say "I don't want anybody but a black man" are saying they're afraid because there are men other than black American men. There are men all over the world. If you can't find one, try another. You could just be out of sync. If you're fat and you're living in Paris, you're going to have a problem with men. Because French men like their women thin. Hey, try the Caribbean, where they like them fat.

I loved *For Colored Girls*. First of all Ntozake is an extremely bright, sensitive, *good poet*. She writes exceptionally well. She has a lot of developing to do and that's not meant as a negative comment. I don't see how anybody could take it as a negative statement. Furthermore, I don't see how anybody can be overly sensitive about her work. It's really a case of if the shoe fits, you simply have to wear it. I mean that's all she's done. She said, *"Here I am."* Ntozake's naked on that stage. She's naked in that book. And if you don't like it, lump it. *For Colored Girls* is not a love poem. I love it. It's one of my favorite poems. But it's not a love poem.

Ntozake's naked on that stage, but not because she's writing from experience. I resent people who say writers write from experience. Writers don't write from experience, though many are hesitant to admit that they don't. I want to be very clear about this. If you wrote from experience, you'd get maybe one book, maybe three poems. Writers write from empathy. We cheapen anything written when we consider it an experience. Because if it's someone else's experience we don't have to take it seriously. We really don't. We could say, "That's what happened to Ntozake. Isn't that a shame?" No, that's not what happened to Ntozake! I don't know whether it did or it didn't. That's not the point. The point is *that's what happened; that's what still happens.* Writers write because they empathize with the general human condition.

I wrote a poem about a black man, and Don Lee wrote the most asinine thing I've ever read. His criticism was that Nikki Giovanni's problem is that she's had difficulty with a man. *Kirkus Review's* critical response to *The Women and the Men* was "Oh she's just in love." If *Kirkus* never reviews another book of mine I'll be more than happy. My life is not bound in anything that sells for $5.95. And it will never be. No matter what you're seeing, it's not me. If I'm not bigger than my books, I have a problem. I have a serious problem. I don't take my books personally because they're not personal. They reflect what I have seen, and I stand behind them because they are about reality, truth. I'm not America's greatest writer, but I'm credible.

The truth I'm trying to express is not about my life. This is not an autobiography we're talking about. *Gemini* is barely one, and it comes close. It was what I said it was, an autobiographical essay, which is very different from autobiography. Even autobiographies are not real because we only remember what we remember. And the truth has to be bigger than that, and if it isn't there's something wrong with your life. What we remember is only a ripple in a pond. It really is. And where does the last ripple go and who sees it? You never see the end of your own life. We put too much emphasis in the wrong places. And what we do to writers, particularly, is we try to get away from what is being said. We brand them. Of course, I'm back to the critics again.

The point of the writer is to remind us that nuclear energy, for example, is not just some technical, scientific thing, not that Pluto is the last planet and it's freezing, but that such things are comprehensible to the human mind.

We've got to live in the real world. If we don't like the world we're living in, change it. And if we can't change it, we change ourselves. We can do something. If in 1956 I didn't like the way the world was, it was incumbent upon me to at least join a picket line. I didn't have to join a picket line happily. I didn't have to join it with full knowledge of what this could mean to me. None of that was required of me. It was only required that I try to make a change so that ten years later I'll be able to go to Knoxville, Tennessee, and I'll be able to walk down Gay Street without having to move aside for some cracker. And in ten years we did. That was a limited goal, but I won. All I'm trying to say is, okay, if you can't win today, you can win tomorrow. That's all. My obligation is to win, but winning is transitory. What you win today, you start from ground zero on the next plateau tomorrow. That's what people don't want to deal with.

You're only as good as your last book. And that's what writers have a problem with. You say you wrote a book twelve years ago. Hey, I'm real glad, but I want to know what you are doing now. I complained about [Ralph] Ellison in *Gemini* in this regard. And I think it's a valid complaint. God wrote one book. The rest of us are forced to do a little better. You can't live forever on that one book. No matter how interesting, or how great, or how whatever, you are forced to continue, to take a chance. Maybe your next book won't be as good as your last. Who knows?

A lot of people refuse to do things because they don't want to go naked, don't want to go without guarantee. But that's what's got to happen. You go naked until you die. That's the way it goes down. If you don't want to play, you're not forced to. You can always quit. But if you're not going to quit, play. You've got to do one or the other. And it's got to be your choice. You've got to make up your own mind. I made up my mind. If you're going to play, play *all* the way. You're going to sweat, and you're going to get hit, and you're going to fall down. And you're going to be *wrong*. Probably nine times out of ten you're going to be wrong, but it's the tenth time that counts. Because when you come up right, you come up right beautifully. But after that you have to start again. We as black people, we as people, we as the human species have got to get used to the fact we're not going to be right most of the time, not even when our intentions are good. We've got to go naked and see what happens.

C.T.:   Do women writers record human experience in fundamentally different ways than men?

GIOVANNI:   I think men and women are different. I think most of these differences have to do with what would have to be considered as conditioning. A woman writer was expected to write little love stories. She was expected to deal with emotions. Women were not really allowed to encouraged to do anything else. So women's published works went down in a certain way. If you were a woman, and you were identifiably a woman, and you sent a manuscript to a publisher, it was not going to be about Buck Rogers because women didn't write science fiction. It wasn't *Executive Suite* [a popular novel published in 1977 by Cameron Hawley], not that *Executive*

*Suite* is a great novel. But women weren't supposed to write business novels. They were supposed to write little homely, lovely novels that were quite safe, and they sold for a quarter and everybody lived happily ever after.

C.T.:   Do you see an evolution in Afro-American writing in terms of theme, craft, perspective?

GIOVANNI:   There has never been a time since we discovered literature that we have not both petitioned white writers and recognized their basic bestiality. As black Americans living in a foreign nation we are, as the wandering Jew, both myth and reality. Black Americans have no home now or ever. We have been here too long to go any place else. I'm not saying we cannot migrate. Twenty of us or 20,000 of us can certainly go to Africa. We can go, but Africa would be a new experience, and we would also be strangers there. This is what black Americans reject. And it's probably human nature to reject the fact that we will always be strangers. But our alienation is our great strength. Our strength is that we are not comfortable any place; therefore, we're comfortable *every place.* We can go any place on earth and find a way to be comfortable.

I'm always saying to the kids—and it's a big joke—that if I were anything from outer space, I would make a point to come into a black community because that's the only place where I would *at least* be given a chance. The first response of black people would not be to shoot me, stamp me out, poison me, or somehow get rid of me. They would be curious about me. They would not do what your average cracker would do which is to wipe me out.

We who are black have to recognize our basic powerlessness, and that's a strength. It's not power; it's strength. We have nothing to protect. What was especially great during the period between '68 and '74 was the mass consciousness that there was nothing for us to protect. We said if the best you have to offer is Richard Nixon, then go to hell! That attitude blew the country's mind. The country said how can we get back to those people. The country sent a lot to us. It sent the women [women's liberation]. It sent "the man." It offered jobs. But you don't hear blacks saying "God Bless America." In fact, nobody cares if the flag goes up or down. When you hear the national anthem, you know we're going to play ball. That's all the anthem seems to be for—to open a ball game. When they finish singing it, the proper expression is "play ball."

Black American consciousness has finally assumed dominance all over the world. I'm serious about this. We're setting the tone. If we function well, we will continue to set it. There's little alternative to the black American consciousness. The alternative is essentially destruction.

We talk about what writers should be doing. Well, we've got to look beyond the block. We've got to do a lot of thinking. You asked a question a while back about my evolution as a writer. A lot has happened. I don't want anybody to think it's just me. It's all of us. It has to do with the way we conceptualize the world. We are earthlings. When Viking II took off we became earthlings. Nobody knows what an earthling is, and how an earthling relates to other earthlings. Is a whale an earthling? If it is, do we have a right to kill it? Is a baby seal an earthling? If it is, is it all right to hit it in the head? And if it's all right to hit a baby seal in the head, which it is, then it's perfectly all right to napalm the Vietnamese. It's also all right to shoot elephants because they're eating up tree bark. We don't have to draw the line. Then it's okay to shoot blacks because they want some land. And if it's not all right, then who's going to stop it?

The choice is between what we do and what they do. As blacks— and I've been consistent on this point—we are not seeking equality. We're seeking superiority. I happen to be a black American chauvinist. I think black Americans are potentially the political tone-setters of the world, though our interest in power has been very low. If black Americans were as interested in power as we are in basketball, we would dominate. There's no question about it. We can do anything we want to do. We ought to quit listening to what people are saying about us. We were talking earlier about *Black Macho*. Hey, they won't even be real. Who will remember? Hey, it's the latest chewing gum. It's Mellow Yellow, the fastest soft drink in the world. So when you look at what we've done as a people, you see we've taken our consciousness and used it for survival.

The fact that we have survived says something for humanity. We are a part of the oldest people on earth, and as black Americans we are also the latest distinct group. Black Americans are different. It's the attitude. The black American attitude is a strange thing. It can really get you. It bothers me sometimes. Everything is so "f---ing laid-back." But that's a black attitude. Laid-back is not a country or

Western attitude. Laid-back is a colored attitude; it always was. It's an attitude blacks have adopted to survive because if we couldn't take it easy, we couldn't take it at all. If we stayed hot, we'd burn up. I'm a hot person and therefore a bit apart from that attitude. I stay hot. I think things can be changed. If you were to look at my personality you'd see I'm always hot. I can't take intolerable situations. Somebody's got to go down. You or me. It "don't" matter. But my attitude, in effect, is not necessarily atypical, if you put me in the group. The group as a whole learns to take it easy. I'm not worried that the white boys are playing with DNA because I'll change them before they change me. I come from a people who learned how to run with hot people.

C.T.:   What makes a poet different from a John Doe who's cleaning gutters?

GIOVANNI:   The fact that I write poetry and do it well makes me different. I dare say I probably wouldn't clean gutters nearly as well. Though if it came to cleaning gutters, I could do it. If I am a better poet, it's because I'm not afraid. If artists are different from ordinary people, that's because we are confident about what we are doing. That's the difference between what I would consider to be a serious artist and those who are in it for the fun. A lot of people are always into thinking they can become famous. Kids are always asking how one becomes famous. Well, I don't know. You know if you're talking fame, you're not a serious person.

If you didn't think this book is important and that you could do it, you wouldn't be here. You think it's important. I don't have to think it's important and I'm part of it. Margaret doesn't; Gwen doesn't. Nobody has to think it's important but you. It's your book; it's not my book. What people have to realize is, the difference between those who are serious and those who are not is simply that the former take it seriously. It wouldn't matter to you if nobody else took your book seriously. If it did, you wouldn't write it. You wouldn't care if all of us wrote you back and said this is not a serious project. You'd just go out and find yourself fourteen other writers. But we didn't respond to you that way because you take it seriously. But if you had written and said what you think we should do, you wouldn't get a response from anybody. You know people write me and say, "I want to be a writer. What should I write about?" How the hell should I know what one should write about?

Nobody's going to tell me what to write about because it's about me dancing naked on that floor. And if I'm going to be cold, it's going to be because I decided to dance there. And if you don't like to dance, go home. It's that simple. So the artistic attitude is that you take your work seriously. However, we writers would all be better off if we didn't deceive ourselves so frequently by thinking everything we create is important or good. It's not. When you reread something you need to be able to say, "Gee, that wasn't so hot. I thought it was really great ten years ago." But sometimes you can say, "Hey, it's not so bad."

c.t.:   What about the prose?

GIOVANNI:   I don't reread my prose because I'm kind of afraid. I suppose one day I will. At least I would like to think so. But I'm very much afraid to be trapped by what I've said. I don't think life is inherently coherent. I think what Emerson said about consistency being the hobgoblin of little minds is true. The more you reread your prose the more likely you're going to try to justify what you've said. I don't really object to being an asshole. I don't take it personally.

If I never contradict myself then I'm either not thinking or I'm conciliating positions and, therefore, not growing. There has to be a contradiction. There would be no point to having me go three-fourths of the way around the world if I couldn't create an inconsistency, if I hadn't learned anything. If I ever get to the moon, it would be absolutely pointless to have gone to the moon and come back with the same position.

That's been a quarrel I've had with my fellow writers of the sixties. If you didn't learn anything what was the point of going through a decade? If I'm going to be the same at thirty-eight as I was at twenty-eight, what justifies the ten years to myself? And I feel that's who I've got to justify it to—ME.

Though I don't reread my prose, I do reread my poetry. After all that's how I earn my living.

c.t.:   How do you polish the poems?

GIOVANNI:   A poem is a way of capturing a moment. I don't do a lot of revisions because I think if you have to do that then you've got problems with the poem. Rather than polish the words, I take the time to polish the poem. If that means I start at the top a dozen times, that's what I do. A poem's got to be a single stroke, and I make it the best I can because it's going to live. I feel if only one thing of mine is to survive, it's at least got to be an accurate picture of what I saw. I want my camera and film to record what my eye and my heart saw. It's that simple. And I keep working until I have the best reflection I can get. Universality has dimension in that moment.

C.T.:   Do you have a particular writing method—a special place, a special time for writing?

GIOVANNI:   One thing for sure I can say about me is that if my book is going to bust, it's going to bust in public. It is either going to be so bad or so good. That's true of most of my books. Nothing is ever half way with me. It's shit or it's great. That's my attitude. I think that's the only way to go. Now other people are much more cautious. They'll do the safe thing and handle it right. Jean Noble put twelve years into *Beautiful Are the Souls of My Black Sisters.* Jean's book is beautiful, and I'm glad she did. Alex put twelve years in *Roots.* I couldn't be happier he did. I'm glad for Alex; I'm glad for me because I've got galleys. But I could no more put twelve years into anything. Nothing is worth twelve years to me. I can't grow a garden. I can't see waiting that long just for some vegetables. Some people can do it; I'm not one of them. I believe in accepting the limits of my competency.

That's a weakness. Yeah, I'll admit it. I just don't get a thrill out of seeing tomatoes grow. I do get a thrill seeing my poems, and I will take the time for them. But if after a year I was working on a poem, not a book but a poem, I would say something's wrong with either the poem or me. That's probably not the best way to be a writer. I wouldn't even want to consider myself an example. I'm essentially undisciplined. I do a lot of thinking, a lot of reading, but I wouldn't recommend my writing method. On the other hand I can't be like Hemingway and get up at six o'clock every morning and write for two hours. He had a wife who got up and cooked his breakfasts. I don't have time to sit there and write for two hours whether I have something to say or not. I write when it's compelling.

I'm not good at moving. I understand why Andrew Wyeth felt that if he left Brandywine he wouldn't be able to paint. It's very difficult for an artist to move. Richard Wright moved to Paris, and people said his work suffered. He didn't live long enough to re-establish his connection with his new place. I think people really overlook this. I never knew Wright, but I'm sure there was a lack of connection. It was very difficult for me to move from Cincinnati to New York. And it was equally difficult for me to move from New York back to Cincinnati. I have to feel at home in order to write. No matter what kind of little shack home is; I have to be at home. I'm very territorial.

C.T.:   How do you regard your audience?

GIOVANNI:   I have always assumed that whoever is listening to a reading of mine, whether it be from my first book [*Black Feeling, Black Talk*] to the most recent, whether a kid or a senior citizen, deserves to hear my best. I think a lot of writers make the assumption that the people in the audience are not generally very bright. So they don't give them their best because they think they won't understand it. I also think there ought to be improvement in every subsequent piece of work.

We were talking about my writing habits. If my next book isn't at least an emotional improvement over my last book, I would never submit it to a publisher. I like to think there's growth. If there's no growth, there's no reason to publish. But I think the people who read me are intelligent. That's one reason I continue to be read because I do make this assumption: if you're reading me, you've got something going for yourself. That's arrogant. Writers are arrogant.

I would really feel badly if somebody said, "Well, I read you in '69 and I'm glad to say, you haven't changed. That would *ruin my day*. That would send me into a glass of something, and I don't drink. I'd have to say who are you and what have you read because I think I've changed. I mentioned Don [Lee] earlier; he doesn't really understand my work. Michele has not read me. There's no way I can be convinced that Michele Wallace has read me. She quoted the wrong books. I have written fifteen books. You can't quote the last book as if it were the first. You can't make a critical judgment based on one book. It doesn't work. She was not only quoting out of context in terms of time, she was quoting out of context in terms of the books. *Black Macho* is bad history.

We were talking about the sixties. I think what happened to a lot of writers—as well as some other people—was they decided what they wrote in '65 was right, and they began to repeat it. If I've grown, and I have, if I share that growth, and I do, then my readers are allowed to grow. I expect growth. I expect a better question from my audience this year than last year. I really do. If I don't get it I'm prone to say, "I'm really bored with you people." I expect intelligence, and I think I have a right to expect it. I don't care if they're paying me. I expect them to be as interested in talking to me, whether they're asking a question or making a statement, as I am in talking to them. And if they're not, one of us is in the wrong place. And since I don't make those kinds of mistakes, it's simple. They can say, "You can't put that on us." I say, "Sure I can, because if I don't who will?"

I have a heavy foot. And the advantage of that is not necessarily that I speed. It's that I will go in the wrong direction fast enough to recognize it and turn around and still beat you. We're going to make mistakes. It's not what so-and-so says that defines a mistake. It's what I decide is an error: that was wrong; that was dumb; that was insensitive; that was stupid. . . . But I've got to go on and try again. That's the only thing we really have to learn.

I'd like to beat the winners. That's the only fun. I wouldn't want to be the only black poet in America. It's not even interesting. I want to be among the best. And it's going to take a lot of poets because we don't even have enough to make a comparison. I'm looking for a golden age, and I would very much like to be a part of it. But there's no race now. In twelve years I produced fifteen books. That's not bad. I would like to have a little more attention.

I'm looking for a golden age, and the only way that's going to happen is for a lot of people to have a lot of different ideas. We don't need just one idea. That's my basic quarrel with some writers, and it remains. We don't need somebody telling us what to think. We need somebody to encourage us to think what we want to think. That was the problem with the black aesthetic. That's why *Negro Digest* went out of business—because it was boring.

On this level you critics do bear responsibility. I'm going to be very clear about this. You critics really praise what you understand. The fact that you understand it is almost suspect. Because once you get the critics all saying, "Well, that's really good," then you have to know something's wrong. If the ideas and concepts of a work are all that comprehensible, then the work hasn't broken any new ground. There has to be something new. That's why Toni Morrison is so great. Alice Walker's *Third Life of Grange Copeland* is great.

That book comes down to Grange, the father, who has to decide that Brownfield is not worth living. Before he will let Brownfield destroy the future, he will kill him. Only Grange could have killed him. He created him and it was an error. That's why pencils have erasers. He said I have made a mistake, but it cannot continue. Now that was a hell of a statement Alice made. A lot of people didn't like it. They can jump on Ntozake, but Ntozake didn't kill him. Alice killed him. She said Brownfield must die. Even *he* recognized that he shouldn't live, but he didn't have the strength to kill himself. It was up to his father. In Toni's *Sula* it is the mother who says, hey, you're a junkie; you've got to go. You're my own and I'm going to take care of you. In *Song of Solomon,* which was comprehensible on most levels, you have Milkman and if anybody should have killed his mother, Milkman should have killed his. Toni made a statement about flying away that people haven't dealt with yet—Milkman's act of wanting to just fly away. We know he didn't. He couldn't have. So where was he? Where is he? That's like the end of a horror movie. Toni made a statement in *Solomon,* but since it is easier to deal with than *Sula* the statement got obscured. *Sula* disturbed the critics because in the beginning there are two women and at the end there is Nel who remarks that "they were girls together." That's a hell of a statement because black women have never been allowed to say they were girls together in print. Critics have not gotten to Toni yet. They just don't understand Toni. That's probably one of the reasons she is very hesitant to talk to people. I don't blame her. If I wrote a book like that I wouldn't give interviews either. Because somebody is bound to ask a dumb question that shows he or she missed the point of the whole book. "Tell me, Ms. Morrison, why do you think Nel missed Sula?"

In terms of American writers, for the three novels Toni's written, let alone any to come, Toni's in. Who else is writing? Who else is doing it? There's no question. It's black women. What's happening with black women is great. Black women are flying. Ask a black woman what is she doing? She'll say, "I'm going to do what I have to do, and I'm really happy for you; I wish you no harm, but I've got to go." I think we are beginning to unleash a lot of energy because there's going to be competition, especially among black women writers. We haven't gotten to the point where black men and women compete, despite what you hear. The competition is among ourselves. What you're seeing in the media isn't important. Very few black women are writing out of respect or concern for what white people think. I don't care whether the [*New York*]*Times* reviews me or not. If it can review Michele, it doesn't need to review me. If the *Times* can review Michele, there's no way it can review Jean Noble. It had to make a choice, so it took what it understood.

If you look through *Cotton Candy* you'll hear a lot of music. 'Cause if you're in trouble, you don't whistle a happy tune and hold your head erect. You hummm. You hum a basic gospel tune. Can you imagine what a slave ship must have sounded like? Imagine what a slave ship must have sounded like to the women. All the slave-ship stories we've heard so far have been from men. All the men heard was the agony of the men. That's valid. But just imagine what a slave ship must have sounded like to a woman. The humming must have been deafening. It had to be there. The hum, the gospel, the call-and-response came over because it's here. The men didn't bring it over. I'm not knocking the men. They brought the drum for sure. But they didn't bring the hum; they didn't bring the leader-call; they didn't bring the field hollers, because they didn't know them. They were not field men. They were hunters. Hunters don't make noise. So what we're hearing in the music is the women. People have just continued to overlook the impact of the women. We women won't. We women were the ones in the fields in Africa. The music is not something we learned on these shores. We were communal even then, and as we got into bigger fields, we would call to one another. If you didn't answer back, we went to see about you. The hum, the holler, the leader-call are women things. The men didn't do them. Black men were out hunting in Africa, but in America they were in the fields with the women. They learned the women things from women. So what you're hearing in our music is nothing but the sound of a woman calling another woman.

# ·KRISTIN HUNTER·

*B*orn *in 1931 in Philadelphia, Kristin Hunter began her literary career at the age of fourteen as a columnist for young readers and a feature writer for* The Pittsburgh Courier. *Since then, she has held a variety of jobs to support her writing, and is now a member of the English department of the University of Pennsylvania, her alma mater.*

*Hunter writes fiction for both the juvenile and adult audiences. Her work is characterized by a striking sense of humor and warm-hearted satire, both originating in her belief that these are more effective in communicating social protest than is direct statement.*

*Her first adult novel,* God Bless the Child *(1964), is about an ambitious young woman, Rosie Fleming, who is determined to leave the ghetto by holding simultaneous jobs. Rosie's action is commendable, even though she works herself into a state of bad health and sets her goals on the false symbols of success. Her second novel,* The Landlord *(1966), is the hilarious story of a wealthy white man, Elgar Enders, who buys an apartment house in a black ghetto and subsequently tries to reform the occupants.* The Survivors *(1975) is about a self-sufficient, middle-aged woman's discovery that love can provide new meaning to life and not, as she once believed, render her emotionally and financially vulnerable.* The Lakestown Rebellion *(1978) recalls the successful struggle of the residents of an all-black town to stop the construction of an interstate highway, which threatens to destroy their community. Her books for the juvenile audience include* The Soul Brothers and Sister Lou *(1968);* Boss Cat *(1971); a collection of short stories, entitled* Guests in the Promised Land *(1973); and* Lou in the Limelight *(1981).*

*Besides teaching, Hunter is also a frequent contributor to* Philadelphia Magazine *and other periodicals.*

◆ ◆ ◆

KRISTIN HUNTER:   I do think the black movement has waned in America. Certainly, I can see a bunch of followers just walking around in circles looking for a leader. From what I hear, the sisters had a lot to do with the disintegration, namely their concern about their men talking black and sleeping white.

I'm not a part of the women's movement, nor do I know anyone who is. It's still growing. I think it has climbed on the back of the black movement along with a great many other social movements: the Gray Panthers, gay lib, handicap lib . . . and almost crushed it. The women's movement has eclipsed many black concerns and diluted black gains. I think we are back where we were before.

As far as the Third World movement goes, that's growing. There's a consciousness that we are a part of a world community of non-whites. That may be where the emphasis is now. I wish I could believe that these movements have brought about higher levels of social consciousness in the general population, but I can't. People are more aware of institutionalized racism now; that's all.

My husband was shot at by the Klan here in New Jersey. After the Klan rally permit was denied in Barnegat, New Jersey, some of the frustrated Klan members congregated with their six-packs in Gloucester County and took a few pot shots at black people. That's how my husband got shot at. They pulled alongside his car, looked at him to see what he was and fired six shots. The same thing happened to the brother behind him; they drove abreast of his car, and fired a few shots. No injuries, just terrorism. Thinking people, not just the intellectuals, are aware that the racial climate is getting worse. Some good might come out of this. Our illusions will be stripped away.

A lot of those Great Society programs, poverty programs— though I admit a lot of them were misused—were only temporary measures, pacifiers to keep people off the streets. Now they are back on the streets. I see too much apathy and black-on-black vandalism. I see sad things happening to our youth, and especially to our young men.

CLAUDIA TATE:   How does being black and female constitute a particular point of view in your work?

HUNTER:   So much of the writing is not deliberate or self-conscious. The contrary might seem to be the case to the critic; but aspects of character, theme come about almost without my intending them to. Of course, being black and female affect my work. Every book has a dominant female character; some have dominant male characters as well, but not all. I don't deliberately set out to do this. My brooding produces these characters. I don't even know who they are, that is, from what part of my subconscious they appear, until long after the book is finished.

Bella [*Lakestown Rebellion*], for example, started out as my mother. My mother's name was Mabel. Bella also started out as a woman named Evabelle. I ended up with Bella, which means both beautiful and rebellious. I was aware of that. Also the novel has a little girl named Cindy who is mute, and all she can do is sing. Then she suddenly starts to talk. I didn't realize until long after the book was done that both characters are extreme aspects of myself. I'm neither as bold as Bella, nor as sensitive as I once was, brought up as I was in a "children-were-seen-and-not-heard household." I literally never got to finish a sentence as a young child. I was not literally mute; I was silenced. So I think the rebellious Bella is an aspect of my own feelings of rebellion, though I was not aware of this at the time I was writing *Lakestown Rebellion.*

In thinking about *The Survivors*, I didn't realize until I was look-ing back that I knew the person on whom I based Miss Lena. This person is very worldly. Miss Lena, on the other hand, is rather prim and proper. I didn't know where I got the name, and then I remem-bered my grandmother, my mother's mother, was named Lena An-derson Manigault, and she too was a dressmaker. Some of the more earthy things that come out of Miss Lena's mouth, when she's deal-ing with the folks instead of her customers, are similar to what my grandmother might have said. But I didn't even think of my grand-mother at the time I was writing the book.

I don't know where I got the bunch of characters in the *Landlord.* That's the honest truth. I do know real people who are actors, that is, they put on real scams, complete with costumes. I know people that, in order to get over—I love that phrase for its multiple mean-ings: success, escape to freedom, achievement of salvation, etc.—have one of a number of facades. They are changing their identities all the time. I see this as a way of going crazy, which is what Charlie eventually does. I actually knew a man who had a charter for a col-lege, and he was a partial basis for DuBois, though he didn't have

DuBois's personality; that, I hope, I pulled from somewhere else. He, too, went around selling degrees. I knew a person like the landlord only very slightly. You know, it's best not to know people well in order to build characters so that the imagination can take over. Characters can then be presented more deeply because you're drawing on the wellsprings of your own imagination—and these are universal springs—rather than copying behavior from life.

The situation in the *Landlord* presented itself to me one day on a street corner. A rich, white person I knew fairly well bought an apartment house and showed me these rent receipt books. He said, "I've got my apartment house. I'll collect my rents. Doc's going to see me next Thursday; he's a truck driver, and he'll be back next Thursday. Minnie's not going to pay me until two weeks from Thursday; that's when she gets paid." I listened to him with a straight face, but inside I was cracking up. I said to myself, "Boy, are you in trouble." I had my story. Of course, those names aren't the same as my characters. I didn't need or want to see him anymore. I never saw any of the characters in his house, but I could tell from what he was saying and from the names that they were inner-city blacks, and everybody was running a game on him. I just knew this rich, white boy was about to be taken. But I'm not sure if many people understand the part about the landlord's babysitting with Walter Gee. The point of the novel is that an immature, white boy, by being pushed into contact with this bunch, is forced to grow up, to be responsible, to see reality. White men are allowed to remain boys until great ages because they're protected. The relationship between himself and Walter Gee symbolizes his growth.

I knew a girl like Rosie in *God Bless the Child*, too. I met her only once, and I knew she was working two jobs in order to buy a house. I went home and said I was going to write a book about her. Of course, nobody believed me.

c.t.:　How do you fit writing into your life?

hunter:　Badly. Very badly. To do a novel one needs a lot of time. I integrate living as a wife and woman, as a person and a teacher, with writing. I'm not complaining about this; I want a full life. But I do pay a price. I said I wanted to get the sequel to *Soul Brothers and Sister Lou* finished in the summer of '79. It was long overdue both in terms of contract and audience. *Soul Brothers* was my most popular book. Kids kept writing me, asking what happened to those characters as if they were real people. I kept putting the book aside. Occasionally, I still try to write after school, on weekends—I plan a chapter every weekend—but that's unlikely. Part of the problem is my discipline. I don't always put first things first. Writing is harder than anything else; at least *starting* to write is. It's much easier to wash dishes. When I'm writing I set myself a daily quota of pages, but nine times out of ten I'm doing those pages at four o'clock in the afternoon because I've done everything else first. This I don't blame on anyone but my reluctance to face the writing. But once I get flowing with it, I wonder what took me so long. That's why I say I don't have my own priorities straight all the time.

As you can see, I've achieved a room of my own—not without determination. There are a couple of growing youngsters around the house and they had taken over this room. One summer I came up here to this room and just like a squaw I sat and said I'm not giving it up. I threw out the television, which started me down the road to victory. My husband jokingly says I don't even allow him in here. Of course, that's not true. He fixed the room up for me. I needed a room, and now I have it. My family's cooperative; so all that's left is to get my own self under control and be able to say, "Let the dishes stay in the sink." That's the hardest part.

C.T.:   What is your responsibility to your audience? Do you consider yourself to be a shaper of human opinion?

HUNTER:   I have never seen myself as a shaper of human opinion. Others do, and I'm beginning to think that I haven't wanted to see myself that way. *Lakestown Rebellion* is based on an all-black town rebelling against a highway construction. It's interesting to note these expressways always come through the black sections of town. It's happening across the country. Black people in the town on which that book is based said they were going to fight the highway with their bodies if necessary, and that was pretty close to what I had written.

Up until now one of my motivating forces has been to recreate the world I know into a world I wish I could be in. Hence my optimism and happy endings. But I've never dreamed I could actually reshape the real world.

I have been optimistic in most of my books, almost compulsively so at the endings, with the exception of the first book and its sequel,

*Lou in the Limelight.* I'm not sorry that's been the case. I feel I'm at a transition though I don't know what direction I'm going in. As I said, as a group blacks must give up their illusions. I think I have lost a lot of mine with just half a year in dear old Dixie. I can't have kids living in a dream world. The boys think they can all be athletes, and the girls think they can all be singers. That's the way to fame and success. That's a delusion. I was compelled to do this book, and yet I wonder what kind of teenage book it is going to be because every chapter I've written has a real shocking event. The ending isn't jubilant optimism, but it isn't absolute horror either.

I have wanted to believe people could make their dreams come true, not necessarily the American dream because my first novel was a negation of that, but that problems could be solved. However, this is a national illness. As Americans, we believe all problems can be solved, that all questions have answers. I learnt to see they don't. I think going south to Emory radicalized me somewhat.

C.T.:    What determines your interest as a writer?

HUNTER:    My themes come to me. I don't think I'll ever run out of ideas. I may run out of energy. Stories are waiting to be written. It's whatever grabs my imagination. It finds form, as a novel, as a short story. What is most urgent I do first. I have a dozen more stories I haven't done yet. You see this box of future projects; it's full.

I am committed to telling the truth. I think I've always been a realistic writer, and I'm not just into the agony and happiness of black women. I'm interested in the enormous and varied adaptations of black people to the distorting, terrifying restrictions of society. Maybe that's why there's cheer and humor in my books. I marvel at the many ways we, as black people, bend but do not break in order to survive. This astonishes me, and what excites me I write about. Everyone of us is a wonder. Everyone of us has a story.

Along with writing *Lakestown,* I was teaching a course on the background of Afro-American literature in which I dealt with the trickster tradition in slave narratives. As a consequence, many of the topics we discussed found their way into my novel. Moreover, I was particularly interested in Zora Neale Hurston, her unique anthropological—"Zoralogical"—work. I used her work extensively as a source while I was teaching the course on "Black Culture and Literature" and while I was writing *The Lakestown Rebellion.* Naturally, her spirit, and that of Langston Hughes, crept into the book. But also, I'm married to a Georgian, John Lattany, and I got some of these trickster stories from him. The people here in Camden, New Jersey, with whom I grew up, are transplanted Southerners, and they've maintained strong continuity. All these things fed into my novel.

c.t.:   Do you see any differences in the ways black men and women writers select their themes, portray their characters?

HUNTER:   I find men place an emphasis on physical violence and actual brutal confrontations. Of course, there are exceptions. With the women there's more sense of personal relationships: family, home-centered dramatic scenes. Perhaps I'm thinking more in terms of what white women writers do. There was a time when there was such a thing as the "feminine sensibility," i.e., sheltered. I don't know if black women were ever sheltered. All this is to say that I basically see more aggression and externalized violence in works by black male writers. Of course, Gayl Jones has this violence too, but her characters are victims, which is somewhat distinct from traditional protagonists.

c.t.:   For whom do you write?

HUNTER:   I write for myself primarily and then secondarily for as many people as possible. One of the strongest forces in my life has been the need to write. I've been writing since I was a tot, and I always knew I wanted to be a writer. There were always a lot of books around the house. So I escaped into books very early. When I picture myself as a child, I see myself somewhere reading, usually hiding and reading. Through an aunt I began a column in *The Pittsburgh Courier* when I was fourteen. I soon branched out to writing feature articles. That went on for six years. During the interim I had some poetry and a short story or two published.

c.t.:   Do you cloak your protest in humor?

HUNTER:   I sometimes think humor and satire are more effective techniques for expressing social statements than direct comment. I've never had to worry about falling into a pathogenic pattern because my mind doesn't run in that direction. I have never felt a placard and a poem are in any way similar. Your question makes it seem as if employing humor as the medium for critical comment is more conscious than it is. I don't sit down and say, "How can I cloak this in humor?" If I'm very angry about something, the anger will come through in the work. When an idea suggests itself to me, it suggests itself in the form in which it should appear. I've written journalistic pieces, as well as prose, poetry, plays, and television scripts. Straightforward anger or humor finds its own way into a character. It becomes that character's anger or humor, not mine.

Furthermore, I don't see any of my characters as totally deprived victims. I don't see black people as victims even though we are exploited. Victims are flat, one-dimensional characters, someone rolled over by a steamroller so you have a cardboard person. We are far more resilient and more *rounded* than that. I will go on showing there's more to us than our being victimized. Victims are dead.

C.T.:   Does university life conflict with your writing?

HUNTER:   They are two totally different activities. I don't get material from the university; in fact, it interferes with writing. I cannot write when I'm carrying two courses a semester. On the other hand, they help me to keep eating and have a roof over my head. I do like working with young people, finding out what's on their minds, seeing them develop. It's a source of energy even though it drains the writing energy.

A few years back my plan was to alternate between writing an adult book and a young adult book. It hasn't quite worked out that way. I think this plan keeps me from getting caught in a rut, keeps me from being one kind of writer only, although there really isn't that much difference between the two categories anymore. There aren't many taboo subjects left. My style so far has been so unembellished I don't have to make any conscious changes in vocabulary, especially since I write for older kids. I want to keep both audiences alive. I'll tell you a secret: juvenile books pay better, not initially, but over the long haul. You see there's always another crop of children for whom schools must buy books; libraries, parents, aunts and uncles continue to buy books. Also, children's books stay in print longer. Adult books have a very short life span. Though most of mine have stayed in print for a long time, the average adult book is off the market if it doesn't make it in three months.

C.T.:   Has the black writer made it to the mainstream of American literature?

HUNTER:   In the last fifteen years or so there's been an enormous flowering of black talent. It was always there. We're an enormously talented and resilient people. But this only saw print in the sixties on a large scale. I think some of the exposure has fallen off now, though a few big names get a lot of media attention. I guess times have improved to the extent that we used to have one big black writer during that writer's lifetime. (It was Richard Wright for a while; then he died so Baldwin took over.) Now we have one big writer a year. This is Morrison's year. Last year was Haley's.

c.t.:   What writers have impressed you?

HUNTER:   At one point it was J. P. Donleavy; then it was Steinbeck. Always I wanted to write like Colette, but I don't. Colette is the one I admire the most. There are other people whom I admire, but I don't even attempt to write like them. I think Ishmael Reed is a genius. I admire his work very much. We have a mutual admiration society. He says he likes my characterizations; I like his being able to take off from this earthbound plane of realism in which I seem to be stuck. Fantasy and fable and power. Morrison does this too, but I don't quite know where she's going with hers. I've come to realize that having yourself rooted in some religious framework gives a lot of power to your writing. Religion has not been deep and permeating in my work or life as it has been with some of these other writers. I was not churched, but I know the Bible. My husband keeps saying I've got to read the entire Bible, not just passages. Now Baldwin was churched. You need to fly, and a spiritual framework provides a departure point. I like Bambara's stories, especially *Gorilla, My Love*. Her language is impressive. I don't try to write like these people; I admire them.

c.t.:   Can black women writers help to resolve the black sexist debate?

HUNTER:   One should be suspicious of the publicity put behind *Black Macho* or any work put out by unknown people that receives an enormous build-up. I'm not saying one should be suspicious of the black people, but one should be suspicious of the society that promotes the works. I think the sexist debate, as you call it, has been a tactic, a divisive ploy that is not set up by black people.

White academia, the white world at large, doesn't see black people as a part of American culture. Literature in this country is an Anglo establishment. And over there are all those exotic things one can deal with, only if one wants to. This is precisely the position black studies programs find themselves in. When something by us becomes an instant overnight success, one should be suspicious of the reasons. These are very undermining forces at work. What we have in *Black Macho,* for example, is black-on-black, male-female divisiveness.

Someone once said what's wrong with matriarchy? It works in certain societies where some things are in the hands of women. For example, I was laughed at in a record shop in Haiti. There the women always keep the money, just like the "market mammies" in Africa. Would you call that matriarchal? I'm not into who is the boss. Anyway, that day in Haiti, John was about a block behind me, and I didn't have any money. We usually split the money when we travel. I selected my record, and I said in French that my husband had the money. Oh, they laughed and laughed.

Whatever matriarchy we have here in America isn't working. It consists of welfare checks. Maybe welfare is a way of keeping us dependent on the system, a way of keeping our people unemployed. The theory behind it is the woman can be more easily controlled, so they send the woman the check. I'm thinking analytically now, and it's a rather unpleasant thought. Black people are fighting back and forth over this matriarchy business, and the real enemy is left alone. I've always had the attitude that if we stop fighting each other just a little bit and help each other, we can watch white society collapse. We should be about pulling out our own survival skills.

I think a lot of black girls go for the strong black woman image, but it becomes a hard thing to live up to. I see a lot of girls behaving as though they believe they can live up to this image. Nikki [Giovanni] once said, "I don't need a husband; I can just have a baby." Then later on she saw, herself, that it's hard to raise a child alone. And she said so. To buy the superwoman myth is no good. And if men believe it, it's even worse. Matriarchy is fine, if it works. But it doesn't work here, probably because we don't have our own land, our own products, our own markets. What we need here is everybody lending a hand, pulling an oar. . . . We don't even have a wheel so we must stop fussing about who's at the helm.

# · GAYL JONES ·

*G*ayl Jones was born in 1949 in Lexington, Kentucky where she lived until she attended Connecticut College and Brown University. Her first novel, Corregidora *(1975), appeared when she was twenty-six years old. It is a bizarre, romantic story exposing the intimate family history of three generations of black women in rural Kentucky from early to mid-twentieth century.* Eva's Man *(1976) is a young woman's recollections of the events leading up to her confinement in a mental institution. A collection of short stories,* White Rat *(1977), depicts brief encounters with seemingly ordinary black people, also in rural Kentucky. Jones's latest work,* Song for Anninho *(1981), is an extended lyrical ballad about a slave revolt in eighteenth-century Brazil.*

*All of Jones's works are carefully wrought narratives developed from her determination to relay a story entirely in terms of the mental processes of the main character, without any authorial intrusion. While this has made many reviewers uneasy, Jones insists her task is to record her observations with compassion and understanding, but without judgment. Her style and method reflect her mastery in combining improvisational storytelling and sophisticated formal techniques, so that the stories do not appear contrived or to be relying on obtrusive narrative devices.*

*In addition to being a writer, Gayl Jones is a professor of English at the University of Michigan.*

◆   ◆   ◆

CLAUDIA TATE:   Gayl, in your discussion with Mike Harper* you said you didn't know what mysterious act Great Gram had performed on old man Corregidora until you got to the end of the novel. Does this mean that your writing is somewhat spontaneous, somewhat open-ended? Would you describe your writing process?

GAYL JONES:   In the interview with Michael Harper I said I didn't know what Great Gram had done to Corregidora when I first mentioned her "mysterious act" in the novel. When I asked myself that question, I didn't know what it was going to be, or even if I was going to resolve it in the book, or whether it was going to remain a "mysterious act." But in the process of writing the question was resolved. Or rather it was resolved in the process of the character Ursa acting out a new situation.

My writing is mostly open-ended, though I make loose outlines of items I want to include: lists of events, themes, situations, characters and even details of conversations. I make notes before and while I'm writing. I find I make more of these notes now than when I was writing *Corregidora* or *Eva's Man,* though this kind of "loose" outlining started with these novels. I like the word "improvisational" rather than "spontaneous"; I think it best describes my writing process.

*Corregidora,* as it appears in the Random House edition, is mostly my first version as I've made a minor revision. It consists of my adding information about Ursa's past, her relationships with Mutt and her mother. My revision method generally consists of asking questions, and then trying to answer those questions *dramatically.* In the case of *Corregidora,* my editor, Toni Morrison, asked an unanswered question: what about Ursa's past? This question required that I clarify the relationships between Ursa and Mutt and Ursa and her mother. So I added about one hundred pages to answer it. Now before I submit anything, I'll ask myself the questions that have not been answered in the course of the manuscript or perhaps pose new questions, which I then answer. Of course, I prefer to answer them dramatically rather than just to make statements.

---

* Michael Harper, "Gayl Jones: An interview," *The Massachusetts Review* XVIII (Winter 1977), pp. 692–715.

*Eva's Man* went through several rewritings. It was first a kind of lyrical novel, then it was a short "dramatic" story, and then it was the *Eva's Man* as printed in the Random House edition. The handling of time, the ordering of events in this novel were primarily improvisational. I wanted to give the sense of different times and different personalities coexisting in memory. I was also trying to do something else I don't think came across very well. I was trying to dramatize a sense of real and fantastic episodes coexisting in Eva's narrative. The question the listener would continually hear would be: how much of Eva's story is true, and how much is deliberately not true, that is, how much of a game is she playing with her listeners, psychiatrists, and others? And, finally, how much of her story is her own fantasy of the past? I try to suggest this in the manner the story begins, and also by the repetition of the same events and situations but with different people involved.

C.T.: The process you just described seems especially well suited for someone who is *telling* a story because a story seemingly doesn't have to concern itself with extreme formal aspects. The story seems to unravel. Do you consider yourself to be primarily a storyteller? If so, what then does that involve in terms of your listener, the evolving story, and especially your narrator for whom you shape ideas?

JONES: I think of myself principally as a storyteller. Most of the fiction I write that seem to work have been those in which I am concerned with the storyteller, not only the author as storyteller but also the characters. There's also a sense of the hearer as well as the teller in terms of my organizing and selecting events and situations.

At the time I was writing *Corregidora* and *Eva's Man* I was particularly interested—and continue to be interested—in oral traditions of storytelling—Afro-American and others, in which there is always the consciousness and importance of the hearer, even in the interior monologues where the storyteller becomes her own hearer. That consciousness or self-consciousness actually determines my selection of significant events.

C.T.: When I read *Corregidora,* I sensed that I was hearing a very private story, one not to be shared with everyone. I felt that the narrator was consciously trying to select events in order to relay her story to me. I also felt it was not just my job to listen to her, but to become so involved in her story that I would somehow share her effort to understand and accept the past. In *Eva's Man* I sensed that Eva's character was not going to be violated by anyone, not even by her selected listener.

JONES:   I think that in the Corregidora story I was concerned with getting across a sense of an intimate history, particularly a personal history, and to contrast it with the broad, impersonal telling of the Corregidora story. Thus, one reason for Ursa's telling her story and her mother's story is to contrast them with the "epic," almost impersonal history of Corregidora.

In *Eva's Man* there is not the same kind of straight confiding, the telling of a history as in *Corregidora*. Although Eva renders her "intimate history," she chooses to do so only in terms of horrific moments, as a kind of challenge to the listener. I wanted the sense of her keeping certain things to herself, choosing the things she would withhold. But I also wanted the reader to have a sense of not even knowing whether the things she recalls are, in fact, true. She may be playing a game with the listener.

C.T.:   In first-person narratives, especially those concerned with self-revelation of experience, the process of characterization is dynamic. A lot of stories, expecially those by black males—I think of *Invisible Man*, I think of the *Autobiography of an Excolored Man*—never tell you anything about the intimate self. They tell you about the self in conflict with external institutions. Your work, and also most of that by women, seems to be concerned with revealing the character's intimate sense of self through very complex relationships. Like those by many black women writers, your stories seem to focus on the revelation of inner character rather than on reporting head-on confrontation with social issues. Do you think that black men write differently from black women in terms of characterization, dramatized themes, elements of craft?

JONES:   Yes. I've been thinking about that mainly in terms of something I call "significant events" in fiction. There is a difference in the way men select significant events and relationships, and the way women make these selections.

With many women writers, relationships within family, community, between men and women, and among women—from slave narratives by black women writers on—are treated as complex and significant relationships, whereas with many men the significant relationships are those that involve confrontations—relationships outside the family and community. In the slave narratives by women, for instance, one often finds personal, particular, "intimate" relationships; whereas those by men contain "representational" relationships. Even when men create heroines, often the relationships selected or given significance are representational rather than personal. For example, let's compare [Ernest] Gaine's *Autobiography of Miss Jane Pittman* and [Margaret] Walker's *Jubilee*. In the former the relationships given attention have some kind of social implication. On the other hand, we really don't have a sense of any kind of personal history for Miss Jane. Her attention is always directed outside of herself, and those events which are described in detail have social, rather than personal or intimate implications. You don't really have any sense of her relationships, let's say with her husband.

The question of one's identity, the power to act seem to determine these differences. Women writers seem to depict essential mobility, essential identity to take place within the family and community. But perhaps for male writers that "place" as well as those relationships are insignificant, restrictive, circumscribed. The questions we are asking are: generally, would the women's actions be considered significant by men? Would the consequences of a man's actions be different from those of a woman? Have the historical consequences of men's and women's actions carried similar weight, and how are these reflected in the works? If you compare the slave narratives written by men with those written by women, you see very delicate and complex interpersonal relationships in the latter, whether they be among members of the same race or between races. With men the focus is on social grievances, with little sense of intimate relationships among the slaves, precluding the desire for freedom.

The question of significant events/actions/relationships in fiction and how one's sex, history, culture, and geography influence them has been something that has interested me—not only in terms of writing, but in terms of how it affects one's critical response to a work. I wrote a story in which a man and a woman participate in the same action, and the consequence for the man is, let's say, death, whereas for the woman it isn't. Although I don't really want to say that women's actions have not carried similar weight, history seems to insist that the burden of consequence rests more heavily on men than on women.

C.T.:   Who or what has had the greatest influence on your work?

JONES:   My mother, Lucille Jones; my writing teachers, Michael Harper and William Meredith; and the "speech community" in which I lived while I was growing up have had the most important influence on my storytelling writing style. Although I can never really say the particular ways writers have influenced my work, I can name some writers I especially like: Hemingway, Joyce, Gaines, Cervantes, [Jean] Toomer, Chaucer. They were probably my first influences. Hemingway, Gaines and Chaucer for me are the "story-tellers"; Joyce and Toomer, the "fictioneers"; Cervantes, both. I say "in terms of writing" because now a new kind of concern has been added: teaching, particularly the course in Afro-American literature that I teach. As a teacher, I have to look at writers, their work, and literary traditions in a way I didn't have to as a reader or writer. As a result of this different perspective, certain themes and concerns crystalize in ways they otherwise would not have for me. For example, classroom discussions about psychohistorical influences on characters is a case in point. This is particularly so when I discuss how these influences enter Zora Neale Hurston's and Jean Toomer's works, or in Alice Walker's or Toni Morrison's. So having to discuss works in this manner forces me to see them very differently.

When I wrote *Corregidora,* psychosexual ambivalences and contradictions in the American experience weren't self-conscious themes, but now they are; these exist in works by Baldwin or Walker or Toomer. Cervantes also has different implications now. When I read Cervantes now, I connect *Don Quixote* with the picaresque Afro-American slave narratives; consequently, *Don Quixote*—which is a favorite book—becomes even more important. Hurston interests me because of her use of folklore and her storytelling; I also think she's important if one wants consciously to crystalize an idea of a heroine, not in a self-conscious way, but in a conscientious way. None of my women are really heroines except in the sense they're storytellers and central figures.

There are also unconscious ways by which people are influenced by speakers and writers, or by an environment or landscape. I realize I'm rambling, and that is because I hesitate to "analyze" influences. The earlier writers—the ones I read at an earlier age—influenced me more stylistically and perhaps the influences now go beyond style to how style can manifest theme, how it contributes or enhances an idea.

C.T.:   Does your writing follow a definite pattern or commitment, or are you telling stories that happen to be in your head?

JONES:   Well, I'm mainly telling stories that happen to be there. But I can look at things I've written up to now and see a pattern in terms of ideas I have been interested in: relationships between men and women, particularly from the viewpoint of a particular woman, the psychology of women, the psychology of language, and personal histories.

C.T.:   Reviewers of *Corregidora* talk incessantly about sexual warfare. What is your response to that? I don't see sexual warfare. I see something I'll call, for lack of another term, the dialectics of love—a synthesis of pleasure and pain. Do you observe this dialectic at work in your novel?

JONES:   I didn't think Ursa was involved in sexual warfare. I was and continue to be interested in contradictory emotions that coexist. There is probably sexual tension in *Corregidora* both in the historical and in the personal sense.

C.T.:   Do you find that relationships which involve contradictory emotions reveal more about human character?

JONES:   Yes. I also think people can hold two different emotions simultaneously.

C.T.:   Do your works attempt to make sense out of the chaos of life or do they just record the chaos?

JONES:   They attempt to record that chaos, but at the same time the artistic process is one of ordering for the storyteller and also a way of dealing with experience.

C.T.:   Can you say what inspired you to write *Corregidora* and *Eva's Man*?

JONES:   Aside from my seeing myself outside of the conventional roles of wife and mother, my interest in Brazilian history, and my wanting to make some kind of relationship between history and autobiography, I cannot. As for *Eva's Man*, I can never really think of any reason why I wrote it. It is easier to talk intellectually about *Corregidora* than about *Eva's Man*. I generally think of *Eva's Man* as a kind of dream or nightmare, something that comes to you, and you write it down. The main idea I wanted to communicate is Eva's unreliability as the narrator of her story.

C.T.:    When I read *Eva's Man*, I was immediately aware of three pervasive symbols: Queen Bee, Medusa, and Eve biting into the apple. These three symbolic personages have been very detrimental to men in our cultural history. How did you happen to select them?

JONES:    Well, they're the kind of images that worked themselves naturally into the story as I was writing it. When I began writing the novel, I focused on Eva's concern that she is different from the way others perceived her. She is bothered by the fact that men repeatedly think she is a different kind of woman than who she actually is.

C.T.:    They think Eva's a whore.

JONES:    Yes. She begins to feel she is, and eventually associates herself with the Queen Bee [the local whore] and the Medusa symbol. I put those images in the story to show how myths or ways in which men perceive women actually define women's characters.

C.T.:    When you selected Eva to tell her story, obviously in a rather incoherent fashion, did you think a character who was not bound by sane responses could tell a story of her relationship with a man, something about life in general, with greater sensitivity than a sane character?

JONES:    An ordinary sane teller might treat a particular incident as insignificant, brush over it, or compress it into a brief narrative package. The person who is psychotic, on the other hand, might spend a great deal of time on selected items. So there might be a reversal in the relative importance of the trivial and what's generally thought of as significant.

In Eva's mind, time and people become fluid. Time has little chronological sequence, and the characters seem to coalesce into one personality. It was an "irrational" process of selecting incidents to be related in the story. In this regard, there was one critic who talked about my not including incidents to round out Eva's life, to make it into less of a horror story. Those things might have happened in her lifetime, but they wouldn't, given her circumstances, have been the things she would choose to tell you.

I'm also interested in "abnormal" psychology and in the psychology of language. Abnormal psychological conditions affect sensitivity to certain things, change the proportions, affect significant events, relationships. . . .

There are some critics who can't or who don't want to separate the character's neurosis/psychosis from the author's psychological autonomy. They feel the character's preoccupations are those of the author's. I don't think this would be as true if the stories were written in the third person, and if there were some sense of the author's responding to experiences, directing how they're to be taken, or if the author wasn't also female and black. There have also been more responses to the neurotic sensuality in the books than to lesbianism. I don't recall lesbianism entering into any critical discussions except as part of the overall sexual picture.

I think the critics are responding to the absence of authorial "judgment." When I write in the first person, I like to have the sense it's just the character who's there. Judgments don't enter unless they're made by a particular character. And oftentimes that character's responses may not be what mine would be in the same situation. Also, I like to have that character as the storyteller without involving myself. It would be, perhaps, more interesting if my position were known. But there would be the same kinds of problems in terms of critics who do not want authorial intrusion. Maybe some of these problems could be avoided if, in my case, there weren't also elements of identity between the characters and myself as a black female. Critics frequently want to make certain correlations.

C.T.:    What kind of responses have you gotten from readers concerning your writing about characters who do not conform to positive images of women or black women? Do they want to castigate Eva and Ursa as some sort of representative black female?

JONES:    Yes. And even if they're not bothered by those things, they're bothered by the fact that the author doesn't offer any judgments or show her attitude toward the offense, but simply has the characters relate it. For example, Eva refuses to render her story coherently. By controlling what she will and will not tell, she maintains her autonomy. Her silences are also ways of maintaining this autonomy. I find the term "autonomy" easier to use with her than "heroism." I like the idea of a heroine, though none of my characters are. That's something I can see working with.

I like something Sterling Brown said: you can't create a significant literature with just creating "plaster of Paris saints." "Positive race images" are fine as long as they're very complex and interesting personalities. Right now I'm not sure how to reconcile the various things that interest me with "positive race images." It's important to be able to work with a range of personalities, as well as with a range within one personality. For instance, how would one reconcile an interest in neurosis or insanity with positive race image? Ernest Gaines can create complex, interesting personalities who are at the same time positive race images. But these can also be very simplistic, so too can negative ones.

C.T.:   When I read your short stories in *White Rat,* I thought about the manner in which James Baldwin tried to vindicate homosexuality. In your works, however, there is no effort to vindicate lesbianism. That it exists seems to be the only justification needed for artistic attention. Is this assessment accurate?

JONES:   Yes. Lesbianism exists, and that's the only way I include it in my work. I'll have characters respond to it positively or negatively, or sometimes the characters may simply acknowledge it as a reality.

C.T.:   Do you feel compelled to relate certain themes or just to dramatize situations?

JONES:   I mainly dramatize situations. My main interest is in characters in relationship with other characters. Theme for me now is a kind of background thing but not something I'm overly concerned with.

What comes out in my work, in those particular novels, is an emphasis on brutality. Something else is also suggested in them that will perhaps be pursued in other works, namely the alternative to brutality, which is tenderness. Although the main focus of *Corregidora* and *Eva's Man* is on the blues relationships or relationships involving brutality, there seems to be a growing understanding— working itself out especially in *Corregidora*—of what is required in order to be genuinely tender. Perhaps brutality enables one to recognize what tenderness is.

C.T.:   Do you take delight in the unusual, or does the unusual event just sort of happen?

JONES:   It's something that happens, but I'm also interested in characters who are unusual. I'm not interested in normal characters. This is related to the whole question of positive and negative images: what does a black writer do who is not interested in the normal?

C.T.:   How does it feel to know critics are dissecting your works?

JONES:   Well, my first response to interviewers and critics was difficult because of the kinds of questions I was asked. The questions seemed to have very little to do with what was for me the process of telling a story. They were curious about my personal life because I have characters who are lesbians.

It feels strange to have people dissect my stories. There's something about it I'm not sure about. I don't know what possible path my writing might have taken had there not been critics. They do make me think of my work in a more self-conscious way. As I write, I imagine how certain critics will respond to the various elements of the story, but I force myself to go ahead and say, "Well, you would ordinarily include this, so go ahead and do it." But I do have a sense of how certain people will take aspects of character, style. Also, I find myself, though not directly, but maybe dramatically responding to certain kinds of criticism, not in ways you might recognize as responses, but in terms of certain kinds of themes. I'm probably taking more notes now than I did when I first started writing. In some ways I like that better. I think some conscientiousness is always necessary when you're writing. This seems even truer now.

C.T.: What is your most recent work?

JONES: I've just finished a new novel, *Palmares*. It's about a man and woman, and it takes place in Brazil in the seventeenth century.

C.T.: Are you working on any short stories?

JONES: A few, but most of them still need a lot of work.

C.T.: Do you write them, put them down and then revise them?

JONES: Yes. There are some stories I've had for more than four or five years now. I recently revised a couple of them. That's pretty much my method. I generally keep the stories for a long time before I decide they are publishable.

C.T.: Do you want to have a reputation, a recognizable name?

JONES: The writers whom I would most like to be like are those whose works have a reputation, but the person, the writer, is more or less outside of it. I would want to maintain some kind of anonymity, like J. D. Salinger. That's the kind of reputation I'd like, where you can go on with what you're doing, but have a sense that what you do is appreciated, that there's quality to what you're doing.

# · AUDRE LORDE ·

*B*orn *in New York City in 1934 of West Indian parents, Audre Lorde received her B.A. from Hunter College and an M.L.S. from Columbia University. She left her job as head librarian of the City University of New York in 1968 to become a lecturer on creative writing, and later that same year, accepted the post of poet-in-residence at Tougaloo College in Mississippi and published her first book-length collection of poems, entitled* The First Cities.

*Describing herself as a "black lesbian feminist warrior poet," Lorde derives the impetus of her poetry's force, tone, and vision from her identity as a black woman who is both a radical feminist and an outspoken lesbian, and as a visionary of a better world. In stunning figurative language she outlines the progress of her unyielding struggle for the human rights of all people.* The First Cities *was followed in 1970 by* Cables to Rage *and* From a Land Where Other People Live *(1973);* New York Head Shop and Museum *(1974);* Coal *(1976);* Between Our Selves *(1976);* The Black Unicorn *(1978);* The Cancer Journals *(1980); and* Zami: A New Spelling of My Name *(1982).*

*Audre Lorde is currently professor of English at Hunter College in New York City, as well as a freelance writer. She lives on Staten Island with her companion and her two children.*

* * *

CLAUDIA TATE: How does your openness about being a black lesbian feminist direct your work and, more importantly, your life?

ED. NOTE: Audre Lorde had preferred that the word "black" be capitalized throughout the interview.

AUDRE LORDE:   When you narrow your definition to what is convenient, or what is fashionable, or what is expected, what happens is dishonesty by silence. It is putting all of your eggs into one basket. That's not where all of your energy comes from.

Black writers, of whatever quality, who step outside the pale of what black writers are supposed to write about, or who black writers are supposed to be, are condemned to silences in black literary circles that are as total and as destructive as any imposed by racism. This is particularly true for black women writers who have refused to be delineated by male-establishment models of femininity, and who have dealt with their sexuality as an accepted part of their identity. For instance, where are the women writers of the Harlem Renaissance being taught? Why did it take so long for Zora Neale Hurston to be reprinted?

Now, when you have a literary community oppressed by silence from the outside, as black writers are in America, and you have this kind of tacit insistence upon some unilateral definition of what "blackness" is, then you are painfully and effectively silencing some of our most dynamic and creative talents, for all change and progress from within require the recognition of differences among ourselves.

When you are a member of an out-group, and you challenge others with whom you share this outsider position to examine some aspect of their lives that distorts differences between you, then there can be a great deal of pain. In other words, when people of a group share an oppression, there are certain strengths that they build together. But there are also certain vulnerabilities. For instance, talking about racism to the women's movement results in "Huh, don't bother us with that. Look, we're all sisters, please don't rock the boat." Talking to the black community about sexism results in pretty much the same thing. You get a "Wait, wait . . . wait a minute: we're all black together. Don't rock the boat." In our work and in our living, we must recognize that difference is a reason for celebration and growth, rather than a reason for destruction.

We should see difference as a dialogue, the same way we deal with symbol and image, in literary study. "Imaging" is the process of developing a dialectic, a tension between opposites that illumi-

nates the differences and similarities between things in apparent op-
position. It is the same way with people. We need to use these differences in constructive ways, creative ways, rather than in ways to
justify our destroying each other.

With respect to myself specifically, I feel that not to be open about
any of the different "people" within my identity, particularly the
"mes" who are challenged by a status quo, is to invite myself and
other women, by my example, to live a lie. In other words, I would
be giving in to a myth of sameness which I think can destroy us.

I'm not into living lies, no matter how comfortable they may be. I
really feel that I'm too old for both abstractions and games, and I
will not shut off any of my essential sources of power, control, and
knowledge. I learned to speak the truth by accepting many parts of
myself and making them serve one another. This power fuels my life
and my work.

C.T.:   Has the social climate of the eighties suppressed the openness of the seventies?

LORDE:   To begin with, all of these things are relative, and when
we speak of the openness of the seventies, we are speaking more of
an appearance than a reality. But as far as sexuality is concerned, it
is true that in the seventies, black lesbians and gay men saw a slowly
increasing acknowledgment of their presence within the black community. In large part this came about because of the number of us
willing to speak out about our sexual identities. In the 1960s, many
black people who spoke from a complex black identity suffered because of it, and were silenced in many ways. In the mistaken belief
that unity must mean sameness, differences within the black community of color, sex, sexuality, and vision were sometimes mis-
labeled, oversimplified, and repressed. We must not romanticize the
sixties while we recognize its importance. Lesbians and gay men
have always existed in black communities, and in the sixties we
played active and important roles on many fronts in that decade's
struggle for black liberation. And that has been so throughout the
history of black people in america, and continues to be so.

In the 1970s some of those differences which have always existed
within the black community began to be articulated and examined,
as we came to learn that we, as a people, cannot afford to waste our
resources, cannot afford to waste each other. The eighties present yet

another challenge. On one hand, there is a certain move towards conservatism and greater repression within american society, and renewed attacks upon lesbians and gay men represent only the cutting edge of that greater repression which is so dangerous to us all as black people. But because of this shift to the right, some voices once willing to examine the role of difference in our communities are falling silent, some once vocal people are heading for cover.

It's very distressing to hear someone say, "I can't really afford to say that or I can't afford to be seen with you." It's scary because we've been through that before. It was called the fifties. Yet more and more these days, "all of our asses are in the sling together," if you'll excuse the expression, and real alliances are beginning to be made. When we talk about "Dykes Against Racism Everywhere," and "Black and White Men Together," which are gay groups who have been doing active antiracist work in a number of communities, when we see the coalition of black community organizations in the Boston area that got together to protest the wholesale murder of black women in 1978 and '79, we are talking about real coalitions. We must recognize that we need each other. Both these trends are operating now. Of course, I'm dedicated to believing that it's through coalitions that we'll win out. There are no more single issues.

C.T.:    Have your critics attempted to stereotype your work?

LORDE:    Critics have always wanted to cast me in a particular role from the time my first poem was published when I was fifteen years old. My English teachers at Hunter High School said that a particular poem was much too romantic. It was a love poem about my first love affair with a boy, and they didn't want to print it in the school paper, which is why I sent it to *Seventeen* magazine.

It's easier to deal with a poet, certainly with a black woman poet, when you categorize her, narrow her down so that she can fulfill your expectations, so she's socially acceptable and not too disturbing, not too discordant. I cannot be categorized. That has been both my weakness and my strength. It has been my weakness because my independence has cost me a lot of support. But you see, it has also been my strength because it has given me a vantage point and the power to go on. I don't know how I would have lived through the difficulties I have survived and continued to produce, if I had not felt that all of who I am is what fulfills me and fulfills the vision I have of the world, and of the future.

C.T.:  For whom do you write? What is your responsibility to your audience?

LORDE:   I write for myself and my children and for as many people as possible who can read me, who need to hear what I have to say—who need to use what I know. When I say myself, I mean not only the Audre who inhabits my body but all those feisty, incorrigible black women who insist on standing up and saying "*I am* and you cannot wipe me out, no matter how irritating I am, how much you fear what I might represent." I write for these women for whom a voice has not yet existed, or whose voices have been silenced. I don't have the only voice or all of their voices, but they are a part of my voice, and I am a part of theirs.

My responsibility is to speak the truth as I feel it, and to attempt to speak it with as much precision and beauty as possible. I think of my responsibility in terms of women because there are many voices for men. There are very few voices for women and particularly very few voices for black women, speaking from the center of consciousness, from the *I am* out to the *we are* and then out to the *we can.*

My mother used to say: "Island women make good wives; whatever happens they've seen worse." Well, I feel that as black women we have been through all kinds of catastrophe. We've survived, and with style.

I feel I have a duty to speak the truth as I see it and to share not just my triumphs, not just the things that felt good, but the pain, the intense, often unmitigating pain. It is important to share how I know survival is survival and not just a walk through the rain. For example, I have a duty to share what it feels like at three o'clock in the morning when you know "they" could cut you down emotionally in the street and grin in your face. And "they" are your own people. To share what it means to look into another sister's eyes and have her look away and choose someone you know she hates because it's expedient. To know that I, at times, have been a coward, or less than myself, or oppressive to other women, and to know that I can change. All of that anxiety, pain, defeat must be shared. We tend to talk about what feels good. We talk about what we think is settled. We never seem to talk about the ongoing problems. We need to share our mistakes in the same way we share our victories because that's the only way learning occurs. In other words, we have survived the pain, the problems, the failures, so what we need to do is use this suffering and learn from it. We must remember and comfort ourselves with that fact that survival is, in itself, a victory.

I never thought I would live to be forty, and I feel, "Hey, I really did it!" I am stronger for confronting the hard issue of breast cancer, of mortality, dying. It is hard, extremely hard, but very strengthening to remember I could be silent my whole life long and then be dead, flat out, and never have said or done what I wanted to do, what I needed to do because of pain or fear. . . . If I wait to be assured I'm right before I speak, I would be sending little cryptic messages on the Ouiji board, complaints from the other side.

I really feel if what I have to say is wrong, then there will be some woman who will stand up and say Audre Lorde was in error. But my words will be there, something for her to bounce off of, something to incite thought, activity.

I write not only for my peers but for those who will come after me, to say I was there, and I passed on, and you will pass on, too. But you're here now, so do it. I believe very strongly in survival and teaching. I feel that is my work.

This is so important that it bears repeating. I write for those women who do not speak, for those who do not have a voice because they/we were so terrified, because we are taught to respect fear more than ourselves. We've been taught that silence would save us, but it won't. We *must* learn to respect ourselves and our needs more than the fear of our differences, and we must learn to share ourselves with each other.

C.T.:   Is writing a way of growing, understanding?

LORDE:    Yes. I think writing and teaching, child-rearing, digging rocks (which is one of my favorite pastimes), all of the things I do are very much a part of my work. They flow in and out of each other, help to nourish each other. That's what the whole question of survival and teaching means. That we keep our experience afloat long enough, that we share what we know, so that other people can build upon our experience. There are many ways of doing that in all aspects of our lives. So teaching for me is in many respects identical to writing. Both become ways of exploring what I need for survival. They are survival techniques. Because as I write, as I teach, I am answering those questions that are primary for my own survival, and I am exploring the response to these questions with other people; this is what teaching is. I think that this is the only way that real learning occurs. Learning does not happen in some detached way of dealing with a text alone, but from becoming so involved in the process that you can see how it might illuminate your life, and then how you can share that illumination.

C.T.:   When did you start to write?

LORDE:   I looked around when I was a young woman and there was no one saying what I wanted and needed to hear. I felt totally alienated, disoriented, crazy. I thought that there's got to be somebody else who feels as I do.

I was very inarticulate as a youngster. I couldn't speak. I didn't speak until I was five, in fact, not really until I started reading and writing poetry. I used to speak in poetry. I would read poems, and I would memorize them. People would say, "Well, what do you think, Audre? What happened to you yesterday?" And I would recite a poem and somewhere in that poem there would be a line or a feeling I was sharing. In other words, I literally communicated through poetry. And when I couldn't find the poems to express the things I was feeling, that's when I started writing poetry. That was when I was twelve or thirteen.

C.T.:   Do black male and female writers dramatize characters and themes in distinctly different ways? Gayl Jones replied to this question by saying she thought one distinction has to do with the kinds of events men and women select to depict in literature. She thinks black women writers tend to select particular and personal events rather than those which are generally considered to be representative.

LORDE:   I think that's true. This reflects a difference between men and women in general. Black men have come to believe to their detriment that you have no validity unless you're "global," as opposed to personal. Yet, our *real power* comes from the personal; our real insights about living come from that deep knowledge within us that arises from our feelings. Our thoughts are shaped by our tutoring. As black people, we have not been tutored for our benefit, but more often than not, for our detriment. We were tutored to function in a structure that already existed but that does not function for our good. Our feelings are our most genuine paths to knowledge. They are chaotic, sometimes painful, sometimes contradictory, but they come from deep within us. And we must key into those feelings and begin to extrapolate from them, examine them for new ways of understanding our experiences. This is how new visions begin, how we begin to posit a future nourished by the past. This is what I mean by matter following energy, and energy following feeling. Our visions begin with our desires.

Men have been taught to deal only with what they understand. This is what they respect. They know that somewhere feeling and knowledge are important, so they keep women around to do their feeling for them, like ants do aphids.

I don't think these differences between men and women are rigidly defined with respect to gender, though the Western input has been to divide these differences into male and female *characteristics*. We all have the ability to feel deeply and to move upon our feelings and see where they lead us. Men in general have suppressed that capacity, so they keep women around to do that for them. Until men begin to develop that capacity within themselves, they will always be at a loss and will always need to victimize women.

The message I have for black men is that it is to their detriment to follow this pattern. Too many black men do precisely that, which results in violence along sexual lines. This violence terrifies me. It is a painful truth which is almost unbearable. As I say in a new poem, it is "a pain almost beyond bearing" because it gives birth to the kind of hostility that will destroy us.

C.T.:   To change the focus, though ever so slightly. Writing by black Americans has traditionally dramatized black people's humanity. Black male writers tend to cry out in rage in order to convince their readers that they too feel, whereas black women writers tend to dramatize the pain, the love. They don't seem to need to intellectualize this capacity to feel, but focus on describing the feeling itself.

LORDE:   It's one thing to talk about feeling. It's another to feel. Yes, love is often pain. But I think what is really necessary is to see how much of this pain I can use, how much of this truth I can see and still live unblinded. That is an essential question that we must all ask ourselves. There is some point at which pain becomes an end in itself, and we must let it go. On the other hand, we must not be afraid of pain, and we must not subject ourselves to pain as an end in itself. We must not celebrate victimization because there are other ways of being black.

There is a very thin but a very definite line between these two responses to pain. And I would like to see this line more carefully drawn in some of the works by black women writers. I am particularly aware of the two responses in my own work. And I find I must remember that the pain is not its own reason for being. It is a part of living. And the only kind of pain that is intolerable is pain that is wasteful, pain from which we do not learn. And I think that we must learn to distinguish between the two.

C.T.:   How do you integrate social protest and art in your work?

LORDE:   I see protest as a genuine means of encouraging someone to feel the inconsistencies, the horror of the lives we are living. Social protest is saying that we do not have to live this way. If we feel deeply, and we encourage ourselves and others to feel deeply, we will find the germ of our answers to bring about change. Because once we recognize what it is we are feeling, once we recognize we can feel deeply, love deeply, can feel joy, then we will demand that all parts of our lives produce that kind of joy. And when they do not, we will ask, "Why don't they?" And it is the asking that will lead us inevitably toward change.

So the question of social protest and art is inseparable for me. I can't say it is an either-or proposition. Art for art's sake doesn't really exist for me. What I saw was wrong, and I had to speak up. I loved poetry, and I loved words. But what was beautiful had to serve the purpose of changing my life, or I would have died. If I cannot air this pain and alter it, I will surely die of it. That's the beginning of social protest.

C.T.:   How has your work evolved in terms of interest and craft? Let's look at the love poetry, for instance, which dominated your early work [The First Cities and New York Head Shop] and which appears in The Black Unicorn.

LORDE:   Everyone has a first-love poem that comes out of that first love. Everybody has it, and it's so wonderful and new and great. But when you've been writing love poems after thirty years, the later poems are the ones that really hit the nitty gritty, that meet your boundaries. They witness what you've been through. Those are the real love poems. And I love them because they say, "Hey! We define ourselves as lovers, as people who love each other all over again; we become new again." These poems insist that you can't separate loving from fighting, from dying, from hurting, but love is triumphant. It is powerful and strong, and I feel I grow a great deal in all of my emotions, especially in the capacity to love.

C.T.:   Your love poetry seems not only to celebrate the personal experience of love but also love as a human concept, a theme embracing all of life, a theme which appears more and more emphatically in your later work. Particularly interesting, for instance, are the lesbian love poems ["Letter for Jan" and "Walking Our Boundaries"]. It didn't seem to make much difference whether the poems depicted a relationship between two women, two men, or a man and a woman. . . . The poems do not celebrate the people but the love.

LORDE:   When you love, you love. It only depends on how you do it, how committed you are, how many mistakes you make. . . . But I do believe that the love expressed between women is particular and powerful because we have had to love ourselves in order to live; love has been our means of survival. And having been in love with both men and women, I want to resist the temptation to gloss over the differences.

C.T.:   I am frequently jarred by my sometimes unconscious attempt to identify the sex of the person addressed in the poem. Since I associate the speaker's voice with you, and since I'm not always conscious that you are a lesbian, the jarring occurs when I realize the object of affection is likewise a woman. I'm certain this disturbance originates in how society defines love in terms of heterosexuality. So if we are to see love as a "universal" concept, society pressures us to see it as heterosexual.

LORDE:   Yes, we're supposed to see "universal" love as heterosexual. What I insist upon in my work is that there is no such thing as universal love in literature. There is *this* love in *this* poem. The poem happens when I, Audre Lorde, poet, deal with the particular instead of the "UNIVERSAL." My power as a person, as a poet, comes from who I am. I am a particular person. The relationships I have had, in which people kept me alive, helped sustain me, were sustained by me, were particular relationships. They help give me my particular identity, which is the source of my energy. Not to deal with my life in my art is to cut out the fount of my strength.

I love to write love poems. I love loving. And to put it into another framework, that is, other than poetry, I wrote a paper entitled "The Uses of the Erotic," where I examine the whole question of loving as a manifestation, love as a source of tremendous power. Women have been taught to suspect the erotic urge, the place that is uniquely female. So, just as we tend to reject our blackness because it has been termed inferior, as women we tend to reject our capacity for feeling, our ability to love, to touch the erotic, because it has been devalued. But it is within this that lies so much of our power, our ability to posit, our vision. Because once we know how deeply we can feel, we begin to demand from all of our life pursuits that they be in accordance with these feelings. And when they don't we must raise the question why do I feel constantly suicidal, for instance? What's wrong? Is it me, or is it what I am doing? We begin to need to answer such questions. But we cannot when we have no image of joy, no vision of what we are capable of. After the killing is over. When you live without the sunlight, you don't know what it is to relish the bright light or even to have too much of it. Once you have light, then you can measure its intensity. So too with joy.

C.T.:  Universities seem to be one major source of income for many writers, that is in terms of writer-in-residence positions. Have you had such appointments? What has been their effect?

LORDE:  I've only had one writer-in-residence position, and that was at Tougaloo College in Mississippi fourteen years ago. It was pivotal for me. Pivotal. In 1968 my first book had just been published; it was my first trip into the Deep South; it was the first time I had been away from the children; the first time I worked with young black students in a workshop situation. I came to realize that this was my work. That teaching and writing were inextricably combined, and it was there that I knew what I wanted to do for the rest of my life.

I had been "the librarian who wrote." After my experience at Tougaloo, I realized that writing was central to my life and that the library, although I loved books, was not enough. Combined with the circumstances that followed my stay at Tougaloo: King's death, Kennedy's death, Martha's accident,* all of these things really made me see that life is very short, and what we have to do must be done now.

* Lorde's close personal friend.

I have never had another writer-in-residence position. The poem "Touring" from *The Black Unicorn* represents another aspect of being a travelling cultural worker. I go and read my poetry. I drop my little seeds and then I leave. I hope they spring into something. Sometimes I find out they do; sometimes I never find out. I just have to have faith, and fun along the way.

c.t.:    Would you describe your writing process?

LORDE:    I keep a journal and write in it fairly regularly. I get a lot of my poems out of it. It's like the raw material for my poems. Sometimes I'm blessed with a poem that comes in the form of a poem, but other times I've worked for two years on a poem.

For me, there are two very basic and different processes for revising my poetry. One is recognizing that a poem has not yet become itself. In other words, I mean that the feeling, the truth that the poem is anchored in is somehow not clearly clarified inside of me, and as a result it lacks something. Then it has to be re-felt. Then there's the other process which is easier. The poem is itself, but it has rough edges that need to be refined. That kind of revision involves picking the image that is more potent or tailoring it so that it carries the feeling. That's an easier kind of rewriting and re-feeling.

My journal entries focus on things I feel: feelings that sometimes have no place, no beginning, no end; phrases I hear in passing; something that looks good to me; sometimes just observations of the world.

I went through a period once when I felt like I was dying. I wasn't writing any poetry, and I felt that if I couldn't write I would split. I was recording in my journal, but no poems came. I know now that this period was a transition in my life.

The next year, I went back to my journal, and here were these incredible poems that I could almost lift out of it. Many of them are in *The Black Unicorn*. "Harriet" is one of them; "Sequelae" and "The Litany for Survival" are others. These poems came right out of the journal. But I didn't see them as poems then.

"Power" was in the journal too. It is a poem written about Clifford Glover, the ten-year-old black boy shot by a cop who was acquitted by a jury on which a black woman sat. In fact, the day I heard on the radio that O'Shea had been acquitted, I was going across town on 88th Street [New York City] and I had to pull over. A kind of fury rose up in me—the sky turned red. I felt so sick. I felt as if I would drive the car into a wall, into the next person I saw. So I pulled over. I took out my journal just to air some of my fury, to get it out of my fingertips. Those expressed feelings are that poem. That was just how "Power" was written.

C.T.:   A transition has to occur before you can make poetry out of your journal entries.

LORDE:   There is a gap between the journal and my poetry. I write this stuff in my journal, and sometimes I cannot even read my journals because there is so much pain and rage in them. I'll put it away in a drawer, and six months, a year or so later, I'll pick up the journal, and there will be the seeds of poems. The journal entries somehow have to be assimilated into my living; only then can I deal with what I have written down.

Art is not living. It is the use of living. The artist has the ability to take the living and use it in a certain way and produce art.

C.T.:   Does Afro-American literature possess particular characteristics?

LORDE:   Afro-American literature is certainly part of an African tradition. African tradition deals with life as an experience to be lived. In many respects, it is much like the Eastern philosophies in that we see ourselves as a part of a life force; we are joined, for instance, to the air, to the earth. We are part of the whole-life process. We live in accordance with, in a kind of correspondence with the rest of the world as a whole. And therefore living becomes an experience, rather than a problem, no matter how bad or how painful it may be. Change will rise endemically from the experience fully lived and responded to.

I feel this very much in African writing. And as a consequence, I have learned a great deal from Achebe, Tutuola, Ekwensi, from Flora Nwapa and Ama Ata Aido. Leslie Lacy, a black American who lived temporarily in Ghana, writes about experiencing this transcendence in his book *The Rise and Fall of a Proper Negro.*

It's not a turning away from pain, error, but seeing these things as part of living, and learning from them. This characteristic is particularly African, and it is transposed into the best of Afro-American literature. In addition, we have the legends of our struggle and survival in the New World.

This transcendence appears in Ellison, a little bit in Baldwin. And it is present very much so in Toni Morrison's *Sula,* which is a most wonderful piece of fiction. And I don't care if she won a prize for *The Song of Solomon. Sula* is a totally incredible book. It made me light up inside like a Christmas tree. I particularly identified with the book because of the female-outsider idea. That book is one long poem. Sula is the ultimate black female of our time, trapped in her power and her pain. Alice Walker uses that quality in *The Color Purple,* another wonderful novel of living as power.

C.T.: The recent writing by many black women seems to explore human concerns somewhat differently than do the men. These women refuse to blame racism alone for every negative aspect of black life. They are examining the nature of what passes between black women and black men—the power principles. Men tend to respond defensively to the writing of black women by labeling them as the "darklings" of the literary establishment. Goodness knows, the critics, especially black male critics, had a field day with Ntozake Shange's *For Colored Girls Who Have Considered Suicide When the Rainbow is Enuf.* And they are getting started on Alice Walker's *The Color Purple.* But there are cruel black men, just as there are kind black men. Can't we try to alter that cruelty by focusing on it?

LORDE: Let me read an excerpt from a piece in *The Black Scholar* for you, which I wrote a while back:

As I have said elsewhere, it is not the destiny of black America to repeat white America's mistakes. But we will, if we mistake the trappings of success in a sick society for the signs of a meaningful life. If black men continue to do so, defining "femininity" in its archaic European terms, this augurs ill for our survival as a people, let alone our survival as individuals. Freedom and future for blacks do not mean absorbing the dominant white male disease. . . .

As black people, we cannot begin our dialogue by denying the oppressive nature of male privilege. And if black males choose to assume that privilege, for whatever reason, raping, brutalizing and killing women, then we cannot ignore black male oppression. One oppression does not justify another.*

* "Feminism and Black Liberation: The Great American Disease" by Audre Lorde, *The Black Scholar,* X, 8–9 (April 1979), p. 19.

It's infuriating. Misguided black men. And meanwhile they are killing us in the streets. Is that the nature of nationhood?

I find this divisiveness to be oppressive and very persistent. It's been going on for a long time. It didn't start with Ntozake. It's been coming more and more to the forefront now. If you ask any of the black women writers over thirty whom you're interviewing, if she's honest, she will tell you. You know there's as much a black literary mafia in this country as there is a white literary mafia. They control who gets exposure. If you don't toe the line, then you're not published; your works are not distributed. At the same time, as black women, of course, we do not want to be used against black men by a system that means both of us ill.

C.T.:   Do you think that had it not been for the women's movement black women would still be struggling to achieve their voice in the literary establishment?

LORDE:   Without a doubt. Black women writers have been around a long time, and they have suffered consistent inattention. Despite this reality, you hear from various sources that black women really have "it." We're getting jobs; we're getting this and that, supposedly. Yet we still constitute the lowest economic group in America. Meanwhile those of us who do not fit into the "establishment" have not been allowed a voice, and it was only with the advent of the women's movement—even though black women are in disagreement with many aspects of the women's movement—that black women began to demand a voice, as women and as blacks. I think any of us who are honest have to say this. As Barbara Smith says, "All the women were white and all the blacks were men, but some of us are still brave." Her book on black women's studies [*Some of Us Are Brave*], which she edited along with Gloria Hull and Patricia Bell Scott, is the first one on the subject.

C.T.:   Are you at a turning point in your career, your life?

LORDE:   I think I have deepened and broadened my understanding of the true difficulty of my work. Twenty years ago when I said we needed to understand each other I had not really perfected a consciousness concerning how important differences are in our lives. But that is a theme which recurs in my life and in my work. I have become more powerful because I have refused to settle for the myth of sorry sameness, that myth of easy sameness. My life's work continues to be survival and teaching. As I said before, teaching is also learning; teach what you need to learn. If we do this deeply, then it is most effective. I have, for example, deepened the questions that I follow, and so I have also deepened the ways I teach and learn.

The work I did on the erotic was very, very important. It opened up for me a whole area of connections in the absence of codified knowledge, or in the absence of some other clear choice. The erotic has been a real guide for me. And learning as a discipline is identical to learning how to reach through feeling the essence of how and where the erotic originates, to posit what it is based upon. This process of feeling and therefore knowing has been very, very constructive for me.

I believe in the erotic and I believe in it as an enlightening force within our lives as women. I have become clearer about the distinctions between the erotic and other apparently similar forces. We tend to think of the erotic as an easy, tantalizing sexual arousal. I speak of the erotic as the deepest life force, a force which moves us toward living in a fundamental way. And when I say living I mean it as that force which moves us toward what will accomplish real positive change.

When I speak of a future that I work for, I speak of a future in which all of us can learn, a future which we want for our children. I posit that future to be led by my visions, my dreams, and my knowledge of life. It is that knowledge which I call the erotic, and I think we must develop it within ourselves. I think so much of our living and our consciousness has been formed by death or by non-living. This is what allows us to tolerate so much of what is vile around us. When I speak of "the good," I speak of living; I speak of the erotic in all forms. They are all one. So in that sense I believe in the erotic as an illuminating principle in our lives.

C.T.:   You've just finished a new work.

LORDE:   Yes. *Zami: A New Spelling of My Name* was just published. It's a biomythography, which is really fiction. It has the elements of biography and history of myth. In other words, it's fiction built from many sources. This is one way of expanding our vision.

I'm very excited about this book. As you know, it's been a long time coming. Now that it's out, it'll do its work. Whatever its faults, whatever its glories, it's there.

You might call *Zami* a novel. I don't like to call it that. Writing *Zami* was a lifeline through the cancer experience. As I said in *The*

*Cancer Journals,* I couldn't believe that what I was fighting I would fight alone and only for myself. I couldn't believe that there wasn't something there that somebody could use at some other point because I know that I could have used some other woman's words, whatever she had to say. Just to know that someone had been there before me would have been very important, but there was nothing. Writing *The Cancer Journals* gave me the strength and power to examine that experience, to put down into words what I was feeling. It was my belief that if this work were useful to just one woman, it was worth doing.

C.T.:   What can you share with the younger generation of black women writers and writers in general?

LORDE:   Not to be afraid of difference. To be real, tough, loving. And to recognize each other. I can tell them not to be afraid to feel and not to be afraid to write about it. Even if you are afraid, do it anyway because we learn to work when we are tired, so we can learn to work when we are afraid. Silence never brought us anything. Survive and teach; that's what we've got to do and to do it with joy.

# · TONI MORRISON ·

*T*oni Morrison was born Chloe Anthony Wofford in 1931 in Lorain, Ohio. She received her B.A. from Howard University and an M.A. from Cornell. She is the mother of two and is a senior editor at Random House.

Morrison's novels are characterized by meticulously crafted prose, using ordinary words to produce lustrous, lyrical phrases and to portray precise emotional perceptions. Her extraordinary characters struggle to understand aspects of the human condition: good and evil, love, friendship, beauty, ugliness, death. While her stories seem to unfold with natural ease, the reader can discern the great care Morrison has taken in constructing them.

Her first novel, The Bluest Eye (1969), depicts the tragic life of a young black girl, Pecola Breedlove, who wants nothing more than to be loved by her family and her school friends. She surmises that the reason she is despised and ridiculed is that she is black and, therefore, ugly. Consequently, Pecola sublimates her desire to be loved into a desire to have blue eyes and blond hair; in short, to look like Shirley Temple, who is adored by all. Unable to endure the brutality toward her frail self-image, Pecola goes quietly insane and withdraws into a fantasy world in which she is the most beloved little girl because she has the bluest eye of all.

Morrison's second novel, Sula (1974), is about a marvelously unconventional woman, Sula Peace, whose life becomes one of unlimited experiment. Not bound by any social codes of propriety, Sula is first thought to be simply unusual, then outrageous, and eventually evil. She becomes a pariah of her community, a measuring stick of what's evil and, ironically, inspires goodness in those around her.

The Song of Solomon (1977) traces, in an epic way, the self-discovery of Macon Dead III. Macon or "Milkman," as he is called by his *friends, sets out on a journey to recover a lost treasure in his family's past, but instead of discovering wealth learns the intricate details of his ancestry. Milkman's odyssey becomes a kind of cultural epic by which black people can recall their often obscured slave heritage.*

*Morrison's latest novel,* Tar Baby *(1981), is about the evolution of an intimate relationship between an unlikely couple. Jade, a jet-set fashion model, falls in love with a young vagrant only to become estranged soon thereafter. He is not discouraged by their breakup but pursues her with the hope of reconciliation. Through the use of elaborate symbol, Morrison suggests that reconciliation between the black man and the black woman can only occur when they mutually understand they are both victims of racial exploitation.*

◆  ◆  ◆

CLAUDIA TATE:  How does being black and female constitute a particular perspective in your work?

TONI MORRISON:  When I view the world, perceive it and write about it, it's the world of black people. It's not that I won't write about white people. I just know that when I'm trying to develop the various themes I write about, the people who best manifest those themes for me are the black people whom I invent. It's not deliberate or calculated or self-consciously black, because I recognize and despise the artificial black writing some writers do. I feel them slumming among black people.

When I wrote *Sula,* I knew I was going to write a book about good and evil and about friendship. I had to figure out what kind of people would manifest this theme, would have this kind of relationship. Nel would be one kind of person; Sula would be different.

Friendship between women is special, different, and has never been depicted as the major focus of a novel before *Sula.* Nobody ever talked about friendship between women unless it was homosexual, and there is no homosexuality in *Sula.* Relationships between women were always written about as though they were subordinate to some other roles they're playing. This is not true of men. It seemed to me that black women have friends in the old-fashioned sense of the word; perhaps this isn't true just for black people, but it seemed so to me. I was half-way through the book before I realized that friendship in literary terms is a rather contemporary idea. So when I was making up people in *Sula,* it was inevitable I would focus on black women, not out of ignorance of any other kind of people, but because they are of compelling interest to me.

c.t.:   Do you consciously select towns like Lorain, Ohio, as settings for your stories?

MORRISON:   Only *The Bluest Eye,* my first book, is set in Lorain, Ohio. In the others I was more interested in mood than in geography. I am from the Midwest so I have a special affection for it. My beginnings are always there. No matter what I write, I begin there. I may abandon this focus at some point, but for now it's the matrix for me.

Black people take their culture wherever they go. If I wrote about Maine, the black people in Maine would be very much like black people in Ohio. You can change the plate, but the menu would still be the same. The barber shop in Maine would still be the same kind of barber shop as in Ohio; there would be the same kinds of people sitting around. They cook a little bit differently, but I know what the language will be like.

c.t.:   Ohio is an interesting and complex state. It has both a southern and a northern disposition. The Ohio River has historically represented freedom. Therefore, the state seems to be especially well suited for staging leaps in *The Song of Solomon* and free falls in *Sula* into freedom.

MORRISON:   Yes. The northern part of the state had underground railroad stations and a history of black people escaping into Canada, but the southern part of the state is as much Kentucky as there is, complete with cross burnings. Ohio is a curious juxtaposition of what was ideal in this country and what was base. It was also a Mecca for black people; they came to the mills and plants because Ohio offered the possibility of a good life, the possibility of freedom, even though there were some terrible obstacles. Ohio also offers an escape from stereotyped black settings. It is neither plantation nor ghetto.

c.t.:   How do you fit writing into your life?

MORRISON:   Time has never really been a problem for me. I don't do much. I don't go out. I don't entertain. And I get off the telephone. Those activities demand an enormous part of what people call time. In addition, I can do two things at once. Most of the things I do, I know how to do so I don't have to concentrate on them, give them my full attention. And they don't suffer as a consequence. There's very little one does that engages the full mind for a long period of time. In a sense we all produce time. But when we compartmentalize our lives, then we complain about time. We say this is the time we do this; this is the time we do that. Then we feel we have to do things in some sort of sequence.

Writing is a process that goes on all the time. I can find myself in any place, solving some problem in the work that I am at the moment working on. I don't have to summon it. It's just a way of life, so there's never a time when I'm writing a book when it's not on my mind. I live with it. But there are times when I have to sit down and write. The difficulty comes in not having sustained periods of time—four or five hours at a clip. I have more of that now, but the trick is to get to where I want to be very fast in the writing so I can avoid three hours of frustrating, clumsy writing. . . . I have done a lot if I produce six pages during such times.

C.T.:    Do you employ particular methods to summon your muse?

MORRISON:    When I sit down in order to write, sometimes it's there; sometimes it's not. But that doesn't bother me anymore. I tell my students there is such a thing as "writer's block," and they should respect it. You shouldn't write through it. It's blocked because it ought to be blocked, because you haven't got it right now. All the frustration and nuttiness that comes from "Oh, my God, I cannot write now" should be displaced. It's just a message to you saying, "That's right, you can't write now, so don't." We operate with deadlines, so facing the anxiety about the block has become a way of life. We get frightened about the fear. I can't write like that. If I don't have anything to say for three or four months, I just don't write. When I read a book, I can always tell if the writer has written through a block. If he or she had just waited, it would have been better or different, or a little more natural. You can see the seams.

I always know the story when I'm working on a book. That's not difficult. Anybody can think up a story. But trying to breathe life into characters, allow them space, make them people whom I care about is hard. I only have twenty-six letters of the alphabet; I don't have color or music. I must use my craft to make the reader see the colors and hear the sounds.

My stories come to me as clichés. A cliché is a cliché because it's worthwhile. Otherwise, it would have been discarded. A good cliché can never be overwritten; it's still mysterious. The concepts of beauty and ugliness are mysterious to me. Many people write about them. In mulling over them, I try to get underneath them and see what they mean, understand the impact they have on what people do. I also write about love and death. The problem I face as a writer is to make my stories mean something. You can have wonderful, interesting people, a fascinating story, but it's not about anything. It has no real substance. I can fail in any number of ways when I write, but I want my books to always be about something that is important to me, and the subjects that are important in the world are the same ones that have always been important.

Critics generally don't associate black people with ideas. They see marginal people; they just see another story about black folks. They regard the whole thing as sociologically interesting perhaps but very parochial. There's a notion out in the land that there are human beings one writes about, and then there are black people or Indians or some other marginal group. If you write about the world from that point of view, somehow it is considered lesser. It's racist, of course. The fact that I chose to write about black people means I've only been stimulated to write about black people. We are people, not aliens. We live, we love, and we die.

A woman wrote a book on women writers, and she has an apology in the preface in which she explains why the book doesn't include any black women writers. She says she doesn't feel qualified to criticize their work. I think that's dishonest scholarship. I may be wrong but I think so, and I took the trouble to tell her that. I feel perfectly qualified to discuss Emily Dickinson, anybody for that matter, because I assume what Jane Austen and all those people have to say has something to do with life and being human in the world. Why she could not figure out that the preoccupation of black characters is this as well startled me, as though our lives are so exotic that the differences are incomprehensible.

Insensitive white people cannot deal with black writing, but then they cannot deal with their own literature either. It's not a question of my not liking white criticism. I don't like most black criticism either. Most criticism by blacks only respond to the impetus of the criticism we were all taught in college. It justifies itself by identifying black writers with some already accepted white writer. If someone says I write like Joyce, that's giving me a kind of credibility I find offensive. It has nothing to do with my liking Joyce. I do, but the comparison has to do with nothing out of which I write. I find such criticism dishonest because it never goes into the work on its own terms. It comes from some other place and finds content outside of the work and wholly irrelevant to it to support the work. You can hear them talking to Northrop Frye, and you can hear his response. You can also hear a novelist talking to *The New York Times* and not to me, the anonymous reader. The criticism may read well, in fact very well, but it's not about the book at hand. It's merely trying to place the book into an already established literary tradition. The critic is too frightened or too uninformed to break new ground.

C.T.:   What is your responsibility as a writer to yourself and to your audience?

MORRISON:   I wrote *Sula* and *The Bluest Eye* because they were books I had wanted to read. No one had written them yet, so I wrote them. My audience is always the people in the book I'm writing at the time. I don't think of an external audience. You can see it when a writer is writing deliberately to educate an audience. You can feel the artifice, not the art, when the writer is getting somebody told.

C.T.:   Do black men and women approach subjects differently in their works?

MORRISON:   I think women probably do write out of a different place. There's some difference in the ways they approach conflict, dominion, and power. I don't find the large differences between male and female writing in terms of intimacy though. But I do think black women write differently from white women. This is the most marked difference of all those combinations of black and white, male and female. It's not so much that women write differently from men, but that black women write differently from white women. Black men don't write very differently from white men.

It seems to me there's an enormous difference in the writing of black and white women. Aggression is not as new to black women as it is to white women. Black women seem able to combine the nest and the adventure. They don't see conflicts in certain areas as do white women. They are both safe harbor and ship; they are both inn and trail. We, black women, do both. We don't find these places, these roles, mutually exclusive. That's one of the differences. White women often find if they leave their husbands and go out into the world, it's an extraordinary event. If they've settled for the benefits of housewifery that preclude a career, then it's marriage *or* a career for them, not both, not *and*.

It would be interesting to do a piece on the kinds of work women do in novels written by women. What kinds of jobs they do, not just the paying jobs, but how they perceive work. When white women characters get depressed about the dishes, what do they do? It's not just a question of being in the labor force and doing domestic kinds of things; it's about how one perceives work, how it fits into one's life.

There's a male/female thing that's also different in the works of black and white women writers, and this difference is good. There's a special kind of domestic perception that has its own violence in writings by black women—not bloody violence, but violence nonetheless. Love, in the Western notion, is full of possession, distortion, and corruption. It's a slaughter without the blood.

Men always want to change things, and women probably don't. I don't think it has much to do with women's powerlessness. Change could be death. You don't have to change everything. Some things should be just the way they are. Change in itself is not so important. But men see it as important. Under the guise of change and love, you destroy all sorts of things: each other, children. You move things around and put them in special places. I remember when I was in elementary school, there were all sorts of people in my class: the mentally defective, the handicapped, and us. To improve that situation, the school removed all those people and put them into special classes. Perhaps they were better cared for, but they were not among us. There's an enormous amount a sighted child can learn from a blind child; but when you separate them, their learning becomes deficient. That kind of change is masculine. Women don't tend to do this. It's all done under the guise of civilization to improve things. The impetus for this kind of change is not hatred; it is doing good works.

Black people have a way of allowing things to go on the way they're going. We're not too terrified of death, not too terrified of being different, not too upset about divisions among things, people. Our interests have always been, it seems to me, on how un-alike things are rather than how alike things are. Black people always see differences before they see similarities, which means they probably cannot lump people into groups as quickly as other kinds of people can. They don't tend to say all Polish people are such and such. They look at one person in order to see what he or she is like.

So-called primitive languages always emphasize differences. You have hundreds of words for yam, but no one word for yam—hundreds of words for every variety. That's not a deficiency in the thought process; it reflects an emphasis on distinctions. It may account for why black people, generally speaking, used to have such difficulty thinking in purely racist terms.

C.T.:   In *The Bluest Eye* and *Sula* there are evocative, lyrical, verbal compression and expansion. In *The Song of Solomon* there is a linear progression of language, a sense of intrigue with subsequent resolution. Does the selection of a hero as compared to a heroine place demands on the quality of your expression?

MORRISON:    The first two books were beginnings. I start with the childhood of a person in all the books; but in the first two, the movement, the rhythm is circular, although the circles are broken. If you go back to the beginnings, you get pushed along toward the end. This is particularly so with *The Bluest Eye*. *Sula* is more spiral than circular. *The Song of Solomon* is different. I was trying to push this novel outward; its movement is neither circular nor spiral. The image in my mind for it is that of a train picking up speed; and that image informs the language; whereas with *The Bluest Eye* and *Sula*, the rhythm is very different.

Every life to me has a rhythm, a shape—there are dips and curves as well as straightaways. You can't see the contours all at once. Some very small incident that takes place today may be *the* most important event that happens to you this year, but you don't know that when it happens. You don't know it until much later. I try to reflect this awareness in my work. In a chapter I may talk about what has already happened so the reader knows what I'm about to say has already taken place, but he or she is moving toward something they don't know yet. The best illustration is in the chapter in *Sula* where Hannah accidentally catches on fire. It starts out with what the second strange thing was, then recalls the first strange thing, so you know to expect something. A black person in particular would know, if I'm going to list strange things, to expect something dreadful. These things are omens. If I'm talking about death, you should know to expect it because the omens alert you. The strange things are all omens; you don't know what's going to happen at the time the omens occur, and you don't always recognize an omen until after the fact, but when the bad thing does happen, you somehow expected it. As the reader, you can take comfort in knowing whatever it is has already happened so you don't have to be too frightened. The author has already experienced it. It's happened; it's over. You're going to find out about it, but it's not going to be a big surprise, even though it might be awful. I may hurt you, but I don't want to tear the rug out from under you. I don't want to give you total surprise. I just want you to feel dread and to feel the awfulness without having the language compete with the event itself. I may want to hold you in a comfortable place, but I want you to know something awful is going to happen, and when it does happen you won't be shattered. When it happens, you expect it, though you did not before.

The language has to be quiet; it has to engage your participation. I never describe characters very much. My writing expects, demands participatory reading, and that I think is what literature is supposed to do. It's not just about telling the story; it's about involving the reader. The reader supplies the emotions. The reader supplies even some of the color, some of the sound. My language has to have holes and spaces so the reader can come into it. He or she can feel something visceral, see something striking. Then we [you, the reader, and I, the author] come together to make this book, to feel this experience. It doesn't matter what happens. I tell you at the beginning of *The Bluest Eye* on the very first page what happened, but now I want you to go with me and look at this, so when you get to the scene where the father rapes the daughter, which is as awful a thing, I suppose, as can be imagined, by the time you get there, it's almost irrelevant because I want you to *look* at him and see his love for his daughter and his powerlessness to help her pain. By that time his embrace, the rape, is all the gift he has left.

C.T.:   Cholly [*The Bluest Eye*], Ajax [*Sula*], and Guitar [*The Song of Solomon*] are the golden-eyed heroes. Even Sula has gold flecks in her eyes. They are the free people, the dangerously free people.

MORRISON:   The salt tasters. . . . They express either an effort of the will or a freedom of the will. It's all about choosing. Though granted there's an enormous amount of stuff one cannot choose. But if you own yourself, you can make some types of choices, take certain kinds of risks. They do, and they're misunderstood. They are the misunderstood people in the world. There's a wildness that they have, a nice wildness. It has bad effects in society such as the one in which we live. It's pre-Christ in the best sense. It's Eve. When I see this wildness gone in a person, it's sad. This special lack of restraint, which is a part of human life and is best typified in certain black males, is of particular interest to me. It's in black men despite the reasons society says they're not supposed to have it. Everybody knows who "that man" is, and they may give him bad names and call him a "street nigger"; but when you take away the vocabulary of denigration, what you have is somebody who is fearless and who is comfortable with that fearlessness. It's not about meanness. It's a kind of self-flagellant resistance to certain kinds of control, which is fascinating. Opposed to accepted notions of progress, the lock-step life, they live in the world unreconstructed and that's it.

C.T.:  Your writing seems effortless. Of course, I know tremendous work is concealed behind effortless writing. No seams show. The garment has marvelous images. Everyday details become extraordinary when flashed through your perception, your craft.

MORRISON:  I try to clean the language up and give words back their original meaning, not the one that's sabotaged by constant use, so that "chaste" means what it meant originally. I try to do that by constructing sentences that throw such words into relief, but not strange words, not "large" words. Most large words are imprecise. They are useful because of their imprecision. If you work very carefully, you can clean up ordinary words and repolish them, make parabolic language seem alive again.

Dialogue done properly can be heard. Somebody in London told me I seldom used adverbs in my dialogue, that I never have a character say such-and-such *loudly*. But that he always knew how something is said. When I do a first draft, it's usually very bad because my tendency is to write in the language of everyday speech, which is the language of business, media, the language we use to get through the day. If you have friends you can speak to in your own language, you keep the vocabulary alive, the nuances, the complexity, the places where language had its original power; but in order to get there, I have to rewrite, discard, and remove the print-quality of language to put back the oral quality, where intonation, volume, gesture are all there. Furthermore, the characters have to speak their own language. Novice writers, even when they get a good dialogue style, frequently have everybody talking the same way. If they didn't identify the speaker, the reader wouldn't know. You've got to be able to distinguish among your characters. Sula doesn't use the same language Eva does because they perceive things differently. If the reader feels he or she can visualize a character, in spite of the fact no one has said what the character looks like, that's it! All I have to do as a writer is *know* it in my mind. I don't have to write every piece of it. I give a few clues, some gestures . . .

I try to avoid editorializing emotional abstractions. I can't bear to read any more of those books where there is this hopeless, labored explanation of a simple thing. If you can see the person experiencing the thing, you don't need the explanation. When Eva looks at the back of the man who abandoned her, she doesn't know how she's going to feel. It all comes together when he diddy-bops down the steps, and she hears the laughter of the woman in the green dress. Her emotional clarity crystalizes at that moment. When you think of how it feels to see a man who has abandoned you, to see him after a long period of time, you can go a number of ways to convey it. You could use a lot of rhetoric, but you don't need to do any of that if you simply see it. You see a person who *is* a simile, a metaphor, a painting. A painting conveys it better because then the reader can identify with that feeling, whether or not he or she has ever experienced it. They can feel it because they see the things that person sees. It's a question of how to project character, experience from that viewpoint.

I don't use much autobiography in my writing. My life is uneventful. Writing has to do with the imagination. It's being willing to open a door or think the unthinkable, no matter how silly it may appear. When Pilate [*The Song of Solomon*] appeared without a navel, that didn't seem to make much sense to me either, so I did some casual research. Of course, everybody told me it couldn't happen because it was absurd, impossible. Just because I didn't know where I was going with it didn't stop me from seeing what use it could be to me in terms of developing the character. The fact that I thought of it at all was of interest to me. If I thought about it, it may be valuable. There are a lot of things I think about that are not valuable, but I don't discard them just because they don't "make sense." It's like the tail end of a dream. You wake up and you remember a few little pieces. Those are the pieces you can concentrate on, just the ones you remember. You don't have to worry about the part you can't remember. If the woman doesn't have a navel, then I have to think what that could mean, not just in terms of her development, her life, but in terms of the whole book. I didn't try to think of some strange thing. I was trying to draw the character of a sister to a man, a sister who was different, and part of my visualization of her included that she had no navel. Then it became an enormous thing for her. It also had to come at the beginning of the book so the reader would know to expect anything of her. It had to be a thing that was very powerful in its absence but of no consequence in its presence. It couldn't be anything grotesque, but something to set her apart, to make her literally invent herself. Of course, it has tremendous symbolic ramifications, but that wasn't uppermost in my mind. What I thought was what would happen if a person was not to have a navel, then other things became clearer.

c.t.:    When did you know you were a writer?

MORRISON:    After I had written *Sula*. I've said I wrote *The Bluest Eye* after a period of depression, but the words "lonely, depressed, melancholy" don't really mean the obvious. They simply represent a different state. It's an unbusy state, when I am more aware of myself than of others. The best words for making that state clear to other people are those words. It's not necessarily an unhappy feeling; it's just a different one. I think now I know better what that state is. Sometimes when I'm in mourning, for example, after my father died, there's a period when I'm not fighting day-to-day battles, a period when I can't fight or don't fight, and I am very passive, like a vessel. When I'm in this state, I can hear things. As long as I'm busy doing what I should be doing, what I'm supposed to be doing, what I must do, I don't hear anything; there isn't anything there. This sensibility occurred when I was lonely or depressed or melancholy or idle or emotionally exhausted. I would think I was at my nadir, but it was then that I was in a position to hear something. Ideas can't come to me while I'm preoccupied. This is what I meant when I said I was in a state that was not busy, not productive or engaged. It happened after my father died, thus the association with depression. It happened after my divorce. It has happened other times, but not so much because I was unhappy or happy. It was that I was unengaged, and in that situation of disengagement with the day-to-day rush, something positive happened. I've never had sense enough to deliberately put myself in a situation like that before. At that time I had to be put into it. Now I know how to bring it about without going through the actual event. It's exactly what Guitar said: when you release all the shit, then you can fly.

c.t.:   Do you take particular delight in the unusual character, the pariah?

MORRISON:   There are several levels of the pariah figure working in my writing. The black community is a pariah community. Black people are pariahs. The civilization of black people that lives apart from but in juxtaposition to other civilizations is a pariah relationship. In fact, the concept of the black in this country is almost always one of the pariah. But a community contains pariahs within it that are very useful for the conscience of that community.

When I was writing about good and evil, I really wasn't writing about them in Western terms. It was interesting to me that black people at one time seemed not to respond to evil in the ways other people did, but that they thought evil had a natural place in the universe; they did not wish to eradicate it. They just wished to protect themselves from it, maybe even to manipulate it, but they never wanted to kill it. They thought evil was just another aspect of life. The ways black people dealt with evil accounted in my mind for how they responded to a lot of other things. It's like a double-edged sword. It accounts for one of the reasons it's difficult for them to organize long-term political wars against another people. It accounts for their generosity and acceptance of all sorts of things. It's because they're not terrified by evil, by difference. Evil is not an alien force; it's just a different force. That's the evil I was describing in *Sula*.

Even when I'm talking about universal concepts, I try to see how people, such as myself, would look at these universal concepts, how they would respond to them. Our cosmology may be a little different, as each group's is, so what I want to figure out is how ours is different. How is our concept of evil unlike other peoples'? How is our rearing of children different? How are our pariahs different? A legal outlaw is not the same thing as a community outlaw. That's why I have the Deweys, Shadrack and Sula; they are all variations of the pariah. The town can accept Shadrack much easier than Sula because he's systematized. They know what to expect from him.

A woman who wrote a paper on *Sula* said she thought Sula's community was very unnurturing for her. That's very strange to me because I found that community to be very nurturing for Sula. There was no other place in the world she could have lived without being harmed. Whatever they think about Sula, however strange she is to them, however different, they won't harm her. Medallion is a sustaining environment even for a woman who is very different. Nobody's going to lynch her or call the police. They call her bad names and try to protect themselves from her evil; that's all. But they put her to very good use, which is a way of manipulating her.

C.T.:   Have your works been misunderstood?

MORRISON:   Of course. That's all quite legitimate. Some people get things in your work you never saw. But that's all right. After all, one reads and gets what one can. Sometimes people talk about the work in a way that is closer to my own feeling, interpretation. I don't know if they're any more right than the people who see it another way. I'm sometimes disappointed that something I think is key is missed, but that's a writer's ego surfacing at that point. I always assume that if it didn't impress the reader, that it has something to do with the writing and not with the person reading it. It's my job to make it clearer, to make it dazzling. If it didn't happen, then I was too timid, too subtle, too clumsy—something was wrong. To make it happen is my job, not the reader's.

C.T.:   Do you talk about your books before they're finished?

MORRISON:   I talk about the little I know, which is always a little risky because I might change my mind or it might change itself. I write out of ignorance. I write about the things I don't have any resolutions for, and when I'm finished, I think I know a little bit more about it. I don't write out of what I know. It's what I don't know that stimulates me. I merely know enough to get started. Writing is discovery; it's talking deep within myself, "deep talking" as you say. The publishing is rather anticlimatic, although I'm in the publishing business. I know all the wonderful things that are made possible by publishing something; but for me, on a very personal level, the publishing is really very secondary.

My students ask me when I'm going to make my books into movies. I tell them I'm not terribly interested in that because the film would not be mine. The book is my work. I don't want to write scripts; I don't want artistic "control" of a film. I don't mean that it shouldn't be done, just that I don't have to do it. What's alarming to me is the notion that the book is what you do before the film, that the final outcome is the film.

There's a difference between writing for a living and writing for life. If you write for a living, you make enormous compromises, and you might not ever be able to uncompromise yourself. If you write for life, you'll work hard; you'll do it in a disciplined fashion; you'll do what's honest, not what pays. You'll be willing to say no when somebody wants to play games with your work. You'll be willing to not sell it. You'll have a very strong sense of your work, your self-development.

c.t.:    What has been the cost of success for you?

morrison:    I don't subscribe to the definition of success I think you're talking about. For me, whatever the cost is, I don't pay it. Success in those terms is a substitute for value in your life. When you say a successful life, you generally mean a life surrounded by material things. I continue to live my life pretty much as I always have, except I may live a little better now because I can make some choices I wasn't able to before. Having more money than I had a few years ago makes it possible for me to have choices and, therefore, make them. But in terms of meaningful things, relationships with other people, none of that has changed. What changes is not always the successful person; other people change.

c.t.:    How do you feel when you've finished a book?

morrison:    I feel something's missing. I miss the characters, their company, the sense of possibility in them. But then I have another idea.

Some people work on several books at one time. I can never do that. So if one's not there, I feel a little lonely, as though I've lost touch, though momentarily, with some collective memory. But each time the waiting period between ideas for books grows shorter and shorter, for which I am grateful.

# ·SONIA SANCHEZ·

*F*or Sonia Sanchez the black consciousness of the sixties is not
something of the past, but continues to play a part in her political
and social participation. Born in 1934 in Birmingham, Alabama, Sanchez attended Hunter College in New York City, receiving a B.A. in
1955. She was first an educator, then became involved with the black
studies movement at San Francisco State College in 1966, which
evolved into a life-long commitment and is a source of her creativity.
She has also assisted in the development of black studies curricula and
has taught black literature and creative writing at several colleges and
universities, including the University of Pittsburgh, Rutgers University
in New Brunswick, New Jersey, Manhattan Community College, and
Amherst College.

Sanchez has a prolific publishing career. Her collections of poems
include: Homecoming *(1969);* We A Baddddd People *(1970);* It's A
New Day: Poems for Young Brothas and Sisthus *(1971);* Love
Poems *(1973);* A Blues Book for Blue Black Magical Women
*(1973); and* I've Been A Woman *(1978). Her stories for children are*
The Adventures of Small Head, Square Head and Fathead *(1973)
and* A Sound Investment and Other Stories *(1980). In addition to
contributing poetry to numerous publications, Sanchez is the editor of
two anthologies,* Three Hundred and Sixty Degrees of Blackness
Comin' at You *(1971) and* We Be Word Sorcerers: 25 Stories by
Black Americans *(1973). She is also a playwright, and is currently
working on a novel,* After Saturday Night Comes Sunday, *which is
evolved from a short story of the same name. She teaches at Temple
University in Philadelphia.*

◆  ◆  ◆

CLAUDIA TATE:    What's happened to the revolutionary fervor of the sixties and seventies?

SONIA SANCHEZ:    I think it's a misconception when people talk about the 1960s and say that the fervor has died down. What people fail to understand is that it has not died down of its own accord but that the country, through the FBI and CIA, began to move against the 1960s' so-called revolution. It took twelve to thirteen years of systematic plotting but the disintegration was pretty much accomplished. This is very serious. What these groups did in Chile and Cuba, for instance, they did here to blacks in this country. This must be understood. The militants of the sixties were not just a bunch of people jumping up saying that they were BAD. They constituted a black social force.

When this country looked up and saw this force coming toward it, it retreated for a while. Of course, it opened up more universities to more blacks in the north, opened up jobs to black professors, opened up the whole area of education in terms of black Ph.Ds, and then waited. Certain people were placed in certain positions; certain people were given more money, positions of power, whatever. Then you began to see other things happening. The country systematically brought in more dope and systematically began to give us something called "disco madness." I'm talking about systematic destruction of the revolutionary thrust through manipulation and infiltration, through death, through dope, through jailing people.

These tactics also resurrected a new kind of writer, and people must understand this. If America says she cannot control this kind of writer, then she must give alternatives to him or her. And so many of us had alternatives made to us. Certain themes were rewarded; others were ignored. And since writers want recognition, many would not talk directly about social change; they would not necessarily talk about what America had done, but would turn inward and begin to talk about victimization. This is especially true of some black women writers. So we get an onslaught of young black women writers who see themselves as victims. The problem with that is that if you see yourself as a victim in a one-to-one relationship, then it's very difficult for you to see yourself getting out from under the yoke of something called America, imperialism, capitalism, racism, or sexism. If you cannot remove yourself from the oppression of a man, how in the hell are you going to remove yourself from the oppression of a country?

This focus on victimization is deliberate, you see. Therefore, we begin to see people who will say, "Yeah, that no-good nigger did this to me, and I can't do anything about it. Or all I can do about it is sit down and talk to you or write about it." He did this to me, he did that to me; but you don't move on it. Or if you move on it, the movement is in discussion. The movement is verbal in that you just lash out at what he did, but you don't focus on *why*. You don't ask why this has happened to us in this country. Why there is this distance that exists between black men and black women. These writers generally do not focus on what has happened to black people in terms of slavery in America; neither do they talk about the kinds of things that are happening to us now as black men and black women in this country. What results is that you have no one to blame; so you begin to turn it back in on yourself.

When I teach writing I get a lot of young women who come in with "victimization" poetry. And immediately I begin to talk about it as "woman-as victim" poetry. I insist that I won't see myself as a victim. That's not to say I've never had, or won't have, a bad relationship with a man. But it is to say I've never seen myself as a victim in a bad relationship, nor do I intend to. If I tried to make the relationship work, and it didn't, you know that I went through all kinds of changes. But I moved on, because I have children; I moved on because I have myself. People tend to lose sight of themselves in a bad relationship. But they must not do this. They must see what must be done, and they must move on it because it's beyond their power to change the situation.

In time, probably in my children's time, we must move past always focusing on the "personal self" because there's a larger self. There's a "self" of black people. And many of us will have to make a sacrifice in our lives to ensure that our bigger self continues. Seriously, there is a danger that we might not continue as a people in this country. If we're not careful, the animosity between black men and women will destroy us.

Moving on. Check out the literacy rates of young black people in high school. You don't survive, if you cannot read. You might as well just have black bodies there tuned in to the television and radio. Watch the young men and women who walk down the streets with radios stuck in their ears, and you know what I'm saying. The bodies will be there, but we'll not have the kind of people for whom our ancestors fought. Our ancestors fought for us to be literate, educated, self-sustaining people who have a future. And there's no future for a group of people glued to a radio.

When I teach literature, I try to make my students understand that the sixties as a literary period is not removed from that which produced the slave narratives. I am not removed from Sterling Brown or Gwen Brooks or Phillis Wheatley. People have said that many of the 1960s writers thought they were utterly important, but I've always taught that they are because we are all part of a tradition of black writers.

So, therefore, I am concerned about young black women who write "victimization" poetry. I'm concerned because other writers will follow them, and they must not be programmed for defeat and victimization.

The writers who celebrate victimization are the writers who get all the publicity. They don't have to struggle. This country systematically chooses people who will make it! And I think that's what we must talk about. We don't seem to understand this. If you say nothing else of what I've said, you must say this, that people don't fully understand the importance of the 1960s. If you go outside America, you understand that what's happening in South Africa is a reflection of the sixties in America. What's happening in the Caribbean is a result of what happened in the 1960s. So what happens in this country is *key*. America understands this perfectly. What happens in this country in terms of its writers will affect the rest of the black world that's waiting. So what happens is that America elevates those writers who will not take political positions. It's happened before. What happened in the sixties is not new. Some years ago I did research on what happened to the Marcus Garvey movement in the twenties. The destruction of that organization reveals the same pattern we've witnessed with the so-called Black Revolution: systematic discreditation and infiltration. The black artist is dangerous. Black art controls the "Negro's" reality, negates negative influences, and creates positive images.

C.T.:    What did, in fact, happen to the writers of the sixties who would not be controlled?

SANCHEZ:    I can't speak for what happened to other writers. I can only speak for myself. The country said that I would not survive; that's what it said to me. While I helped to organize the black studies program at San Francisco State, the FBI came to my landlord and said put her out. She's one of those radicals. I then went on to Pittsburg to help with that black studies program. I stayed there a year and came home and taught at Rutgers for a year. Rutgers had a serious problem. People were just walking in off the street on hard drugs. As a result, hell was let loose on that campus. Some of us were threatened by people who were dealing drugs—veiled threats. So I resigned. Well, I intended to return, but then I thought about the threats. I had no protection. So I just decided to leave it be and move away. Then I taught at Manhattan Community College in New York City, and I stayed there until my record was picked up. You know how you have your record on file, and you can go down and look at it. Well, I went down to look at it, because we had had a strike there, and I had been arrested with my students. I went to the dean to ask for my record, and he told me that I could not have my record because it was sent downtown. That's when I began to realize just how much the government was involved with teachers in the university. I then tried to get another job in New York City—no job. I had been white-balled. The word was out, I was too political. Sonia Sanchez was too political; do not hire her. So institutions would hire people who barely had a degree and who had no experience. People were teaching writing courses who didn't even have a book. I went to a place called Amherst, Massachusetts. That's how I ended up at Amherst College, because I couldn't get a job in my home state. That's what they do to you. If they can't control what you write, they make alternatives for you and send you to places where you have no constituency.

The chosen people are nurtured very carefully and given direct exposure. The media forces will say, "Hey, you really don't need to hear Sonia Sanchez. We have so-and-so who's even more militant!" It's more than just about "militancy." What it is, and I try to teach this to my students wherever they be, is about the total you. We're talking about how you not only see yourself and your work, but how you see the country and the world, and how you fit into those contexts. Many of us are blessed to be privy to the collective unconsciousness of one's people which resides in the world. We get information from it: poems, stories, novels. . . . And we give something back. There's nothing new under the sun. The same ideas have been here before; another generation will pick up on what has already been said and put it in new terms. We have, as writers, a responsibility to use that information to change injustice.

The first time I stood on a stage and said, "We are an oppressed people," some people in the audience got up and left. Because blacks didn't see themselves in the early sixties as an oppressed, enslaved people. They had cars, clothes, stereos. . . . But the majority of black people in America don't have houses; they are enslaved. There are a few of what I'd call "exceptional niggers." That's not a negative comment. We are in a sense "exceptional niggers," you and I. But I don't make money to acquire a big bank account. When I work, it means that a couple of other people I know who also don't necessarily work regularly, can live. That's what I owe. I owe my ancestors this. Therefore, I don't have any money in my bank account; my money is put into real things.

C.T.:   What's happened to black studies programs across the country?

SANCHEZ:   Many have closed down. They were established because of this great black social force that said, "How can you have a university and not have courses on black people and no black professors?" This assertion was fought, which tells you how threatening something called "black studies" *could be.* It's not necessarily threatening as it's generally taught. Some of the programs had some very important people in them; others didn't give a damn. Some of the programs became elitist and cut themselves off entirely from the community. They brought in people who said, "I am a scholar, so therefore I have nothing to do with the masses." They brought in people who deliberately antagonized black students. When I say "they" I don't necessarily mean the black people in the programs because very few programs were in fact controlled by black people. They were not the source of power, so they couldn't say who was to be hired or fired. They didn't have any power to keep the programs true to the ideals of black studies. So, when some people came in who just wanted jobs because they couldn't enter through the history department, for example, and when the programs had no power to exercise control, havoc was let loose. The universities knew what was happening and very often the administrations just sat back and let the "niggers" kill each other.

C.T.:   How does being black, female, and a one-time member
of the Nation of Islam constitute a particular perspective in your
work?

SANCHEZ:   I wrote as a child. When I first started to write, I stuttered. Always at the core of my being was the realization that I was
black, not that I knew I was oppressed, but that I knew I was black. I
might have said "Negro" years ago. I knew something was wrong,
but I didn't know the terminology to explain it or what to do about
it. I was in Alabama then. There were simple things, like going to a
house where my grandmother worked, and we were in the kitchen
and heard the way she was talked to. But I could not verbalize my
feeling. When we went into elevators in stores, white people always
wanted to touch us and say, "Aren't they some nice little children." I
would always draw back because I knew something was wrong, but
my stepmother allowed this to happen, and I was always very angry
about that. Because I knew they had no business touching me. I
somehow knew that because she was black, she let that happen. I remember asking my stepmother four times why she couldn't try on a
hat she wanted to buy, and each time I didn't get an answer. That I
remember.

I also remember an aunt who spat in a bus driver's face—that was
the subject of one of my first poems—because he wanted her to get
off as the bus was filling up with white people. In the South black
people sat in the back half of the bus when it wasn't crowded. As it
got crowded the bus driver would move them back. And when it got
even more crowded whites would sit on the back seats and blacks
would stand. But when it really got very crowded they would ask
blacks to get the hell off the bus. Well, my aunt would not get off the
bus, so she spat, and was arrested. That was the first visual instance I
can remember of encountering racism.

Coming north to Harlem for "freedom" when I was nine presented me with a whole new racial landscape. Here was the realization of the cornerstore, where I watched white men pinch black
women on their behinds. And I made a vow that nobody would ever
do that to me unless I wanted him to. I continued to live in the
neighborhood, went to that store as a nine-year-old child, and continued to go there as a student at Hunter College. When I was sixteen to eighteen they attempted to pinch my behind. I turned

around and said, "Oh no you don't." They knew I was serious. I can't say that this was ever discussed; it wasn't. Something made me understand that that was not to be. So I made sure that it would not happen to me.

Although I was a very shy child, a very introspective child, one who stuttered, one who was not very self-confident, there were some things that I was sure of. One of the things which has propelled me all my life is when a principle is violated. America has violated many principles as far as black people are concerned and that's why I do battle with her. I do battle not because I think it's cute or militant but because America has violated a race of people. This means that my whole life has been dedicated toward the eradication of those violations.

I went into the Nation of Islam in 1972. I had been in New York for a couple of years, and had watched a lot of people who were "in the Nation." When I joined I didn't change my basic lifestyle, my writing. I had children, and I thought it was important for them to be around people who had a sense of nationhood, a sense of righteousness and morality. I wanted them to be exposed to this behavior. You cannot talk about progress for people unless you also talk about morality. The Nation was the one organization that was trying to deal with the concepts of nationhood, morality, small businesses, schools.... And these things were very important to me.

It was not easy being in the Nation. I was/am a writer. I was also speaking on campuses. In the Nation at that time women were supposed to be in the background. My contribution to the Nation has been that I refused to let them tell me where my place was. I would be reading my poetry some place, and men would get up to leave, and I'd say, "Look, my words are equally important." So I got into trouble. I wanted them to understand, without causing schisms, by continuing to BE. One dude said to me once that the solution for Sonia Sanchez was for her to have some babies, and I wrote a long satirical poem called "Solution to Sonia Sanchez," which was my response. I already had two children. The solution for women is not babies. The solution for black people is not children. It's much more complex than that, and we women are also much more complex. I fought against the stereotype of me as a black woman in the movement relegated to three steps behind. It especially was important for women in the Nation to see that. I told them that in order to pull this "mother" out from what it's under we gonna need men, women, children, but most important, we need minds. I had to fight. I had to fight a lot of people in and outside of the Nation due to so-called sexism. I spoke up. I think it was important that there were women there to do that. I left the Nation during the 1975-76 academic year.

I was at Amherst while I was a member of the Nation and that was very difficult. The professors in no way wanted to deal with "that" and the influence that I might have on students. Though among black professors we had political disagreements, I always moved with them on positive issues. We were never disunited on anything. Despite this effort at unity, I had all kinds of students coming into my classroom prepared "to jump me," to disagree. The white students, especially, would tell me they had been advised not to take my course because I was a racist teacher, because I was in the Nation. These same students stayed the year and later on thanked me.

c.t.:   Did your involvement with the Nation change your poetry?

SANCHEZ:   I did three books before joining the Nation: *Homecoming* (1970); *We a Baddddd People* (1970); and *It's a New Day* (1971). I only completed one book, and some of the poems in *Love Poems*, while I was in the Nation—*A Blue Book for Blue Black Magical Women* (1974) which I began in 1972. It was in process for a long time because I thought it was important to do a book about a woman who had been in the struggle. *Blues Book* is about my motions and observations as a child, as a young black woman, and about how society does not prepare young black women, or women period, to be women. It just says, "Oh, oh, you're sixteen, seventeen, eighteen. You have boobies, a fresh little behind, good. Okay. You're a woman." But there's no preparation for womanhood. There's a section in *Blues Book* about how all of a sudden here I was a woman, and I didn't know what that meant. There's a section which deals with a black woman's political involvement—my CORE [Congress of Racial Equality] days. In those days I would be listening to Malcolm, who insisted that America would always label me as black no matter how smart, how rich, how this and that I am.

He seared the mind. I tried to ignore what he had said, and then I'd be talking to some of my integrationist friends and something Malcolm had said would suddenly come out of my mouth, and they'd say "WHAT?" "What?" So I found myself alone, as I said in *Blues Book*. Then I began to search for people who were like me. I said there must be someone out there experiencing this. So I looked for people wearing naturals.

When I got my hair cut: there was a natural. I went to my father's house and people in the house said, "My God, Sonia, what are you doing? Why don't you just get married and have some babies?" So I left the house angry. I crossed the street, 135th Street. A taxi stopped. He had the light, but he stopped the car and pulled over. When the light changed, and I began to cross the street, he pulled his car up and said, "ugaa, booga booga." Then I realized how much work had to be done. My father told me later on that he was afraid I'd lose my job, and one would. He was just trying to prepare me for what would happen.

Sisters tell me today that when they go out for jobs they straighten their hair because if they go in with their hair natural or braided, they probably won't get the job. So I say, "How can you let someone dictate to you how you're going to look?" The reason we went through what we did is so that one group of people would no longer dictate to another group. Because if a country can tell a people, the way it used to tell black people a few years ago, you must look a certain way, then it has complete control over you. I don't care how many Ph.Ds. you have. Who else does this country dictate to? Granted, people say that if you want to work for IBM you have to wear a suit. That's everybody. Hair has nothing to do with a job, clothing yes. People must begin to bring this up again.

C.T.:   How do you fit writing into your life?

SANCHEZ:   One year I taught five courses and finished two books. I work from midnight to around three every morning on my writing. At that time the house is quiet. The children are asleep. I've prepared for my classes; I've graded my papers. I've answered letters. I get a lot of unsolicited manuscripts from people. At a quarter to twelve all that stops. Then my writing starts. If the work is not going well, then I sit at my desk. If I'm rewriting then I tend to do that in bed. When I'm beginning something, and it's not going well, I have some favorite people whom I might read: Gwen, Sterling. . . . That's a relaxation process. Then I'm loosened up and I'm ready to begin. I work in two or three notebooks; I still have all the notebooks from the ten books I've done. I do everything long-hand. I hate to see first drafts. I read them out loud. They're terrible, and then I read successive drafts, and the students can see the change. Then the final draft. I don't know how it happens; all the steps cannot always be seen in the final draft. All of a sudden there is the poem. I sometimes literally jump up and down. I might go cover up the kids and kiss them because I want to share my joy. It's a joy that I have never duplicated; perhaps the closest comparison is sex.

C.T.:   For whom do you write?

SANCHEZ:   I write because I must. I write because it keeps me going. I probably have not killed anyone in America because I write. I've maintained good controls over myself by writing. I also write because I think one must not only share what one thinks, or the conclusions one has reached, but one must also share to help others reach their conclusions. Writing might help them survive.

My audience has always been a black audience. But I have also found that other people have picked up on my writing. Therefore, I might say that I write for progressive people. My work has been translated into European languages. White people write to me about my work, and say that I have touched them, that it's been painful, but it's made them grow. I've always known I have whites in my audience. America has tried to say that that's not true and has tried to isolate people. But I've always known that if you write from a black experience, you're writing from a universal experience as well. People try to tell you not to write "blackly," but universally. I can feel a woman's pain, be she Italian or whatever, because I have felt pain. So when people speak about being universal, I crack up and laugh, because I know what being universal means. I know you don't have to whitewash yourself to be universal.

C.T.:   Do you see a difference in how black male and female writers dramatize their themes, characterize their heroes/heroines, give tone to their personae?

SANCHEZ:   In prose perhaps. But in poetry I would almost say no. Look at Sterling's work. Look at Gwen's work. Look at Margaret Walker's work. There is the same thread in those people's work. There's oppression against blacks, the love of black self in all their work. Their work is very progressive because it speaks to the positive movement of our people.

I think there are differences between male and female writing. I don't want to get into men seeing women differently and women seeing men differently. That's unimportant. I think men are different from women and, therefore, the emphases might be different. Men tend to write in what I would call an objective mood. Women tend to write in a subjective mood. Critics and reviewers think subjective writing is personal writing, but it isn't. I think some men can write like women, and vice versa. Some men can write some very loving and tender things that you might have thought were written by a woman, and some women can write some damned rough stuff.

When I think of the black men and women writing poetry in the sixties, I think there was a similar voice, almost a communal voice, because the themes were so similar. A woman writer might have talked about a woman in a particular situation with a man. A man did not tend to do that. Many women understood that you could not talk about a nation unless you talked about group relationships, that a nation could not evolve from people talking about what should be without involving the two of them, without acknowledging that what will be comes from their working together. You can fully understand revolution if you can fully understand what it is to love a man. Because in order to be a true revolutionary, you must understand love. Love, sacrifice, and death.

A short story like "After Saturday Night Comes Sunday" is really a revolutionary story but it's personalized. Many people see it only as a love story. But look at its textures: it talks about love between a man and a woman; a woman's love for children, and about responsibility. Ultimately, the story says that you hold on to people as long as you can. If you're going out to say something, your house must be in order, because there's so much disorder outside. That's why some people fell by the wayside during the sixties. Some people didn't understand fully that in order to do battle, you must have a sense of place, a sense of well-being between two people or between an adult and a child or children.

That's why a lot of people could only write stories of what was;

whereas some people tried to show what could be. I hope that's what *After Saturday Night Comes Sunday* does.

The story is set in seven days, though we focus only on the first two days. The days overlap—Friday/Saturday, Saturday/Sunday. It is about a woman who goes out and talks to people about social change. Personal problems are oppressing her and she literally goes crazy, but no one on the outside knows it. In one instance, the woman is giving a talk. As she's talking, she's hearing other words. She's hearing the chaos. There's a whole chapter on this woman's disintegration, as it occurs onstage with the irony of applause. People are commending her; she's autographing books, but meanwhile she's going insane. She later goes home and goes to pieces. She waits until then because she understands that you cannot go to pieces in front of people who need you.

People see that kind of writing as personal writing, but it's not. There's a difference. Granted, I show the movement of a particular woman from madness to rising alone without falling into the trap of blues or wine. The difference between personal writing, in which you're either victim or just recording the pain, and subjective writing is one of focus. *After Saturday Night* focuses on the maintenance of some kind of strength that can be shared.

It's too easy to make generalizations about black female and male writers. There are common themes we all hit upon. But I think that quite often men might objectify them, and women might have made them personal or subjective. We're finding that even some of these victimization works have also been objectified by the very fact that they've moved from the subjective and personal and flung themselves out to people, insisting that they deal with the works. They demand that we look at what they're saying, and internalize it. They suggest that maybe we'll be stronger people for doing so.

So, therefore, the story might be my personal story but without just being my burden. In fact, it's not just a personal story. It might be a personal experience but the whole world comes into it.

I don't like to pigeon-hole people. Some men tell a story just like Lucille Clifton or like Louise Meriwether. I do think it's important to say that more than likely women writers move in a much more subjective mood—from a house, a place—and that they move out from there. However, this is not necessarily subjective because the house is the society.

C.T.:   Do your children interfere with your writing?

SANCHEZ:   I don't write in spite of my children. I'd write even if I didn't have children. I write because of them, and they don't interfere. In other words, I might be doing something and if they have needs, I might say damn it and close the book. I might be annoyed but they do not see that annoyance. Most of the time I don't put them in that situation. Most of the time I will write around them. They should not feel guilty about interfering with my writing.

Some of the things I've written they like. I wrote *A Sound Investment and Other Stories* for them. I wrote *Fathead* for them. I do think that it's important to leave a legacy of my books for my children to read and understand; to leave a legacy of the history of black people who have moved toward revolution and freedom; to leave a legacy of not being afraid to tell the truth, which you must accept the consequences for, but you do not have to be afraid. We must pass this on to our children, rather than a legacy of fear and victimization.

When I used to take the children to my readings—they've been going since they were two- and three-months old—they never cried. I'd say, "Yes, I'll come for free to read, but I'm bringing my children, and you must have someone to help me take care of them." At a very early age they had a sense of what it was I was doing. They used to listen so carefully to me reading that when they were two or two-and-a-half, they would know some of the poems by heart. In the midst of doing one poem, the poem that ends *Blues Book*—"In the beginning there was no end"— Mongu came up on stage with me. He was around two and as I chanted he chanted just a little behind me. Somewhere someone has that on tape, and I wish I could find it. In fact, once when he was two, he asked me if he was going to read with me the next time. Those are memories that I keep. I smile when I think of them now.

I write because I must. I also write because I know they will read it. And there's nothing that I've ever written that I'm ashamed of, that they cannot read, and that includes the curse words. The children know that their home is not a home of cursing. So, if I cursed in a poem, it was done on purpose.

Someone asked me about a poem which says, "My old man tells me I'm so full of sweet pussy . . .":

Short Poem

*my old man*
*tells me i'm*
*so full of sweet*
*pussy he can*
*smell me coming.*
*maybe*
    *I*
*shd*
*bottle*
*it*
    *and*
*sell it*
*when he goes.*
        —from *I've Been A Woman*

I've explained that poem to the children. It came out of this situation. I was on 125th Street in Harlem, and there was a black man and a black woman standing on the corner of Amsterdam Avenue. I can never forget it; I can still see them now. She looked up at him and said, "Man, why, why did you ask me to do that?" He had his back to me and she was facing him. I saw her eyes. Here I was rushing to the post office on Saturday. I could see her eyes and they were staring fat zeros. She said, "Man, why did you ask . . ." and he said, "But you didn't do it baby, you didn't do it baby. So there's no problem. . . . It's cool. . . ." She said, "But why did you ask me to do that?" I stood there looking and the poem came. I was on that corner fifteen minutes and never made it to the post office. I just watched her face and her eyes. Meanwhile a car came and he jumped into it, but she stood there. I went home and wrote that poem. That's what the poem is about. That's what I told my children. I had to use the terminology I used because I knew those feelings. I couldn't make it nice. People read that poem and say it's vulgar. My response is, "There's vulgar stuff out there." One has got to talk about it in order for it not to be.

C.T.:   Who influenced your writing?

SANCHEZ:   A lot of people. I used to read a lot of poetry. In the South we were given a lot of black poetry in school to memorize, mostly works by Paul Lawrence Dunbar and Langston Hughes. When we moved north, I used to go to the library. The librarian would always see me moving around the poetry section. She was the one who turned me onto Langston Hughes and Gwen Brooks. She was the one who made me go back and examine the poets of the twenties and thirties. She also told me about Pushkin. One day this woman said to me, "This book is by a black man who lived in Russia." I read his poetry and just went crazy. I was twelve or thirteen. In high school I mostly read white writers. No one gave me any literary work by black writers to read. I did not get back to black writers until I got out of Hunter. That's really a terrible commentary on education. I went to the Schomburg Library. I'd just come from a job interview and got on the wrong train and got out at 135th Street and Lenox Avenue. It was hot, so I went inside to cool off. The librarian said that I couldn't take any books out. My response was, "What kind of library is this?" And she said that the books in there were by and for black people. I looked around and told her I didn't believe her. She gave me a personal tour.

I had been educated to think that Gwen Brooks and Langston Hughes were exceptions. In high school and college American Literature contained no black writers. As a consequence, the only time I saw "me" was in sociology courses, and then I was an aberration. To make a long story short, I came back to that library for a week or two and I just read and read. I couldn't believe it. That's when I started buying books. I went down to 125th Street and met Mr. Michaux who owned a black bookstore. He told me what books to buy. I went back to the Schomburg and told the librarian that one day I'd have a book in there. I really meant it. I don't know what made me do that.

C.T.:    Do you have any works that have been misunderstood?

SANCHEZ:    I don't think my work has been misinterpreted. I do know that people have been frightened by my work. I know that *The New York Times* said it would not review a book of mine because I was too political. That much I do know.

I didn't just write I'm black, I'm black. There have been people, some of the older writers, who have tried to criticize some of us by saying all we were writing was blackblackblack. But if they really read our work, they would see that was not true. They were frightened by what we said. I've always understood this. They felt threatened by us. But I've always said that if I were just like them I would not be doing what I'm supposed to be doing. Each generation builds on a higher level. They were supposed to produce us in spite of themselves. We came from them, and when we came they were frightened. Fathers and mothers were frightened of their sons and daughters, and they tried to deny us. We are the thoughts they were afraid to utter, the things they said about white folks to each other in the barber shop, on street corners, at home.

I know that Don Lee (Haki Madhubuti) did not understand *We a Baddddd People* when he did *Dynamite Voices*. He liked *Homecoming*, but he didn't understand what I was trying to do with *We a Baddddd People*. I was experimenting a lot with language, and that book was a necessary book for me. He didn't understand the satirical point and black humor of the "Suicide Poem." He didn't understand the Coltrane poem, and the poem for my father, or the necessary hard-hitting words of revolution.

I know that I've come. Before me there were Brown, Walker and Brooks, among others. Before them, there were others. Otherwise Sterling would not have been. You don't come out of a vacuum. We're not like Topsy; we don't just grow. The joy of writing for me has been that I have been able to be innovative on many levels.

C.T.:   Let's turn to your revolutionary theater pieces. Would you talk about the conception of "Sister Son/ji?"

SANCHEZ:   The character is *woman* of all ages. I'd promised Ed Bullins the play. I had just given birth to the twins—they were about three months old—when he called. I said that I'd just given birth, that I was teaching, that I was tired and depressed. He said, "Don't tell me your problems; I just want that play." I got so mad at him that night I sat down and finished that play at five in the morning. In "Sister Son/ji" I portray a woman who has come through; she's lost children, husbands; she's been through pain. She's been to college; she's been militant; she's been in love; she's fought. She has seen death. But she's come through them all. She ages on the stage, but her spirit is ageless. She is Harriet Tubman, a woman.

# ·NTOZAKE SHANGE·

*B*orn in 1948 in Trenton, New Jersey, Shange has been writing since she was a child. Her literary career, however, began as part of her involvement with the black and women's movements and her style evolved from pieces prepared for public readings in San Francisco and New York. She received a B.A. from Barnard College in 1970 and an M.A. in English Literature from the University of California in Los Angeles.

Shange changed her name from Paulette Williams as an act of protest against her Western roots. The Zulu names she embraced, ntozake ("she who comes with her own things") and shange ("she who walks like a lion") emphasize both the independence and potential strength of the young black women for whom she speaks. Her works are characterized by an intense rendering of their emotional lives, frequently painful, sometimes ecstatic, but always ruthlessly honest. Shange works from the anger she feels at the roles forced upon black women by American society and highlights the havoc caused by superficially imposed sexual attitudes upon all intimate relationships.

Although the 1976 Broadway production For Colored Girls Who Have Considered Suicide When the Rainbow is Enuf fell victim to a media blitz and was, thus, transformed and exploited, much of the controversy it aroused was due to its honest appraisal of black women's emotional vulnerability, at a time when only positive images were acceptable to the black media. Shange has consistently been one of the few writers to pursue this theme and has several dramatic works to her credit, including: A Photograph: A Study of Lovers in Motion and A Photograph: A Study of Still Life with Shadows/A Photograph: A Study of Cruelty, both produced in 1977, Boogie Woogie Landscapes (1978), Spell #7 (1979), and an adaptation of Bertolt Brecht's Mother Courage in 1980.

*While her writing started as a part-time activity and Shange had originally planned to teach, she is now a frequent contributor to many national magazines and is the author of several works: the novella* Sassafrass *(1976); a collection of poetry and prose,* Natural Disasters and Other Festive Occasions *(1977); a volume of poetry,* Nappy Edges *(1978); a collection of plays,* Three Pieces *(1981); and a recent novel,* Sassafrass, Indigo and Cyprus *(1982).*

*Ntozake Shange lives in New York City with her young daughter Savannah.*

◆  ◆  ◆

CLAUDIA TATE:   What has success done to you? Do people recognize you in the street? Do they get defensive?

NTOZAKE SHANGE:   All of those things happen. David Franklin is my lawyer now; when we had our first meeting, he said I was crazy for not taking advantage of my sudden fame and sudden wealth. I told him that I couldn't take advantage because I was totally devastated. It took me five years to do anything at all. As much as other people thought they had problems with my public persona, I had more problems than they could ever imagine. I had never tried to do anything but keep a part-time job and write whenever I felt like it. That was my ambition: to keep doing that for the rest of my life. I had no intention of becoming involved with anything related to institutional theater.

People whom I love dearly don't treat me oddly anymore. But we went through four years of trauma and high drama. I'm talking about very close friends and family going through high drama, envy, sibling rivalry, etc. We've worked through this for the most part, at least to the point where we can again have enriching relationships.

I have three ways of dealing with strangers. Either I don't talk at all, or I try as politely as I can to explain that I'm not working now, that I'm not going to sign autographs now, and that I'm not going to discuss what critics say because I don't like to talk about critics. So, please, just leave me alone, or be a nice person. Or else, I lie and say I'm not who they think I am. People always tell me, "You look just like her! Isn't it fascinating?"

C.T.:   How did you deal with Broadway and *For Colored Girls*?

SHANGE:    I left the Broadway show of *For Colored Girls* after three weeks. I didn't want to go in the first place because Broadway to me always represented something tawdry and tacky in American theater. I said, "Take the show up there without me." The producers said, "We can't do that." They tried to convince me that it would be good for me and for black people if I went to Broadway. I said, "All right. I'll open it, but I have to be out within a month." What happened was that my unconscious really got on the move and gave me strep throat in twelve days, so I was really out in twelve days. I had a fever of 104°; I couldn't talk. That was the end of my Broadway career.

I generally handle theater transitions very well. But that's only in terms of rehearsals and performances. I'm not good at all about sitting in an audience that is looking at something I did. I feel very self-conscious. I can look at or rework a piece in rehearsal, or I can be in a piece of mine. I just don't like going to performances of my work. It's as if I were watching people watch me.

C.T.:    There seems to be very little distance between you, the author, and the dramatic character on stage or the speaker of your poem.

SHANGE:    I'm committed to the idea that one of the few things human beings have to offer is the richness of unconscious and conscious emotional responses to being alive. That to me is one of the most important things anybody could bring to another soul, and that's what's so wonderful about living. The kind of esteem that's given to brightness/smartness obliterates average people or slow learners from participating fully in human life, particularly technical and intellectual life. But you cannot exclude any human being from emotional participation.

C.T.:    There seems to be a wealth of writing about emotional participation in works by women as opposed to those by men.

SHANGE:    It would be difficult for men to have this focus, inasmuch as they generally have so little true intimate contact with other human beings. It seems perfectly reasonable that if one were raised in a patriarchal environment and accepted that as one's definition of one's manhood, then a struggle would evolve against patriarchy because it is antihuman. But if you don't have any other value system, then, of course, you are at a loss for a vocabulary. Men don't have an emotional vocabulary that is as highly developed as women's because women have been taking care of other people all their lives. Therefore they are able to know *immediately* how they're feeling and what they're feeling; whereas men, certain men, not all men but some men, are unable to express such feelings—unless it's related to humiliation or anger or pride or revenge or their domination over some other being. Things of that nature men, generally, can do pretty well with. But there's so much more going on in the world.

C.T.:   Are you aware that your poetry is so very personal that it seems very self-conscious?

SHANGE:   I see my self-consciousness in terms of battling with myself to let go of something. For instance, "the white girl" piece in *Spell #7,* a play written for the New York Shakespeare Festival in 1979, "the black and white two dimensional planes" in *Boogie Woogie Landscapes,* even "Allegre" in *Photographs,* or the "no more love poems" in *For Colored Girls,* were written following highly vulnerable times. I had fought through very difficult emotional tasks in order to allow myself to say: "Okay, as weird as *this* is, *this* is truly how I feel. Therefore, if I write anything else, it would be a lie. So as long as I'm thinking about *this,* and I know how I feel about *this,* you have to see *it, too.*" In other words, my self-consciousness has nothing really to do with other people. It has to do with whether or not I'm going to confront what I'm feeling.

One day I did "battle." I wrote this very peculiar piece, and it made me so angry. I said: "This is the weirdest piece in the world. How could you ever think such a thought?" But it went on for about two hours. I kept walking around the house. I wept and finally said that this is stupid, stop crying. I washed something. I cleaned up the apartment. Finally, I shed my last tear, and I said: "You already know the end of the story, so why don't you just go on and finish it? Because if it stays in your head, it's just going to keep coming."

The story is about this girl, Marta, who doesn't want to see anymore. She covers her eyes with a blindfold and goes to the Lighthouse to learn how not to see. She goes there to learn how to walk with a cane and how to touch her way around. She doesn't want to see anymore because she decides she has seen enough. She has made contact with her memory, and her memories are so intense that every new thing she sees becomes a part of these memories. Every year there are more and more and more memories, and they are overwhelming her. That's why she doesn't want to see anymore, so as not to add to these memories. There are particular things she doesn't want to see: hypocrisy, abuse of children and women, and so on. There are also a lot of social and sexual issues she specifically names that she doesn't want to know anymore about.

In the beginning it was perfectly fine. It was sort of witty, and I was having fun writing it. Then the implications of her not seeing really upset me because I knew she was in danger if she refused to see. I knew I had to send her out into the street where she would not be able to see that there were two men in a vacant lot who eventually would rape and beat her virtually to death. The last line of the piece is: "I don't know if they took the blindfold off before or after." If she lives, will she have the guts to remember? I kept saying, "This is an awful story. I don't want to write *that*." But then, on the other hand, I had to write *that* because I just had to.

Many of my poems are by-products of my journal-keeping. I made a list, just yesterday, of all these wonderful, delightful stories I was going to write. I thought I was going to start on one of these highly fanciful fables with all kinds of imaginary creatures who were vehicles for something emotionally important. I was just about to do that. I went to write in my journal, and this girl came up who couldn't see. I was really very angry with her because I didn't want to deal with her. I wanted to write these pretty things. But I knew whatever else I wanted to do was not going to be right because whoever this weirdo was, she was going to find her way to the piece I really wanted to do and ruin it. She'd make the happy character somber or bizarre.

I'm not saying that none of the women whom I write about are strange because that's what I like about my women characters— they're all a little strange. I feel that as an artist my job is to appreciate the differences among my women characters. We're usually just thrown together, like "tits and ass," or a good cook, or how we can really "f---." Our personalities and distinctions are lost. What I appreciate about the women whom I write about, the women whom I know, is how idiosyncratic they are. I take delight in the very peculiar or particular things that fascinate or terrify them. Also, I discovered that by putting them all together, there are some things they all are repelled by, and there are some things they are all attracted to. I only discovered this by having them have their special relationships to their dreams and their unconscious.

C.T.:   Is your journal the source for most of your work?

SHANGE:   I carry my journal with me almost all the time. If I have poems that just come, I write them in there as if they were journal entries. I try to keep my journal on a day-to-day basis. I stopped for a year because I was in production all the time. When I'm working on a production, I find it best to stay with just that because if I try to write something for myself, the piece in production insinuates itself into whatever I'm doing, even if it's somebody else's work.

My work is difficult for actors to perform because I demand all kinds of emotional commitment that they don't necessarily have to give to other playwrights. If they don't do it for me, I'll either take the part out or I'll get somebody else. If they do, in fact, enact whatever the trauma is that I put the characters through, I make them do it maybe four or five times a week to make sure that when it happens to them on stage we don't lose them as people, that their traumas don't overtake them. As a director, I have to get actors accustomed to all kinds of strange sufferings. So now the playwright in me has a little more respect for the character or actor's emotional commitment to the piece than I used to have. I didn't used to know, since I didn't have to direct these actors, what I was really demanding of them. Now I have a different type of respect, not only for the actors but also for my characters.

I was always able to give my characters emotions, but what I'm more conscious of doing now is handling them a little more gently so that they don't injure themselves or create inordinate havoc in the soul of the reader or the viewer. For example, last night when I was describing this girl who couldn't see to Jayne Cortez, I said something like: "Well, Marta went to the Lighthouse and then because she couldn't see, she got raped and beaten, and she died." Jayne was appalled. "What else could I have done?" I said. About an hour later, Jayne said, "Yeah, I guess that is the only way you could have ended the story." "Yeah, I know," I said, "but it was so morbid." And Jayne said, "Yes, it was." So treating my characters or actors gently is like finding a way to do what I did with Jayne. I want to show what happens, but I don't want it to happen in a way that disgusts people. In other words, I have to have the story unfold so that the observer/listener/reader cares about whomever the character is. And that's something I learned in rewriting *A Photograph: Lovers in*

*Motion.* The sexual and verbal violence occurring in that piece is as violent as I ever had it, but it also allows the audience to care about some or all of the characters so that they all don't seem to be half mad and vicious. I already care about them. I care about anybody who's in pain. I don't care about why they're in pain. Most people respond to somebody in pain as someone being very irrational, as opposed to someone feeling pain and suffering. I didn't know that. I just thought that if somebody were suffering, you would see that he or she were suffering. So my task is to make you, the viewer, care also. In a way, I resented having to rewrite so as to do this, but the characters are fuller people as a result.

C.T.:    What is your responsibility to yourself and your audience? Or is your writing your effort to maintain a dialogue among your many selves?

SHANGE:    I really resent having to meet somebody else's standards or needs, or having to justify their reasons for living. When I started writing, I wrote for myself, to help myself better understand what was going on around me. I thought it was really great if other people could understand what I was saying, but it didn't really matter that they did. On the other hand, I don't like being misunderstood, but if they genuinely don't understand what I'm saying, that's perfectly all right, too. It's dangerous for me to invite the audience into my house, to sit on my typewriter, to read my manuscripts unless they're finished, and then they can have them. By then, I'm okay, but I can't allow them inside while I'm writing.

I was laughing rather cynically when I was trying to do the "Marta" story. I said: "Okay, you're the person who is *so* ruthlessly honest. Why don't you go on and do it? You're supposed to have the veracity of a child. Why don't you go on and do it? Are you afraid?" Those are quotes from critics. So I said to myself: "That's what you are, so why don't you go on and do it." I think that's probably the one thing I can do. I think it was Adrienne Rich or Susan Griffin who said that one of our responsibilities as women writers is to discover the causes for our pain and to respect them. I think that much of the suffering that women and black people endure is not respected. I was also trained not to respect it. For instance, we're taught not to respect women who can't get their lives together by themselves. They have three children and a salary check for $200. The house is a mess; they're sort of hair-brained.  We're taught not to respect their suffering. So I write about things that I know have never been given their full due. I have to do that. These are the moments in life that are important to me. I want people to at least understand or have the chance to see that *this* is a person whose life is not only valid but whose life is valiant. My responsibility is to be as honest as I can and to use whatever technical skills I may possess to make these experiences even clearer, or sharper, or more devastating or more beautiful.

The reason I wrote *Sassafrass* with what they call "no punctuation"—which is very bizarre to me because I think it's highly punctuated—is because I didn't want the reader to be able to put the book down. If you put it down, you had to start all over again. I did not want the book to be something you could put down when it got too emotional. I don't enjoy books like that. I don't like being given the opportunity to stop and say: I've had enough; I want to go do something else. How can you have enough of someone's life? They're living it. As far as I'm concerned a character's living a life. She can't stop and go do something else; so you can't stop and do something else. Of course, this is very demanding. That's one of the reasons why the piece is so short, so that it can be read in one sitting. The language has been thoroughly standardized in the St. Martin's Press edition [*Sassafrass, Indigo and Cyprus*, 1982]. Obviously, I think it's important not to abort an emotional breakthrough. That's something English-speaking people have a lot of difficulty with. Aborting emotional breakthroughs allows one to keep one's decorum at all moments. Our society allows people to be absolutely neurotic and totally out of touch with their feelings and everyone else's feelings, and yet be very respectable. This, to me, is a travesty. So I write to get at the part of people's emotional lives that they don't have control over, the part that can and will respond. If I have to write about blood and babies dying, then fine, I'll write about that. As you can see from my work, I'm primarily interested in evoking an emotional response. I do have intellectual moments, but I'm not so aware of them.

I'm trying to change the idea of seeing emotions and intellect as distinct faculties. Many of the pieces, in *Nappy Edges,* in *For Colored Girls,* and especially in *Spell #7,* refer to all kinds of intellectual disciplines and topics, such as psychotherapy, philosophy, music, literature, foreign languages and countries. Obviously, I read a lot; I travel a lot, and I think a lot, but I have not segmented thinking from feeling. For instance, there's a piece in *Spell #7* called "flying song" which is a love poem, and it's about poverty, racism and imperialism, and about the death of Europe, but it's a love poem. It's not a didactic love poem. It's simply that when I love somebody, I want my beloved in a world where those things aren't occurring. So I have to tell my beloved: these are the things I don't want you to have to deal with. When people used to make fun of women writing love poems, they didn't see that we see the world in a way that allows us to care more about people than about military power. The power we see is the power to feed, the power to nourish and to educate. But these kinds of powers are not respected, and so it's part of our responsibility as writers to make these things important. If we can't do that, then we at least have to put it on record that in the twentieth century somebody did, in fact, care about other human beings. This does not imply that I'm a pacifist by any means. I have never suggested that caring does not include struggle in the way men would term struggle. I'm not saying that we don't have to struggle in physical ways but, of course, that should be a last resort.

c.t.:    How did your parents respond to your writing ambitions?

shange:    My parents were very enthusiastic about my writing. They thought it was wonderful. The implications of writing were what troubled them. My parents have always been especially involved in all kinds of Third World culture. We used to go to hear Latin music, jazz and symphonies, to see ballets. . . . I was always aware that there were different kinds of black people all over the world because my father had friends from virtually all of the colonized French-, Spanish-, and English-speaking countries. So I knew I wasn't on this planet by myself. I had some connection with other people.

My parents respected my writing. They respected what I was trying to do, but at the same time they didn't realize that being a writer meant not being and not doing what everybody else is being and doing. This is what threw them. I don't think my craft threw them so much as why I couldn't look like so-and-so. Or why I didn't go to this dance with them. Or why I didn't join the NAACP. These things were totally abominable to me at the time and still are. I don't do those things. What upset them was a difference in values, which I could have had if I were a physician, so it wasn't my being a writer per se.

C.T.:    Have your parents been able to adjust to the critical attacks hurled your way?

SHANGE:    My parents adjusted far better than I did. They don't see their persons being attacked. For them it's an article in *Ebony* or an article in *The New York Times*. My mother will immediately jot off a very intelligent and rational letter about why this article is wrong; whereas, I will either not read it, or I'll just be vitally damaged because what I write is an offering of myself to the world. When somebody attacks that, then they're saying I'm not alive, or that I'm not doing what I'm doing, or that I didn't see what I saw, or that I couldn't have felt what I felt, or that I don't know who I know. One time a critic said that the people I had written about couldn't possibly exist. That would mean that everybody I knew did not exist. That kind of response totally disorients and upsets me. I've gotten better about it, but generally, I don't read what critics write.

As long as I have a stable peer group of other writers and a stable audience, I'll be fine. There's no reason to be around people who don't love my work. It's never been my premise to proselytize among people who don't want to listen. It's fine if you like my work—great. If you don't, that's great, too. The problem with critics is if they don't like you, they can, in fact, either close your show or not get your book distributed. This can happen simply because they don't like your work. Therefore, people who do want to read me and who do like my work can't have it. That's what makes me resent critics so much.

C.T.:    Why did you have to tell about Beau Willie Brown?*

SHANGE:    Because I have to live around people like him. I can't live around a whole bunch of lies. There are enough lies around as it is. I cannot sustain lies. My critics can say that he doesn't exist. Then they can try to explain to me why there are two million American children who are abused by their parents every single year.

I got really upset one night. A man was interviewing me for *The New York Times*. He used to be a war reporter, of all things, and he had been reassigned as a theater critic. He told me he had never

---

* Beau Willie Brown is a major character in *For Colored Girls*.

raped anybody. My response was: "You know, every man I meet who wants to talk about rape always wants to talk about how he never did it. Maybe we should have a congressional hearing to find out if it's the UFOs who are raping women. Maybe we should go to the zoo and find out if it's the crocodiles or giraffes because I really would like to know, and I don't want to blame anybody who's not doing it." By that point I was on the verge of tears. After all, that is a denial of reality. It does *not* matter if you did or did not do something. If you didn't do it, does that mean it didn't happen? When is someone going to take responsibility for what goes on where we live? People were running around sending two million Christmas cards to fifty people in Iran who were being fed and housed every night. There are women and children, especially young boys here, who are living in abominable conditions. They didn't get no Christmas cards. And they're right here in this country. Those kinds of things don't make any sense to me. That's why I write about it. I refuse to be a part of this conspiracy of silence. I will not do it. So that's why I wrote about Beau Willie Brown. I'm tired of living lies.

"With No Immediate Cause" [*Nappy Edges*] was based directly on quotes in *The New York Times,* and people got upset with me. I said, "Why get upset with me when I'm simply telling you what's in the newspaper? Don't you read the newspaper?" It's not my fault that they reported these things.

It's like if it's a statistic, it's not a woman! Let me make it very clear to you; it's a woman that this has happened to or a child. Oh, I just can't stand it. See that's what upsets me: the slow erosion of our humanity so that we don't even know that we're supposed to care about one another. That's going on because these technocrats have almost convinced us that a machine can do anything better than a person. So he or she doesn't have to worry about what he or she is doing.

A while back *The Black Enterprise* suggested what might happen in the year 2000. The article goes on and on about how people would have virtually nothing to do but push buttons. Their major problem, in fact, their only problem would be interpersonal relations. My God! What other kind of problems could there be? It was covered in just one little sentence. The article then went on and on about what kinds of equipment these people would have. Jesus Christ, I don't ever want to live in a world where you can just dispense with interpersonal relations in a little phrase. For me, there's nothing else for human beings to do. There's just nothing else to do! You want some more machines so you can put your psyche away? This repression of feelings is why the homicide rate has increased 300 per cent in ten years in New York City. Nobody knows what to say to anyone, so they just kill. Some people don't know how to deal with a problem so they just kill. That's the danger of living the way we're living. When you're living lies, you don't know what's real.

C.T.:   Have you noticed differences in the ways in which black men and women writers approach their creative work in terms of selecting themes, characters and events?

SHANGE:   I have a problem with a lot of male writers in that there is always *the idea*. I never really feel the person; I'm always getting the idea that we're either going to beat the white people or the white people have beaten this man to death. . . . He is the leader, and he is besieged by racism. . . . In works by men there's usually an *idea* as opposed to a *reality*. So that the main character sometimes just embodies a notion or a philosophical perspective, as opposed to being a feeling and thinking person. Men also generally approach the conflicts involved in the sexual or political identity of a male character in a way that allows them to skim over whatever the real crisis is. In [Amiri] Baraka's *The Toilet,* for instance, or in Wesley Richard's *The Mighty Gents,* or in Baraka's *Sidnee Poet Heroical,* there are sexual innuendoes respectively about homosexuality, getting raped, and fear of women; but they are just skimmed over, when the whole play could have been about those things. Respect for that focus is going to take a lot more emotional growth.

I have to fight with myself. I hit my head against the wall because I don't want to know all the terrible things that I know about. I don't want to feel all these wretched things, but they're in me already. If I don't get rid of them, I'm not ever going to feel anything else. When our culture, as a whole, realizes that the act of *not* saying something does not mean that you're not living it, when this happens, we're going to have dramatic pieces, all kinds of art, that are so rich. Now we just dash ahead to the finale and, as a result, we have an idea instead of meeting and knowing a new person. A play or a book should bring a new person into your life, somebody to whom you can refer, even have a conversation with, because you ought to get to know them very well.

One of the male writers whom I love dearly, whose work is not as well known as I would like, is Bill Gunn. He has two incredible male characters with whom I feel very close in *Black Picture Show*. But I think their honesty scares the general public because here are two grown men being absolutely honest with themselves. This kind of honesty questions the public's perception of what "a man" is supposed to be. As a result, the public rejected the piece. Sean David in *A Photograph: Lovers in Motion* is another example. The first year he appeared with us, two or three people came up to me and said that the only man who could talk that gently or that beautifully would have to be gay and was he gay? "What? Was he gay? No, he's got three lovers who are women in the piece. He's not gay." That's the response! He couldn't possibly exist because "real men" don't feel, act, or talk like that. My God, I know men who feel, act and talk like that. There's a general misconception that a gentle man must have some kind of sexual problem. This is very, very tragic for us all. It's tragic for men, and it's sad for women because it means that half of the tenderness and intimacy we could have we just don't get.

C.T.:   Women's writing tends to focus on very vivid emotional descriptions of sexual intimacy; whereas, that of men tends to focus on physical movement in the sense of an oncoming train. In women's writing you have the sensation of psychic contact among people.

SHANGE:   That is because women are more in touch with their feelings; therefore, they're able to identify what it is they're doing and feeling. I also think that women use their feelings to a greater degree and in more varied ways than men do. Then, on the other hand, I know so many men—poets, painters, among others—with whom I feel perfectly comfortable in any situation, as friends, as lovers and as peers.

C.T.:   Do you have a special audience for whom you write?

SHANGE:   I collect dolls and the reason I collect dolls is because there's a person in me who's still a little girl and she loves them. I also collect dolls because I want to give the person in me who's a little girl things that I should have had and never got. The reason that *For Colored Girls* is entitled *For Colored Girls* is that that's who it was for. I wanted them to have information that I did not have. I wanted them to know what it was truthfully like to be a grown woman. I didn't know. All I had was a whole bunch of mythology—tales and outright lies. I want a twelve-year-old girl to reach out for and get some information that isn't just contraceptive information but emotional information, so that the great disillusion I experienced on my first wedding night, for instance, would never happen or would not be so great. Perhaps there's not too much you can do if you've been raised to be virginal and to believe that this great thing is going to happen to you on your wedding night. But I don't want them to grow up in a void of misogynous lies. If there is an audience for whom I write, it's the little girls who are coming of age. I want them to know that they are not alone and that we adult women thought and continue to think about them.

In Adrienne Rich's book, *Of Woman Born,* and also in Susan Griffin's book, *Women and Nature,* it's the silence of mothers that is so shattering. The mothers know that it's a dreadful proposition to give up one's life for one's family and one's mate and, therefore, lose oneself in the process of caring and tending for others. To send one's daughter off to that kind of self-sacrifice in silence with no preparation is a mortal sin to me. To do this without telling her that this is a sacrifice is so unnecessary. To break this silence is my responsibility, and I'm absolutely committed to it. When I die, I will not be guilty of having left a generation of girls behind thinking that anyone can tend to their emotional health other than themselves. We see women who at fifty look back at their lives; they are either very bitter or very childlike because their development was arrested. It is not incumbent upon us for this to happen as it was incumbent upon our mothers.

C.T.:   The title *Nappy Edges* brings back memories.

SHANGE:   Most people act like they don't know what nappy edges are, or they act like they don't know what I'm talking about. Those that do just giggle, but most of the time it seems like the title just goes over people's heads. Maybe it's a sign of my age. A lot of young people who are now fifteen to twenty haven't really had to experience nappy edges, because they grew up with the Afro or permanent hair straighteners. Straightening hair and being told not to dance with boys after 10:30 at night evidently didn't happen to them.

I really like the title. I think it has something to do with how I feel and how I see the world. It's the roughness and the rawness of it that is the wealth of it. As crude and as painful as this rawness is, it is still the crux of human life. It's the sweat from work, from fear, from anger, from love, that is the basis of whatever it is that makes us different from plants and other animals. We can do all these things, and we do them on purpose. We don't do them because we're driven or because we're in heat. We make love because we want and need to. We work because we love. These activities make us human beings. And there is a certain amount of wear and tear in being human.

C.T.: Who or what influenced the way your work looks on the printed page?

SHANGE: My lower-case letters, slashes, and spelling. . . . I think I was really influenced by LeRoi Jones's *The Dead Lecturer* and *The System of Dante's Hell* and Ishmael Reed's *Yellow Book Radio*. I like the kinds of diction Ishmael uses, and I like the way LeRoi's poems look on the page. I'm not referring to what LeRoi's describing. I'm talking about his syntax and structure—the way the poem looks. It bothers me, on occasion, to look at poems where all the first letters are capitalized. It's very boring to me. That's why I use the lower-case alphabet. Also, I like the idea that letters dance, not just that the words dance; of course, the words also dance. I need some visual stimulation, so that reading becomes not just a passive act and more than an intellectual activity, but demands rigorous participation. Furthermore, I think there are ways to accentuate very subtle ideas and emotions so that the reader is not in control of the process. This means that I have to have more tricks than everybody else because I can't let you get away with thinking you know what I mean. After all, I didn't mean whatever you can just ignore. I mean what you have to struggle with, and in this transition the piece becomes special.

The spellings result from the way I talk or the way the character talks, or the way I heard something said. Basically, the spellings reflect language as I hear it. I don't write because words come out of my brain. I write this way because I hear the words. It's as if somebody were talking to me. I don't mean to sound as if I'm out of my mind but I do hear my characters. It's really very peculiar because sometimes I'll hear very particular rhythms underneath whatever I'm typing, and this rhythm affects the structure of the piece. For instance, if I'm hearing a rumba, you'll get a poem that looks like a rumba on the page. So the structure is connected to the music that I hear beneath the words.

It annoys me when people think that my writing isn't intellectual. That to me is a denigration of Afro-American culture. I have an overwhelming amount of material I could footnote if I wanted to. I could make my work very official and European and say the "Del Vikings" were a group of singers . . . the "Shorrells" were a group . . . but why should I. I'm not interested in doing an *annotated Shange.* I could let a European do that, but I'm not going to. Either you know us or you don't. If you don't, then you should look it up. The Del Vikings and the Brown and Fergerson decisions [see "just as the del vikings stole my heart" in *Nappy Edges*] were two cultural events that have importance to black people. If you can't get that together, then I guess you just can't get it together. I cannot teach and write poetry at the same time. Therefore, I'm not going to annotate these things. If you're ignorant, you're ignorant. If I refer to Pacheco and Rodriguez, or if I refer to Roland Young or David Murray, or if I refer to *l'Arche de Triomphe,* that's because black people have all these things.

There's been systematic cultural attack on black people that has propagated the misconception that we only have this little thing over here: this bottle top and this piece of gum. So when people read my stuff, Thulani Davis's things, June Jordan's things, or even Ish's [Ishmael Reed's] things, the folks propagating this myth get all confused because they are not the "black people" whom they know. Well, isn't that unfortunate. I've had black students trying to correct Paul Lawrence Dunbar's dialect poetry. So it's not just white folks. They actually tried to read it in "good" English. That just hurt my feelings so much. So it's important for me to keep writing these things that refer to our culture, even though in the U.S. it's called "popular culture" or "vernacular culture." For me James Brown, Earth, Wind and Fire, the Art Ensemble of Chicago, Cecil Taylor, Pacheco and Rodriguez are all *high* art. I will stick to my guns about that. We do not have to refer continually to European art as the standard. That's absolutely absurd and racist, and I won't participate in that utter lie. My work is one of the few ways I can preserve the elements of our culture that need to be remembered and absolutely revered.

C.T.:    Have you noticed an evolution in terms of your creative interest?

SHANGE:    My work has changed significantly. One of the reasons I agreed to have this interview, because I actually hate interviews, is that I thought it would be a good project for me to figure out exactly how I felt and what I thought. There are two or three things that have happened. I'm a little bit less flippant than I used to be. I can write and did write very pernicious, nasty, awful, terrible, cruel, virtually sadistic things. I have stopped doing that because I was on the receiving end of this kind of cruelty. So I'm a little more careful about castigating people. When I get the urge to castigate someone now, I say to myself: what did they really do that makes me feel this way? Can I voice my criticism without openly attacking them? Can I present their case and suggest the castigation without saying they're full of shit, and I can't stand their guts? Can I just show that a person is full of shit without having to say it, and then let the audience decide? That way I don't have to be a bull whip. I've been working on this method of expressing criticism just because I don't want to do to anybody else what was done to me. This task is very personal, and it may not be a literary issue.

The other change concerns language. I got all confused about what language I wanted to write in. For a while there would be lines in English, in French and in Portuguese. I said, "Nobody would be able to understand this but me and my sister." So I said, "This is ridiculous. I can't do this." So I had to get rid of the multilingual stuff. But I didn't really get rid of it. I realize that I have some responsibility for this position in literature I have now; I kept this stuff because some scholar at some time might want to see it, but basically I just stopped myself from writing in this fashion. That phase lasted maybe eight months.

Then I got all involved in writing what I call "not-poetry." Other people call it poetry, but I say they're stories. People keep talking about the poems in *Spell #7*. I didn't know there were any poems in *Spell #7*. I was having difficulty understanding what people were saying I was doing. I decided that I wouldn't pay any attention to what they were saying. I'll just call these pieces "things." When I settled that, I started having all these character people show up. I had to decide whether I should write a novel about this person, whether this other one needed two more stories about her. Should I, for instance, carry on with the character because I know she has a life? Or should I let her stop because I have a nice finished product? This is a technical problem I'm working through because in *A Photograph: Lovers in Motion* there are really five plays, one for each of those characters; there is no main character. Five full-length plays would be a wonderful thing to do . . . a quintet. But should I do it? Or shouldn't I go on to some other people whom I don't already know? I have been worried about this.

Of course, I still want to do what I've always wanted to do, but *how* I do it is different now. I seem to be eluding landscapes almost entirely. Sometimes I have no idea where these people are, and the novelist in me resents that but the poet in me loves it. The stories just take place inside of somebody. They satisfy me, but sometimes I miss the environment. For instance, in "Allegre" [*Photographs: A Study in Cruelty,* an unpublished manuscript] I have no idea where she is. There's no mention of her house. There's no description of what she wears. I have no idea what she looks like. I just don't know. I don't know what city she lives in. It just didn't matter. She is just telling us what she dreamt about, so that other stuff isn't important. Whereas with "Sue Jean" [*Photographs*] we know that she lives somewhere in West Virginia up in the hills in some little dinky town. She has a bar with sawdust on the floor, and she has a house with specific items. "Crystal Lee" [*Photographs*] apparently lives in an old part of a big midwestern city because she has a yard and a tree. They're all different, but they still bother me because I love lushness; I love trees. I love beautiful things, but living in New York prohibited me from having that. The reason *Sassafrass* is one of my favorite books is because she lives somewhere; there is space and greenery. She has all these beautiful things I can tell you about because I lived in California then, and I could see them. In New York I only see what's in my house. So what you get is the inside of a person because there's nothing for me to see of any interest on the outside. It's all man-made, and it's really all very uninteresting.

I don't have any relationship to the earth here in New York. When I lived in Houston while *A Photograph* was in rehearsal, I felt incredible. I was writing fifteen pages a day. It was so easy to do because I had trees and grass; there were rustling leaves and singing birds, and I could smell dirt when I went outside. That's really important to me. It bothers me that my environment affects what I'm able to give, so much so that I've decided that in order to preserve the quality of the work that I like to write—I'm not saying I don't like the work that I write here, but it's different from what I want to write—I must move. It's what I have to do. If I lived in Connecticut, I wouldn't write about Marta. In the recent past I wrote all the ugly stuff I could think of. It's not that I'll stop writing ugly stories, but at least I'll be able to put in a patch of decency when I get out of here. I really need that. So that's what's changed in my work. It's gotten much starker.

I wrote this in my journal yesterday: "I want others to see what I see, but how? Lyrically as landscape or as a verb, as colored or non-ethnic, whatever that is. And I wonder if they, the omnipresent others, will ever understand, even if I do preen and crop each line leaving only what I have distilled, if I leave only the smell of a person, her eyes, will the others understand that that was the point?" Everything I write here in New York seems to me to have more to do with verbs; the work talks about constant doing. Whereas, outside of New York the texture of somebody or something is more available to me. Here in the city, it is she *went*. In the country, it is she *is*. There you can *have* it, as opposed to *getting* it here. In the New York stories I think I *get* it, whereas in the California stories I *have* it, and I love it. I would never spend the time on a character here in New York as I did with Sassafrass because a New York character doesn't have that kind of time. She doesn't have the time to do what Sassafrass did. She doesn't have the time to make all these recipes. "Fay" [*Photographs*] had [only] one night when she could go out and that was it. Whereas, we must be with Sassafrass for months. I would never allow myself to stay with a New York character for months. It would drive me crazy. I wouldn't even want to know about her. Beaten up, raped and left is the symbol for this city, just like Marta.

C.T.:   Can you describe your writing process?

SHANGE:   I go to the typewriter if I absolutely have to go to the typewriter. This would occur in two situations: when I have a poem that I have to write because I know enough about it so that it can just come out on the typewriter. Or when I have a deadline, and I have to get some poems some place; then I go to my journal and type them out. Usually I wait until I feel I've got a lot of stuff ready;

then I feel very gratified when I sit at the typewriter and type, though generally I write in longhand.

I write whenever I get up. I also like to go to one of the cafés that I frequent and write during off-hours between 2 and 4:30 in the afternoon and between 6:30 and 8 in the evening. I'll have a glass of wine and Perrier water, and I just sit and write in my journal for an hour-and-a-half or two hours. That's very good for me to do because that environment is very protected. I'm not here at home by myself; so whatever my demons are, they're not going to be able to overwhelm me because I'm alone and vulnerable. If I have a real scary piece to write, I might go outside and do it; it would be too much for me to do alone because then these character people would get all over the place and I'd be afraid. Whereas, if I go outside and I know I'm around people, I feel very secure. Then I can write about all kinds of weird or scary things. The demons must control themselves. I wrote "with no immediate cause" [*Nappy Edges*] in a café. I wrote "the white girl story" in a café. I wrote "it's not so good to be a girl"* in a café. There I can write about things that are frightening or even about my own emotional development, which can also be very scary. I go in there, sit down, have a glass of wine, have some Perrier water. I sit there for hours and write and have a grand time. I might see some people whom I know, but they know me well enough not to bother me. But I'll be in communication with other living people so these weird character people who are coming out have to behave. When I'm in the house alone, I've got to tackle these demons. Sometimes they appear at five in the morning. I'm not going to go anyplace then.

I wrote "Beau Willie" at home. I typed it out because I just knew it. I had it so it was not frightening to me. I was angry about it. Angry things I can do here at home. I have to go outside to do things that threaten me. Things that are very joyous to me I do both outside and at home. They can be done anywhere. I don't ever like to be afraid in the house; I'll always go out because home is supposed to be a safe haven. Things aren't supposed to run me here. I run them.

Have I done something really scary here? I did the "black & white two dimensional planes" girl here. I did her in a way I haven't done anything before. I did her a section at a time over a two-week pe-

* This appeared in *The Black Scholar*, vol. 10, no. 8–9, May–June 1979, pp. 28–29.

riod. If I have a "scholarly" poem, I think she's probably it. She's very specific; she's paced. She's all those things "academic" poetry is supposed to be.

C.T.: You refer to your poems, to your work as a whole, in the feminine—as "she."

SHANGE: That's right. That's why I don't like having the weird ones get out of control. When I was directing *A Photograph: Lovers in Motion* there were five of these weird characters living with me. As the director, I was responsible for all of them emotionally. I had to share them with the actors. Sharing my life with them really was making me quite "insane" because they were really five wanton and uncontrollable creatures. That was just very difficult. I was really glad when the show opened because I could just place them over *there*.

C.T.: Is the transition between creating the work and directing it a big jump for you?

SHANGE: Not really. I've been in every piece I've ever written including *A Photograph*. I was in *A Photograph* in closed rehearsal for two weeks. I was in the advertisement for *Spell #7*. I know about the acting end. But there was a transition in the sense that I really had to direct the pieces as well as write them. Thus, I had to see my work in two very different ways. I don't generally believe in doing this, but I had to because of circumstances, not by choice. I was not able to get the directors [for *A Photograph*] I wanted because they were all working. Somebody had to do it, so I did it. I felt confident and competent to do so because I had just finished Wesley Richards's *The Mighty Gents* and June Jordan's *The Issue,* but I don't believe nor would I ever suggest that writers should direct their own work. I'll never do it again, but at that time it had to be done.

My major problem as a director was easing up my actors so that they wouldn't give up. After all, I'd been living with the characters for three years; they had them for three weeks. So I could not push the actors into different kinds of emotional climaxes and discoveries at a pace faster than they could handle. That was my major area of restraint. I had to see that I had been very selfish and narcissistic because I wasn't looking at other people's needs. These people couldn't possibly be where I was in terms of understanding these characters; so I had to stop pushing them. The first day of rehearsal I saw that the actors didn't understand anything and it was awful.

Then I said, "My God, Zaki, this is the first day they have it, so just lighten up." I also had a lot of help, not just from the theater people themselves, but from my family and my coterie of friends.

C.T.:    It's been five years since the sensational productions of *For Colored Girls.*

SHANGE:    For years I wouldn't discuss *For Colored Girls.* I also wouldn't see it. If you mentioned it to me in an interview, I would say, "If you talk about *For Colored Girls,* I'll leave."

People say they saw my play and I respond by saying, "Which one?" I'm being very serious when I say that; I'm not being haughty at all. I am not a one-shot artist; I've done five shows, all of which have been received well. I'm basing my relationship with the world on that and not just on *For Colored Girls.* I was between twenty-four and twenty-six when I wrote it. Why would I want to base my thirty-four-year-old person on that? That would be absurd! That was the piece that was commercially available to people, which is unfortunate because that's all they were able to get. That's one of the reasons I resent Broadway: one cannot become a national writer in the United States, at least not in theater, unless one's either been an underground hero or heroine for years and years or unless one has had a smash hit on Broadway. Then nobody wants to deal with anything else you do except what's been on Broadway. You might want to do a piece in Detroit just because you love the piece, and people respond by saying when is it going to Broadway, as if Broadway has something to do with the piece.

C.T.:    Was *For Colored Girls* a victim of media manipulation?

SHANGE:    Of course, it was. People look at what will serve their interests best. People who want to read my work have the responsibility to read it. I do not have a responsibility to be famous, but they have the responsibility to go look for the books. They have a responsibility even to buy theater books. Sure, it would be great if *Spell #7* were on Broadway, or if *Sassafrass* were a musical, or if "Carrie" [Boogie Woogie] were a movie, or if *A Photograph* were a movie. These things are all possible, but they're not probable right this minute. That doesn't prevent people from reading these works. I am at least still being published. So that's not a problem.

Reading, to me, is simply the expansion of one's mind to include some people whom you just didn't get to meet before.

This reminds me of another point. I was very upset with a few people whom I must respect—real knowledgeable theater people—who asked me what was the point of *Spell #7*? What was the point of *Boogie Woogie*? What was the point of such-and-such? I kept saying: "Didn't you have some feelings while you were reading it?" And they said that they had a lot of feelings. So I said, "That was the point!" One of my major problems with black theater at this time is that I really resent the idea that we still have to have not "race" plays but "issue" plays, or "point" plays. *For Colored Girls* for me is not an issue play. It is an exploration. All my work is just an exploration of people's lives. So there isn't any point. There are just some people who are interesting. There's something there to make you feel intensely. Black writers have a right to do this.

The commercial people tell me that one of the reasons the rest of my work hasn't been as commercially successful as *For Colored Girls* is that it has *no point* that they could sell. That's because there's going to be *no more point*. I'm not writing about a point. *For Colored Girls* doesn't have a point either, but they made a point out of it. Those girls were people whom I cared about, people whom I offered to you for you to see and to know. Black and Latin writers have to start demanding that the fact we're alive is point enough!

Half the plays in *The New York Times* today don't have a point. *Babes in Toyland* doesn't have a point. *Sugar Babies* doesn't have a point. *Bent* doesn't have a point. *Elephant Man* doesn't have a point. They're just people—white people. They're people and we experience their lives. That is the point. But with black people, our being alive is not enough of a point. Well, it's enough of a point for me.

C.T.: When did you first know you were a writer?

SHANGE: I wrote when I was a child. I wrote stories. Then it became very difficult for me to get through school because somebody told me that "Negroes"—we weren't "black" then—didn't write. Some racial incident blocked my writing, and I just stopped. I can't remember exactly when it was. I started writing again in high school. I wrote some poetry, and it was published in a high-school magazine. That same year I'd been writing a lot of essays in English class, and I would always write about black people. Then I was told that I was beating a dead horse, so I stopped writing again. I started back at it when I was nineteen.

C.T.: Do you intend to include white people in your work?

SHANGE: I would never have a white person in a story I wrote with the possible exception of "the white girl" [*Spell #7*] piece. I have no reason to do it. I was writing this real funny thing last night in my head. It was about my putting a story in a time capsule so that people in the year 20,000 could find it. It was a conversation with a white director: "Yes, I think it's wonderful that you think it's so good that you think it should be all white. Yes, I think it's fine that you think, even though the character is black, a white actress could do it so much better because you know black people really can't talk, although I remember that when my mother was speaking to me in my house, I never heard her talk like the white girl you're going to hire is going to talk like a black person. Then again, I'm only black, so how would I know how best to do it? Yes, I think it's wonderful that you think that because it's a black character you absolutely have to have this white actress play her because she's so good. And where in the world could you find a black person who could play her? I mean, after all it is a black character, and you know a black actress isn't perfectly trained to do this. So, yes, I think you should take my name off it and give me my money. Yes, it's perfectly all right if you use the story as is, but remember nobody in the world will believe that these people were really white. I mean, after all, they sweat."

This business is very sick. The theater is very sick. I feel really badly about it, though I'm compelled to keep working in this medium. What keeps me in theater has nothing to do with an audience. It has to do with the adventure that's available in that little, three-dimensional stage. I can see a character who exists for me in one way become a real human body. That's a great adventure for me. I don't care if anybody comes. My artist-self, the person who writes these things, doesn't care. Theater gives my stuff what I cannot give it. Actors spend as many years learning how to act as I've spent learning how to write. Actors spend many years trying to give me something that I don't have. They make the piece come alive in a new way. For example, writers think they know how their characters sit. But if you give a piece to Avery Brooks or Laurie Carlos or Judy Brown or Mary Alice, how they sit can change everything. The timbre of their voices, how they walk, what they do, become available as a communal experience. You cannot read a book with somebody. Whereas, when you have a character there in front of you, that's somebody you know and anybody else sitting there with you would know also. Theater helps me, as a writer, know where I didn't give a character enough stuff, or where I told a lie. It's just a glorious thing to see actors make my characters come alive. But I don't like it when my artist-self has to be confined so that other people can understand. In the theater you have to do this; otherwise, they call your work "performance pieces," which means that you should be a white person and live downtown. Obviously, I can't do that.

Taking risks in a performance is virtually prohibited in this country. I think I take a lot of risks. It was risky for us to do the minstrel dance in *Spell #7*, but I insisted on it because I thought the actors in my play were coming from pieces they didn't want to be in but pieces that helped them pay their bills. Black characters are always being closed up in a "point." They decided, for instance, that *Spell #7* by Zaki Shange is a feminist piece and therefore not poetry. Well, that's a lie. That's giving me a minstrel mask. That's forcing me to fulfill somebody else's idea. So I put that dance in there because that's how I felt. I felt trapped, and I felt parodied and ridiculed and exploited. I had the minstrel dance because that's what happens to black people in the arts no matter how famous we become. They still refer to Alvin Ailey as if he were a freak; he's had a company for twenty years. They still act as if Carmen De Lavallade was the last Afro-American ballerina, and she has trained at least fifty people herself. It's this box, these stereotypes, that people expect, so I put them in a minstrel dance.

Black Theater is not moving forward the way people like to think it is. We're not free of our paint yet! The biggest moneymakers— *The Wiz, Bubblin' Brown Sugar, Ain't Misbehavin'*—are all minstrel shows. So that's why I did the minstrel piece

C.T.: How did you go about integrating feminist activity with black responsiveness to it?

SHANGE: I didn't. I was simply writing, and the people who wanted to hear what I was writing were women. I didn't start out to write feminist tracts. I was writing what I had to write. The places where I'd been asked to read in San Francisco were women's places. My first feminist experience was the book that Thulani Davis and I did, called *Fat Mama*. It's a woman's book, an anthology which we did in 1969 at Barnard with a grant from the school and donations from our friends. We went from there to California where we belonged to a Third World Women's Cooperative, which was very supportive and instrumental in our development. So, I didn't really do anything about integrating feminism and black consciousness. We met together in groups by ourselves: black, white, Asian, and Native-American women. We did our work for our own people, and all of my work just grew from there.

# · ALICE WALKER ·

*L*ike *many of her fictional characters, Alice Walker was born the daughter of a Southern sharecropper, in rural Georgia, and was active in the civil rights movement. She attended Spelman College on a scholarship and graduated from Sarah Lawrence in 1965.*

*Walker began her literary career as a poet with the collection* Once: Poems *(1968), followed by* Revolutionary Petunias *(1973), and in 1979,* Good Night Willie Lee, I'll See You in the Morning. *She also edited an anthology of Zora Neale Hurston's writing, entitled* I Love Myself When I'm Laughing *(1979).*

*At the time of publication of her first novel,* The Third Life of Grange Copeland *(1970), Alice Walker said in* Library Journal *that for her, "family relationships are sacred." Indeed, much of Walker's work portrays the spiritual and physical devastation that occurs when the family trust is violated.* The Third Life of Grange Copeland *centers around the life of a young black girl, Ruth Copeland, and her grandfather, Grange. After brutalizing his own family because of the overwhelming racial circumstances of early twentieth-century rural Georgia and his own personal inadequacies, Grange learns that self-respect and family esteem can only be gained by assuming absolute responsibility for one's actions.*

*In* In Love and Trouble *(1973), a collection of powerful short stories, this theme is continued but broadened to include personal relationships in general. Walker's second novel,* Meridian *(1976), recounts the valiant life of a civil rights worker, Meridian Hill. Her strength for enduring hardships originates, ironically, in guilt arising from violating the family bond.* You Can't Keep A Good Woman Down *(1981), her second collection of short stories, dramatizes the resiliency of black women in the face of racial, sexual, and economic oppression.* The Color Purple *(1982), Walker's most recent novel, shows a woman's determination to survive the cruelties of her life by recording every detail in letters, first to God, and then to her long-lost sister.*

*Alice Walker's essays and stories appear frequently in* Ms. *where she is a contributing editor. She resides in San Francisco.*

◆ ◆ ◆

CLAUDIA TATE:   Critics have frequently commented about the nonlinear structure of *Meridian.* Did you have a particular form or symbolic structure in mind when you wrote this novel?

ALICE WALKER:   All I was thinking of when I wrote *Meridian,* in terms of structure, was that I wanted one that would continue to be interesting to me. The chronological structure in *The Third Life of Grange Copeland* was interesting as a one-time shot, since I had never before written a novel. So when I wrote *Meridian,* I realized that the chronological sequence is not one that permits me the kind of freedom I need in order to create. And I wanted to do something like a crazy quilt, or like *Cane* [by Jean Toomer]—if you want to be literary—something that works on the mind in different patterns. As for the metaphors and symbols, I suppose, like most writers, I didn't really think of them; they just sort of happened.

You know, there's a lot of difference between a crazy quilt and a patchwork quilt. A patchwork quilt is exactly what the name implies—a quilt made of patches. A crazy quilt, on the other hand, only *looks* crazy. It is not "patched"; it is planned. A patchwork quilt would perhaps be a good metaphor for capitalism; a crazy quilt is perhaps a metaphor for socialism. A crazy-quilt story is one that can jump back and forth in time, work on many different levels, and one that can include myth. It is generally much more evocative of metaphor and symbolism than a novel that is chronological in structure, or one devoted, more or less, to rigorous realism, as is *The Third Life of Grange Copeland.*

*The Third Life of Grange Copeland* is a very realistic novel. I wanted it to be absolutely visual. I wanted the reader to be able to sit down, pick up that book and see a little of Georgia from the early twenties through the sixties—the trees, the hills, the dirt, the sky—to feel it, to feel the pain and the struggle of the family, and the growth of the little girl Ruth. I wanted all of that to be very real. I didn't want there to be any evasion on the part of the reader. I didn't want the reader to say, "Now, I think she didn't mean this." I wanted him or her to say, "She has to mean this. This is a mean man: she *meant* him to be a mean man." I had a lot of criticism, of course, about Brownfield, and my response is that I know many Brownfields, and it's a shame that I know so many.

I will not ignore people like Brownfield. I want you to know I know they exist. I want to tell you about them, and there is no way you are going to avoid them. You are going to have to deal with them. I wish people would do that rather than tell me that this is not the right image. You know, they say this man Brownfield is too mean; nobody's this mean.

C.T.: Brownfield's meanness is balanced against Grange's third life of compassion and understanding. So the statement is not entirely negative.

WALKER: The people who criticize me about Brownfield rarely even talk about Grange. Loyle Hairston is the only black male critic who understood the balance between Grange and Brownfield. Frankly, I think it's because he has read a lot. I'm not convinced that many of the reviewers have read very much literature, and as a result they seem to think you don't put in negative characters, period. But I think Loyle's background in Russian literature, which I like very much—where you get "meanies" and "goodies" and everything—helped him to deal with that book. But it didn't help him at all when it came to *Meridian.* I know because he told me that he just didn't understand it and would have to read it again. And I said, "Sure, go right ahead."

When you asked about critical response to *Meridian,* I must in all honest humility say I don't know of any critics who could do it justice because I can't think of anyone. The reviews I've seen have taken little parts of the book, never treating it in its entirety. For example, there was a wonderful review by Griel Marcus in *The New Yorker,* but he concentrated totally on the influence of Camus on the work. His whole thing was guilt and expiation. Somebody else talked about the strictly social and political issues of the sixties. Someone else talked about the Indians! And somebody else talked about the invention of legend in the first section where the women's tongue is buried under the tree and the tree grows miraculously and all that.

Oh yes, then there are the people, mostly Jewish "girls," who get to the part about Lynn. And every Jewish "girl" I meet under fifty is Lynn or thinks she is. And they claim a) Lynn's a stereotype, or b) she's just like them. And then there's the whole dilemma about black men and what their responsibility is to black women and vice versa. Some Spelman students even called me up and said, "We've been all over the campus looking for the tree. Where is it?" So I said, "Where is there a reviewer who can put it all together?"*

But anyway, the first novel is easy for the critics to deal with. It's real. The realism is there even though people do not want to accept Brownfield as a real character. But with *Meridian,* there's just a lot going on. And when people tell me they just read it once, I do have to smile because I just don't see how you can read it once, and understand anything.

So, what I feel about *Meridian* is that I knew while I was writing it, it remained interesting to me, and that is very important because often when you write things, they're no longer interesting to you halfway through. Then the best thing to do is to throw them away because they don't hold up. But *Meridian's* structure is interesting, and it's really very carefully done. It's like the work of one of my favorite artists, Romare Bearden. In some ways *Meridian* is like a collage.

Another reason I think nobody has been able to deal with *Meridian* as a total work is the whole sublayer of Indian consciousness, which as I get older becomes more and more pronounced in my life. I know this sounds very strange, but I had been working very hard, but not consciously really, to let into myself all of what being in America means, and not to exclude any part of it. That's something I've been working on, on a subconscious level. I've also been trying to rid my consciousness and my unconscious of the notion of God as a white-haired, British man with big feet and a beard. You know, someone who resembles Charlton Heston. As a subjected people that image has almost been imprinted on our minds, even when we think it hasn't. It's there because of the whole concept of God as a person. Because if God is a person, he has to look like someone. But if he's *not* a person, if she's not a person, if *it's* not a person. . . . Or, if

---

* Barbara Christian in her book *Black Women Novelists: The Development of a Tradition, 1892-1976* (Westport, Conn.: Greenwood Press, 1980) does an incredibly rich and full interpretation of *Meridian.*

it is a person, then everybody is it, and that's all right. But what I've been replacing that original oppressive image with is everything there is, so you get the desert, the trees; you get the birds, the dirt; you get everything. And that's all God.

I don't know how to explain this really, but sometimes it's like when you hear voices. Well, I don't really hear voices, you'll be happy to know. But sometimes I have something like visitations, and I know they come from what is Indian in me, and I don't necessarily mean Indian blood because I'm not getting back to that; you know my grandmother was such-and-such, although I'm sure the Cherokees were very thick with black folks in Georgia, until they got run out. But anyway, I had this visitation, and it was about smoking grass, which I had been smoking, and he said, "It's okay to smoke grass to help you temporarily forget or ease your problems, but you must go through a time when you engage with your problems without the smoke; otherwise, they will not be worked out, but only become layer on layer, like crisscross webs."

I like that. I like these visitations popping into my mind. I don't know any Indians. When I was in the desert, not long ago, I saw Indians. But I don't know them except on a level of longing. In Georgia there are so many remnants of their presence that there is a real kinship with these people who were forced off the land that was theirs.

C.T.:   How did you go about characterizing *Meridian*?

WALKER:   I think it started when I became aware that the very brave and amazing people whom I knew in the civil rights movement were often incredibly flawed, and in a way, it was these flaws that both propelled them and "struck" them. I mean they were often stricken because of their flaws which at the same time kept them going. I was fascinated by the way you hardly ever saw their flaws. And yet, they were there, hidden. The image you got on television showed their remarkable control, their sense of wholeness and beauty. In short, they were heroic. It's just that the other side of that control was the cost of their heroism, which I think as black people, as Americans, we don't tend to want to look at because the cost is so painful.

To most people Meridian's illness seems sort of exotic, and they can't quite figure out why she gets ill. But the fact is that when you are under enormous stress, as most of the civil rights people were, the things that the body will do are just incredible. I fully expect that the people who were very brave and who had endured racial brutality and intimidation ... I fully expect that throughout their lives they will have some sort of physical disorder. Because suffering is not all psychological. The body and the mind really are united and if the central nervous system is crucially unbalanced by something, then there are also physical repercussions.

Guilt is also stress, and if it is compounded by intense political activity in a dangerous situation and compounded further by the giving away of your child, the losing of someone you love, then that stress becomes so intense that physical problems result.

I think Marge Piercy was right in one way in her review of *Meridian,* although in another way she was very humorous. She said that what the book needed to end it was a marriage or a funeral. Marriage is absurd. Meridian is not interested in marriage, but I can see that the expected end of that kind of struggle is death. It's just that in addition to all of her other struggles, her struggle is to not die. That's what she means when she's talking about martyrs not permitting themselves to be martyrs, but at some point just before martyrdom they should just go away and do something else.

She talks about Malcolm and King going off to farm or raise Dalmatians or doing something else other than permitting martyrdom. This impulse to flee represents her struggle to break with Christianity because Christianity really insists on martyrdom. She can see that the life of Christ is exemplary. It truly is. It's a fine life. But just before the crucifixion, according to Meridian, Jesus should have just left town.

C.T.:   Does Truman assume Meridian's struggle at the end of the novel?

WALKER:   Oh yes, Meridian's struggle is in this sense symbolic. Her struggle is the struggle each of us will have to assume in our own way. And Truman will certainly have to assume his because his life has been so full of ambivalence, hypocrisy and obliviousness of his action and their consequences.

C.T.:   Are black women writers more concerned with dramatizing intimate male-female encounters than social confrontations with white society?

WALKER:   I can't think of any twentieth-century black woman writer who is first and foremost interested in what white folks think.

I exempt Phillis Wheatley and all the nineteenth-century black women writers who *did* have that problem. Twentieth-century black women writers all seem to be much more interested in the black community, in intimate relationships, with the white world as a *backdrop*, which is certainly the appropriate perspective, in my view. We black women writers know very clearly that our survival depends on trust. We will not have or cannot have anything until we examine what we do to and with each other. There just has not been enough examination or enough application of findings to real problems in our day-to-day living. Black women continue to talk about intimate relationships so that we can recognize what is happening when we see it, then maybe there will be some change in behavior on the part of men *and* women.

When you see *For Colored Girls Who Have Considered Suicide When the Rainbow is Enuf,* for example, and you see what the behavior looks like on stage and you recognize it, you are recognizing it as behavior you've seen in the real world and you can judge the consequences of it. This recognition has to become very ordinary for all black people. We must be able to see what is happening, recognize such behavior and *make a judgment.* Judgment is crucial because judgment is lacking in black people these days.

Let's see if I can explain what I mean by that. There was a time when behavior was judged much more strictly than it is now. If you were walking down the street and some black man felt he was perfectly right to accost you and say sneaky, nasty little things to you, there was a time when the community rose up and said, "That's wrong! You can't do that. This is Miss so-and-so's child." There was a time when the community looked at this kind of behavior with the eyes of judgment. But today black people see, without judgment. They think that to be nonjudgmental is progress. But in fact, it isn't when your non-judgment means that people suffer. And they do because there is no one saying with the whole authority of the community that what you are doing is hurting us as a community.

c.t.:    Do you think that black women are capitalizing on an antagonistic press, as Ishmael Reed said not too long ago?

WALKER:    I read somewhere that Reed said he had sold only eight thousand copies of his last book, and he was upset. He felt that if he had been a black lesbian poet he would have sold many more. But I have bought nearly all of Reed's books, and I did not buy them because he is a black lesbian poet. I bought them because he is writing about the black community, presumably from inside it. Since I *am* the black community, I represent his audience. And it is this audience that is ultimately important.

In any case, I think anybody can *only write.* Writing or not writing is not dependent on what the market is—whether your work is going to sell or not. If it were, there is not a black woman who would write. And that includes Phillis Wheatley. Think of *her* antagonistic market! I mean if you really thought about the market, you would probably just take a job canning fish. Even the most successful black women writers don't make a lot of money, compared to what white male and female writers earn just routinely. We live in a society that is racist and white. That is one problem. Another is, we don't have a large black readership; I mean, black people, generally speaking, don't read. That is our *main* problem. Instead of attacking each other, we could try to address that problem by doing whatever we can to see that more black works get out into the world—which, for example, Reed does with his publishing company—and by stimulating an interest in literature among black people. Black women writers seem to be trying to do just that, and that's really commendable.

This brings to mind Ntozake Shange's book, *Nappy Edges,* which I just read and liked a lot. It has a wonderful introduction where she refers to a speech she made at Howard. She talked about how black people should try to relate to their writers and permit them the same kind of individuality they permit their jazz musicians. It's beautifully written, and funny, and I'm sure the audience loved what she was saying. Black women instinctively feel a need to connect with their reading audience, to be direct, to build a readership for us all, but more than that, to build *independence.* None of us will survive except in very distorted ways if we have to depend on white publishers and white readers forever. And white critics. If Reed only sold a few thousand copies of his book, he might look at who *controls* publishing first, and then he might look at who is buying his stuff or not buying it, in order to determine whether there is some serious breakdown in communication between him and his potential readers. Although I have all of his early books, it gets harder to lay out money for books that speak of black women as barracudas. As black women become more aware of sexism—when, in fact, they are as sensitive to sexism as they are now to racism, *and they will become so*—then a lot of black male writers are going to be in serious trouble. You notice we do not buy books by William Styron in droves, either.

In any case, to blame black women for one's low sales is just depressing to think about, considering the sad state of our general affairs. Skylab is falling; the nukes are leaking; we're running out of oil and gas; there's a recession. People don't have jobs. Most writers I know, white and black, live with an enormous amount of anxiety over just getting by. That black male writers, no less than black men generally, think that when they don't get something they want, it is because of black women, and not because of the capitalist system that is destroying us all, is almost too much irony to bear. Capitalist society. Racist capitalist society. Racist, sexist and colorist capitalist society which doesn't give a damn about art except art that can be hoarded or sold for big bucks. It doesn't care about art that is crucial to our community because it doesn't care about our community— which is perhaps its only consistency.

If the black community fails to support its own writers, it will never have the knowledge of itself that will make it great. And for foolish, frivolous and totally misinformed reasons—going directly back to its profound laziness about the written message as opposed to one that's sung—it will continue to blunder along, throwing away this one and that one, and never hearing or using what is being said. That is basically what happened with Zora Neale Hurston. The time has to come when the majority of black people, not just two or three, will want their own novels and poems, will want their own folk tales, will want their own folk songs, will want their own whatever. There is so much that is ours that we've lost, and we don't even know we're missing it: ancient Egypt, ancient Ethiopia, Eatonville, Florida! And yet there's no general sense that the spirit can be amputated, that a part of the soul can be cut off because of ignorance of its past development. But I know one thing: when we really respect ourselves, our own minds, our own thoughts, our own words, when we really love ourselves, we won't have any problem whatsoever selling and buying books or anything else.

Look what happens with Jews and books. Jews make Jewish books bestsellers. Whatever is written by and about them they cherish and keep it going. When we feel *we* are worth money, when we feel that *we* are worth time, when we feel that *we* are worth love, we'll do it. But until we do, we won't. And that's that! This whole number about depending on white people for publicity and for this and that and so forth. . . . All I can say is I hope it will soon be over. I am tired of it.

By and large black women writers support themselves, they support each other and support a sense of community much more so than any other group I've ever come in contact with, except for the civil rights era when people tended to be collective. That was true of them, and it is true of us. And I like that.

C.T.:    What is your responsibility to your audience?

WALKER:    I'm always happy to have an audience. It's very nice because otherwise it would be very lonely and futile if I wrote and had no audience. But on the other hand, although *I'm willing* to think about the audience before I write, usually I don't. I try, first of all, to know what I feel and what I think and then to write that. And if there's an audience, well, fine, but if not, I don't worry about it.

Had I ever written a story with all white characters? Well, of course I have. Years ago I wrote a wonderful story which I must find, if it's not packed in a trunk somewhere back in Brooklyn. It's a good story, and I know I'll publish it one day. But at the time I wrote it, nobody would buy it because it was a very chilling view of white people, of these particular white people. I had written what I saw. I had written what I thought. I had written what I felt, but this was a view that was totally unacceptable to everyone. Nobody wanted this particular view.

So what I do generally is write, and if there's an audience, there is one, but if there isn't one, I just pack it up and wait.

C.T.:    Have people asked you whether *Meridian* is autobiographical?

WALKER:    Oh yes. I don't think people really understand that a book like *Meridian* is autobiographical only in the sense of projection. Meridian is entirely better than I am, for one thing. She is an exemplary person; she is an exemplary, *flawed* revolutionary because it seems to me that the revolutionary worth following is one who is flawed. When I was talking about the flaw before I didn't mean that it made these people less worthy of following. It made them more worthy of following.

My life has been, since I became an adult, much more middle-class than Meridian's. Although what happens often when I write is that I try to make models for myself. I project other ways of seeing. Writing to me is not about audience actually. It's about living. It's about expanding myself as much as I can and seeing myself in as many roles and situations as possible. Let me put it this way. If I could live as a tree, as a river, as the moon, as the sun, as a star, as the earth, as a rock, I would. Writing permits me to be more than I am. Writing permits me to experience life as any number of strange creations.

C.T.:   Are you drawn toward the folk hero/heroine as the focal point of your work?

WALKER:   I am drawn to working-class characters as I am to working-class people in general. I have a basic antagonism toward the system of capitalism. Since I'm only interested in changing it, I'm not interested in writing about people who already fit into it. And the working-class can never fit comfortably into a capitalist society.

I think my whole program as a writer is to deal with history just so I know where I am. It was necessary for me to write a story like *The Third Life of Grange Copeland*, which starts in the twenties and has passages that go back even further, so I could, later on, get to *Meridian*, to *In Love and Trouble* and then on to *The Color Purple*. I can't move through time in any other way, since I have strong feelings about history and the need to bring it along. One of the scary things is how much of the past, especially our past, gets forgotten.

C.T.:   You've often written that some of your stories were also your mother's stories:

> Yet so many of the stories that I write, that we all write, are our mothers' stories. Only recently did I fully realize this: that through years of listening to my mother's stories of her life, I have absorbed not only the stories themselves, but something of the manner in which she spoke, something of the urgency that involves the knowledge that her stories—like her life—must be recorded. . . . She had handed down respect for possibilities—and the will to grasp them. . . . Guided by my heritage of love and beauty and a respect for strength—in search of my mother's garden, I found my own.
>
> —"In Search of Our Mothers' Gardens,"
> *Ms.,* May 1974, p. 70

WALKER:    Yes, some of the stories in *In Love and Trouble* came out of my mother's stories, for instance, "Strong Horse Tea." She often talked about how poor people, "in the olden days," had to make up home remedies for sick people. She used to crack me up with the story about my brother who stuttered and how he was stuttering and stuttering and they couldn't figure out what to do about it. So finally someone told her to hit him in the mouth with a cow's melt. As far as I can figure out, it's something like the spleen. Anyway, it's something raw and wet and bloody, and you get a grip on it and just hit the stutterer in the mouth with it. That would make anyone stop stuttering or stop talking altogether. But anyway, she did that; she hit him in the mouth with the cow's melt and he stopped stuttering.

Anyway, my mother would ramble on and tell about how she would make tea out of the cow's hoof when one of us felt ill. Years later when I was living in Mississippi, when I wrote most of those stories, her world was all around me.

People tend to think that life really does progress for everyone eventually, that people progress, but actually only *some* people progress. The rest of the people don't. There's always somebody using "strong horse tea" in the world; this day, this minute, there's some poor woman making strong horse tea for a child because she's too poor to get a doctor. Now that may not be the case in California; it may not even be in Georgia or Mississippi; it might be in India. But somewhere it is current. This is what I started to understand while I was in Mississippi. So I made up the story about the woman who tried to save her baby because the doctor wouldn't come. You know that the baby died and most of the people around the mother, the white people especially, could not even comprehend that she suffered, that she suffered as any mother would suffer.

"The Revenge of Hannah Kemhuff" in *In Love and Trouble* is also based on one of my mother's stories about a time during the Depression when she went to a local commissary to get food and was refused. I carried the germ for that story of hers with me for years and years, just waiting for an opportunity to use it where it would do the most good.

I wrote "The Child Who Favored Daughter" [*In Love and Trouble*] in 1966, after my first summer in Mississippi. I wrote it out of trying to understand how a black father would feel about a daughter who fell in love with a white man. Now, this was very apropos because I had just come out of a long engagement with a young man who was white, and my father never accepted him. I did not take his nonacceptance lightly. I knew I needed to understand the depth of his antagonism. After all, I was twenty or so, and couldn't quite understand his feelings since history is taught in the slapdash fashion that it is taught. I needed to comprehend what was going on with him and what would go on with any black man of his generation brought up in the South, having children in the South, whose child fell in love with someone who is "the enemy."

I had been writing the story for, oh I guess, almost six months and I took it with me to Mississippi. Ironically, it was over that story, in a sense, that I met the man I did, in fact, marry. We met in the movement in Mississippi, and I was dragging around this notebook, saying "I'm a writer." Most people think when you say you're a writer, and especially when you're twenty, that you can't be serious. Well, I read the story to him and he was convinced.

"To Hell with Dying" [*In Love and Trouble*] was the first story I wrote and it was also my first published story. I wrote that story when I was still at Sarah Lawrence. It is my most autobiographical story. But again, the way autobiography works for a writer is different from what you'd think of as being autobiographical. It's autobiographical though, in fact, none of it happened. The *love* happened.

The story is created out of a longing. There was this man I really loved, not in the romantic sense, but I loved, cared about him, and he died while I was away at school. I didn't have any money to go home for the funeral. So the story was my tribute. It was what I could give. Referring to your question about audience, this story really wasn't about having an audience at all. All the audience I gave a damn about was dead. *He* was the audience. I would have been happy if he had known this was what I was thinking about when I couldn't go to his funeral.

# · MARGARET WALKER ·

*M*argaret Abigail Walker was born in Birmingham, Alabama in *1915. She received a B.A. from Northwestern University and an M.A. and Ph.D. from the University of Iowa. At the age of twenty-six in 1942, Margaret Walker received the Yale Younger Poet Award for her collection* For My People, *which brought her instant recognition.* For My People *was subsequently published by Yale University Press; it proclaimed pride in the Afro-American heritage and signalled a militant call for racial dignity.*

*Walker began her first novel* Jubilee *when she was nineteen and spent thirty years completing it. In an inspiring tale for all black Americans struggling for freedom and equality, Walker in* Jubilee *(1966) incorporated actual historical events into the fictionalized life of her maternal great-grandmother, Margaret Duggans, from slavery to the Reconstruction. Walker's other book-length publications include* Ballad of the Free *(1966),* Prophets for a New Day *(1966), and* October Journey *(1973).*

*Retired from teaching at Jackson State University in Jackson, Mississippi, Walker now devotes full-time to writing. She has recently completed the definitive biography of Richard Wright, entitled* The Daemonic Genius of Richard Wright, *and a new collection of poems concerning contemporary events, entitled* This is My Country. *She is at work on a number of projects. These include* Minna and Jim, *a sequel to* Jubilee; Mother Broyer, *a novel; and her autobiography. Walker has also written numerous scholarly articles on Afro-American literature and culture.*

◆  ◆  ◆

MARGARET WALKER:    I would like to read this excerpt from my
forthcoming autobiography from Howard University Press, which
speaks for itself:

> I graduated from Northwestern and [worked for] the WPA.
> After three years I went to graduate school in order to get a
> master's degree to enhance my teaching. Getting my master's
> in one school year nearly killed me. I was on NYA [National
> Youth Administration] and had so little money I ate lunch
> only once a week when a friend bought it. Like my college
> days at Northwestern, I went hungry unless friends fed me.
> When I went home in August, my father lifted me from the
> train. I was in a state of collapse. For eighteen months I was
> unable to work and could not find a job anyway. Meanwhile,
> one of my sisters graduated from music college and got a job
> teaching music at a small school in Mississippi. Her salary was
> forty dollars a month. Like my mother, she worked seven days
> a week, including playing for vespers and church on Sunday
> and practicing with the choir. She said the only time she had
> for herself was at night close to midnight until dawn. After
> teaching for two years in Mississippi, she went to Knoxville,
> Tennessee for a larger salary; but she had the same back-
> breaking schedule.
>
> As for myself, my teaching career has been fraught with
> conflict, insults, humiliations and disappointments. In every
> case when I have attempted to make a creative contribution
> and succeeded, I have been immediately replaced by a man. I
> began teaching over thirty years ago at Livingstone College in
> Salisbury, North Carolina, for the handsome sum of $135 a
> month. I was very happy to get it. I had a master's degree but
> no teaching experience. They would not have had a man for
> less than $150 to $200 a month. I arrived in Salisbury one cold
> February morning at two o'clock. Although I was expected,
> there was no one at the station to meet me. I finally found a
> taxi to take me to the campus, and I banged on the door of the
> girls' dormitory for a full half hour before anyone opened the
> door. Less than three hours after I went to bed, the matron
> ordered me out for breakfast at six o'clock and told me I had
> an eight o'clock class. My life was arranged for me hour by
> hour and controlled by half-a-dozen people. I was resented in
> the town and by some faculty and staff people because I was
> replacing one of their favorites. And I didn't know this person
> from Adam's cat. I had absolutely no social life; I spent most
> of my afternoons and evenings in my room writing.

That summer I won the Yale award and began getting job offers from everywhere. I felt strong pressure to stay at Livingstone, but when I went home my mother had accepted a job for me at West Virginia State College. It paid the grand sum of $200 a month. My dear mother thought it her duty to grab it before somebody else did. While I was there I never had a stable living situation. The night I arrived I had no place to go. . . . Five places in one school year. I had had it. If I had been a man, no one would have dared to move me around like that.

But the real harrowing time of my life came at Jackson State College. In September 1949 when I began teaching in Jackson, Mississippi, I was married and was the mother of three children. My youngest was nine-weeks-old. For nine months everything went well, and they kept saying that they were honored to have me until I moved my family and furniture. When they saw my husband was sick and disabled from the war, that I had three children all under six years of age, that I was poor and had to work, then they put their foot on my neck. . . . If I had been single, I would have quit that day; but I had three children and a sick husband, and I had just moved. So I bowed my head and decided to stay on. Perhaps I should have taken another job. . . .

A year later I was ordered to produce a literary festival for the 75th anniversary of the college. I was told to write some occasional poetry and to write and produce a pageant for the occasion. I said, "If I succeed I must leave here, and if I fail I must leave here." I succeeded through much stress and strain and much public embarrassment. Then I secured a Ford Fellowship and left. I stayed away for fifteen months and when I returned with a substantial raise, I also had another child.

While at Jackson State from 1954 until 1960, my salary remained well under $6,000. Meanwhile, I had devised a humanities program to suit the needs of black students in Mississippi, which not only raised the cultural level 75 percent, but also provided credits on race in the modern world and on the great contributions of black people to the modern world. . . .

Then began the death struggle for me to return to graduate school. I contended that I was no longer content to be classified as the equivalent of a Ph.D. because I was a poet. My salary was not equivalent. I was determined to go back and get the degree that everybody worshipped. Then they would be forced to pay me more money. After all, my children were growing up and getting ready for college, and my husband was disabled. I absolutely needed the money. I was tired of living on borrowed money from one month to the next.

I borrowed $500 from the credit union, got another $300 from the college as salary, plus money from my husband and my mother. I took my two younger children, ages six and eleven, and went back to Iowa to summer school. There I inquired about my chances of returning for the Ph.D. degree and using my civil-war novel for my dissertation. I also inquired about financial assistance. In the fall I went back to Jackson State College for another hellish year, but in September 1962 I managed to get away.

I had two children with me who were in college during those three years. One graduated a week before I did. When I returned to Jackson with my degree, I asked not to be involved with the humanities; instead I tried to formulate a new freshman English program of writing themes from relevant reading. After a year, the college administration did not so much as give me the courtesy of saying they would not require my services in that capacity the next year; they simply replaced me with a man, and not a man with superior training, rank or ability. I returned to an old interest in creative writing and taught courses in literary criticism, the Bible as literature, and Afro-American literature. After another so-so year, I devised the black studies program. Three years with that program have been the happiest of my teaching career at Jackson State College.

CLAUDIA TATE:    What was it like to live with *Jubilee* for thirty years?

WALKER:    You just become part of it, and it becomes part of you. Working, raising a family, all of that becomes part of it. Even though I was preoccupied with everyday things, I used to think about what I wanted to do with *Jubilee*. Part of the problem with the book was the terrible feeling that I wasn't going to be able to get it finished, since I was sick so much of the time. And even if I had the time to work at it, I wasn't sure I would be able to do it the way I wanted. Living with the book over a long period of time was agonizing. Despite all of that, *Jubilee* is the product of a mature person. When I started out with the book, I didn't know half of what I now know about life. That I learned during those thirty years. After all, I started writing *Jubilee* at nineteen, and I couldn't have dealt with, for instance, the childbirth problems. I couldn't have known about them then, not until I had become a mature woman who had her own problems. There's a difference between writing about something and living through it. I did both. I think I was meant to write *Jubilee.*

C.T.: *For My People* appeared in 1942, and [Gwendolyn] Brooks's *A Street in Bronzeville* in 1945. Was there any competition between these two works?

WALKER:    I'll give you some historical background on the two pieces. I wrote the title poem of *For My People* in July of 1937, around my twenty-second birthday. It was published in *Poetry Magazine* in November of that year. I went out to Iowa in the fall of 1939 and got my master's degree in the summer of 1940 when I was 25. I then went South to teach, though I actually didn't begin teaching until 1942. I met Gwendolyn Brooks in 1938, after I had written the title poem "For My People." Margaret Burroughs, a mutual friend, introduced us. I don't think Gwen had published in national magazines at that time. I'm two years older than Gwen.

*For My People* won the Yale award in the summer of '42. Yale had rejected it three times. Stephen Vincent Benet, the editor at that time, wanted to publish it the first time I sent it to him from the University of Iowa. Anyway, he kept it from February until July in '39, and he wrote to me telling me he thought the poems were as near perfect as I could make them. He asked me to resubmit them the following year, and I did. He said he'd keep them while he was trying to make up his mind. I didn't really know what was actually happening at Yale until I won. That year, 1942, was the last year Benet edited the Yale Younger Poet Series. I think he simply confronted his colleagues with the fact that if they wouldn't give the award to me, he wasn't going to name anybody else. In other words I think he was telling them he was through with them if they didn't give it to me. After all, he had repeatedly said the piece was as near perfect as I could make it. I think he felt they were refusing purely on the basis of race. I didn't know how much the issue had gone back and forth between them until I went up there. The woman with whom I'd corresponded said that they had "to come begging" because they had to ask for the manuscript. I hadn't submitted it that year because I got tired of sending it.

Three years after *For My People* was published, *A Street in Bronzeville* appeared in 1945. It was a very good book. I remember saying to Langston that the poetry was promising, technically and

intellectually; the work had great potential. *Annie Allen* [1949] ful-
filled that potential. I think *Annie Allen* is a superb book. Technically it is stunning. The subtleties come through it much better than
they did in *A Street in Bronzeville.*

Getting back to your question . . . I never felt that I was in competition with Gwen. But I had this feeling; I may be very wrong, and
I've been told I was wrong. I said in the book with Nikki [*A Poetic
Equation: Conversation Between Nikki Giovanni and Margaret
Walker*] that it was ironic that all the forces that had dealt negatively with my work dealt positively with Gwendolyn Brooks's
work. I named them in that book. First, Gwen won a poetry prize at
Northwestern. That never happened to me. Northwestern later gave
me a lot of recognition. But when I was a student there, they didn't.
Paul Engle was my teacher, and he was fighting mad with me for
sending *For My People* to Yale. For years he was annoyed about it. I
think he helped Gwen. Second, Richard Wright was a man whom I
knew very well for three years. We were never intimate, but we were
very dear and close friends. After we broke up and our friendship
ended, he helped Gwen. I'm certain that Gwen got published at
Harper because Wright was there. Nobody ever told me, but I think
he interceded for her. Paul Engle, Northwestern, Richard Wright
and the Friends of Literature on the North Side, with whom my
teachers at Northwestern were involved, all helped Gwen. Paul did
do two things for me: he helped me to get a job and helped me find
the ways and means to study at Iowa both times, in 1939 and in the
sixties. But to answer your question—I never figured for one day I
was in competition with Gwen.

I hope the new collection of poems, *This Is My Century,* will be
published. I think I've got a good book. I haven't seen anything like
it. The power is more sustaining than *For My People.* I've wanted to
do it for a long, long time. It's been in me for half a lifetime. What I
have here is a complete indictment of our present-day society, our
whole world. What's wrong with it is money, honey, money. Infla-
tion blues is what we got. What I have tried to do in this piece is integrate what [Alex] Haley did to me to show that it's just part of the
same corrupt scene.

c.t.:    What's happening with the Wright biography?

walker:    I sometimes get very frightened because I know so
much. I know I've been on the "black list" for a long time. Every-

time I pick up the Wright stuff, I get frightened. I realize that I'm dealing with very sensitive material. Sometimes I just turn away from it and wonder will I be signing my death warrant if I do what I know has to be done with that book. You see there are several very sensitive areas. One is communism itself, which concerned the great intellectual debate between black nationalism and the Communist Party: its dictates and policy on Negroes. If you tell the story the way it needs to be told, you're in trouble with both sides—the U. S. Government and the Communist Party. Neither one of them is a friend to black people. When Wright realized that, he got out of the Party.

Do I look like a crazy, foolish, superstitious woman to you? Well, I may be. I've fooled with astrology for forty years. When I first met Wright in 1936, *Horoscope Magazine* was published for the first time. I bought some of the first issues for a dime. I know how to set up charts. When Martin Luther King was killed in Memphis, I was in the Leamington Hotel in Minneapolis, Minnesota. I sat down and made his death chart. The chart shocked me. I didn't understand it at the time because what I saw all over King's chart was not so much death—I saw the gun, the government—as nothing but money—millions and millions of dollars. Money of all kinds, from all countries. Nothing but money.

Getting back to Wright . . . I remember the news flash on television about Wright's death. I was fixing breakfast. It upset me so that I sat down and began to tremble. Wright was just like somebody in my family. I had been that close to him. All that day I kept thinking about it, and I said to Eubanks, "They said he had a heart attack, but I believe it was tied up with his stomach." Because he had a delicate stomach. I know because I had cooked for him, and I knew he had to have simple foods. I didn't think about foul play. I didn't know his death had been kept out of the press for two days. No autopsy was ever performed. *Ebony* came out with an article, "The Mystery Around Richard Wright's Death." And John A. Williams's *The Man Who Cried I Am* suggested in a very symbolic fashion that Wright might have been murdered.

I felt Wright wanted me to write his biography because nobody is going to be more sympathetic and understanding than I. I was in love with him, and he knew it. He could not marry me. I was not what he could marry. That's the whole truth of that. You can't say he didn't love me; I know he did.

People think that Wright helped me and my writing. But I was writing poetry as a child in New Orleans. I had published in *Crisis* even before I ever met Wright. He had a lot of influence on me, but it wasn't on my writing. It concerned social perspective—Marxism and the problems of black people in this country. I helped Wright. He couldn't spell straight; he couldn't write straight. I had just graduated from Northwestern with a major in English literature. Do you believe that I was just being introduced to literature by Wright?

Michel Fabre, Wright's biographer, recognized Wright and I had a literary friendship. He wrote not too long ago on behalf of Yale, asking if I'd donate Wright's letters. Yale wants my letters. Harper & Row called and told me I had a debt to literary posterity. I said, "I'll pay the debt in the way I choose."

They know what I wrote to Wright, but they don't know what he wrote to me. Here's one of Wright's letters. You notice he lived in a different place with every letter: Gates Avenue, Carlton Avenue, Rutledge Place, 136th Street ... he lived at a dozen different addresses in three years' time.

You know, "Goose Island" was the story that Wright took from me for *Native Son*. I had written it for a project, and he read it. It was a slum story. The main character was a girl who went into prostitution. It was very much like Studs Lonigan stuff. I started writing that story in the writer's project, and I took three years. I was supposed to enter my story in the same contest Wright entered *Uncle Tom's Children*.

I remember Wright wrote me a Special Delivery letter, requesting that I send him all the newspaper clippings on Robert Nixon's trial. I sent him enough to cover a nine by twelve foot floor. Then he came to Chicago and asked me to help him for a day or so. We went to the library, and on my card I got that [Clarence] Darrow book, and I took him to the office of [Ulysses] Keys, who had been the lawyer on the case. I asked Keys for the brief. Those were integral parts of *Native Son*. I still didn't know what his story was about. When he did tell me, I said, "Oh, we're writing about the same thing, only your character is a man and mine is a woman." My character was a very talented girl, a musician who became a prostitute. That's what the environment did to her. Of course, I didn't have the violence and murder.

Wright returned to New York. From then on the relationship began to deteriorate. It still hadn't ended until the week he sent the manuscript to the publishers, and then he said that he didn't have any further need of me. He had used me to the fullest extent. He didn't intend to marry me, not ever. I'm glad of that because it wouldn't have worked.

Well, Wright's violence comes out of his anger. I gave a speech at Amherst in which I said the keys to Wright's fiction and personality were: anger, ambivalence and alienation. In the biography I start with him as a child and show how this anger builds up. If you knew him, you would not know how much of that anger was seething inside of him. He was always angry. I didn't understand it. He was like a demon possessed. One of my theses is that Wright was angry as a child. The Farnsworth piece [*Richard Wright: Impressions and Perspectives,* edited by David Ray and Robert Farnsworth] revealed how well I knew him and that I was the one to do the biography. It also revealed the literary content of our friendship. I didn't start out to do a definitive biography. What the editors discovered when I quoted from the letters was that I have a psychoanalytic treatment of Wright. Furthermore, I tied it in with the writing. I did what nobody could do. I dealt with Wright's formative environment: his family background with the broken home, the poverty, the racism, the hunger, and their effects. Horace Cayton was to write the biography. He collected interviews with people who knew Wright, and in '68 was on his way to Paris to complete the research. Vincent Harding suggested I should do the book, also Charles Rowell. I quit teaching with the full intention of writing full-time. I received a Ford grant in 1979 and completed the book in the fall of 1980 just two weeks before my husband died.

I organized it into five or six parts. In the introductory statement I state why I'm writing the book. I have a section on the psychic wound of racism the first nineteen years of his life. I took a quote from Wendell Berry who said: "If the white man has inflicted the wound of racism on black men, the cost has been that he would receive the mirror image of that wound into himself. I want to know as fully and as exactly as I can what the wound is and how much I am suffering from it. And I want to be cured." I did the research. I talk about what's wrong with Constance Webb's book and Fabre's book. Fabre's book was written in the shadow of the widow. She determined what should go in that book. He was indebted to her. He wanted to please her. If he discovered something, he couldn't do anything with it. Then again, he never knew the man. He never saw him in his life. Constance Webb may have seen him, but that book is so disorganized. She talks about "Dear Richard," and anybody who knew Wright either called him Dick Wright or Wright. They didn't call him Richard. She's off-base. In '73 everybody felt that Fabre wrote the definitive biography. I beg to differ. A definitive biography should recreate the man for you so you see him and you know him. Neither one of those books did that. I knew the man, and neither book is Wright.

I went down to Natchez [Mississippi]. I made some contacts with his father's side of the family. That has never been treated. The Wrights still exist all over that area, in Mississippi, Louisiana, and in California. They are just as middle-class as the mother's side. As a matter of fact Blyden Jackson found out that one of Wright's relatives on the father's side had an advanced degree and taught at Southern [University, Baton Rouge, Louisiana]. Yet you are given the impression that his father's side is just a bunch of "dumb niggers."

Wright wasn't really born in Natchez. Fabre found that out, too. Wright was born twenty-five miles from Natchez on a plantation. I found out that he was not really born in Roxie. Wright was born before records were kept in Mississippi. They weren't kept until 1912 on anybody in Mississippi, certainly not on black people before then. All people had then were baptismal records. When I was born records were being kept in Alabama. I had a birth certificate, but Wright was seven years older than I. But there are people down there in Natchez and Roxie who remember the family.

As I said, it was at the Richard Wright symposium at Iowa in '71 that Allison Davis called my attention to Wright's neurotic anger. He talked about the anger that had a realistic basis—the anger that Wright had toward society and toward his family. Then Davis talked about the neurotic anger that Wright could neither understand nor control. He said nobody can tell what the wellsprings of any man's creativity are. You can only guess. The more I thought about it, being a creative person myself, the more I understood. That's why I selected the title, *The Daemonic Genius of Richard Wright*. There are different kinds of geniuses: demonic, intuitive, brooding, and orphic. Perhaps Faulkner had all four. Wright was definitely demonic. It's more than an idea of devils. It's the idea of creativity coming out of anger, madness, out of frustration, rage. Creativity comes out of the madness that borders on lunacy and genius. Allison Davis said that Wright's genius evidently came out of neurotic anger arising from his formative environment, and from the fact that Wright felt his mother didn't really love him. He felt rejected by his mother as well as deserted by his father. This rejection was combined with the cruelty and religious fanaticism within his household.

I talk about the lynchings Wright depicts in his work. There's the poem "Between the World and Me," and the story in *Black Boy* of a man in Memphis being lynched and dismembered. We also know that Aunt Maggie had two husbands killed by white people in Elaine, Arkansas. At the very time and place he's talking about in *Black Boy* there was, in fact, a race riot. One of those uncles [one of Aunt Maggie's husbands] was killed in that riot. Then Wright wrote "Big Boy Leaves Home," which is a story of a lynching. There's another lynching in *Eight Men*. So he's got three substantial pieces dealing with lynching.

When Wright was working on *12,000,000 Black Voices,* he asked where he could find some real, poor, black people in slums. The answer he got was: "Go home, poor nigger, go home."

When I knew Wright he lived at 3836 Indiana Avenue. They have now torn that part of Chicago down. That was a very bad slum when I knew it in the thirties. I was living then in what was considered to be the nice section, Woodlawn—6337 Evans—out there near Cottage Grove and 63rd Street. Now that is a slum. You talk about depravity! The building in which Wright lived had "La Veta" written over the door. Oh, God, what La Veta was like. I went to see Wright and found him in a room that only had one door. I kept trying to figure out what kind of room it was; there was no window; it was not as big as my bathroom. Afterwards, I realized that it was originally built as a closet. He and his brother both were sleeping in it. Don't tell me he wasn't living in abject poverty. I can remember just as clear as I'm sitting here, seeing Wright look in a paper bag and take out a sandwich that was two slices of white bread and a piece of bologna sausage that looked like it was turning green, without mayonnaise, mustard, or anything on it. He would just look at it and throw it over into the wastepaper basket. . . .

The second part of the biography is the period covering the Chicago years, when Wright began to sing his broken song. The Chicago years were ones in which he learnt to write, and his consciousness was raised. Then came the New York years—the Medusa Head. You know Louise Bogan's poem "The Medusa Head?" It's about the whole idea of psychological frustration. Every time you look at the Medusa's head you turn to stone. The psychological analogy is that you freeze and cease to grow. The New York years were the years in which Wright had success: publication, fame and fortune. But it was also the time he broke with everybody. He had started that in Chicago. Now he had no close friends. People like Baldwin weren't the only ones. I wasn't the only one. Neither was Ellison. He broke with the Communist Party. He broke with his family. He spent nineteen years in the South, ten years in Chicago, ten years in New York, and fourteen years in Paris.

He moved from "New York and the Medusa Head" to Paris where we have the "Twisted Torch and the Political Paradox of Black Nationalism v. Internationalism." Wright's marriage and children were just one part of his expatriation. The break with the Communist Party was another. The Communist Party had been the only life he had that was meaningful after he left the South. Now he was outside of that. He had always cultivated black scholars and writers. He always had friendships like the one we had, in Chicago, New York and Paris. No matter what he thought about them, he had them. But they always got to a point when he would cut them off. He could not maintain close, meaningful relationships. It was part of his sense of alienation, his lack of trust. As he had said, it was his protective covering from being hurt because he had been hurt so badly.

The Paris years were the years of the international man; he made an effort to pull together a philosophy that will include black people everywhere: Africa, Asia, America, the Caribbean, and South America—Pan-Africanism. He wanted to be the spokesman for black people all over the world. He also wanted to say, "Workers of the world unite," but he could not reconcile black nationalism with "red" internationalism. During the Presence Africaine conference this dilemma became apparent. He denied what he had said in '37 in "The Blueprint for Negro Writers." He got up at the conference and said he hoped that such dictates were no longer necessary. It wasn't that he was saying that we were no longer brothers. As he talked, he alienated his audience by saying that he hoped the black writer was beyond the point of prescriptive writing. The Africans got mad; the West Indians and the black Americans got mad. Every black person there was infuriated, which meant that the very thing he was struggling to accomplish, he had destroyed: the unity of black brotherhood. He was an outsider again. He would not go to the Rome conference.

Wright was a strange person. We could talk all day or all night. I never kissed him in my life, and we spent hours, days and weeks together. I can remember only one time, when he came back to Chicago and we just had a brief embrace. I could feel him freeze.

C.T.:    You organized a symposium on black women writers.

WALKER:    The Phillis Wheatley Symposium. I'm not going to do any of that again. That phase of my life is over. I don't have energy for it anymore. I've got to write for the rest of my life, no matter how short or long it is. I've got to write. Teaching was never what I intended to do. Sometimes it might appear as though I have wasted so much of my life, but the classroom wasn't a waste. I enjoyed teaching; I was a good teacher. When I began to lose interest and enthusiasm for teaching, I quit. I never just sat there and drew the money, though I taught school to make a living. Moreover, I have never prostituted my writing. I toyed with the idea of being a writer-in-residence. But I don't think I will do it. I realized it's late in the day for me to make a list of priorities, but I must.

Writing is the first thing on my list, and I can't live long enough to write all the books I have in me. The sequel to *Jubilee* starts with Minna marrying in 1877, and ends with Vyry's death. Vyry died a month before I was born. Minna's first child was born in 1878, and that's when the family came to Mississippi. The sequel is the story of Minna and Jim. It's the story of the black church and the black school. It's about black benevolent societies, about jazz and blues. It's about Alabama, Mississippi and Florida.

I have another story which concerns a plot that's just recently become sensational. I haven't worked on it in ten years, though I've done over a hundred pages. It's a folk story entitled *Mother Broyer*. It's about a black woman who is a faith healer and a cult leader. Two things have happened that make that story sensational. One is the Jonestown incident; the other concerns Satanic cult activity here in Mississippi. A lot of black people in Mississippi have become involved in it. It breaks up homes, kills people, drives them insane. It's psychosexual stuff, and it frightens me. My mother told me the story about forty years ago. It starts in New Orleans, moves to Los Angeles, Harlem and ends up on the south side of Chicago, involving Jews, Catholics and black people. The main character is a girl who starts out as a Catholic, goes to the Holiness Church and then a Pentecostal church, and then ends up in jail in New York.

I would have done for black people what Faulkner did for the South. Wright wanted to do that, and he didn't. In recent years I've had to decide that nothing is as important as my writing. I've had to look at the effect of the Haley business on my audience, but I know I'm still on top where the audience is concerned. I know that anything I write will have an audience waiting to read it. That's why it's so important for me to do what I started out to do and not to be sidetracked.

About my autobiography . . . I remember something Lawrence Reddick said to me. He asked whether I was going to tell the whole truth. I said I'm not writing a confession. I don't have to tell anything I don't want to tell. I respect people being honest. Nikki is a very honest person; I don't think I have that kind of honesty. I don't believe in flouting what is contrary to the conventional. In "Being Black, Female and Free," I said I have never felt like I could just defy convention to the point that I went out there all alone. That's a kind of brazen honesty I don't have.

America has a tendency to praise the rags-to-riches phenomenon, the self-made man image. When you talk about being self-made, that's a bubble I intend to burst with the Richard Wright story. The white man in America, the white world, caters to the black person who didn't go to school. I represent education, family, and background. I represent scholarship. I don't see why I must go out and be an entrepreneur. Everybody has help. Richard Wright didn't just learn all by himself. There's no such thing as Topsy just grows.

Being classified as a middle-class black woman has been my undoing. I'm considered a black snob. I have to face the fact that I inherited a tradition—I'm a third-generation college graduate. Society doesn't want to recognize that there's this kind of black writer. I'm the Ph.D. black woman. That's horrible. That is to be despised. I didn't know how bad it was until I went back to school [to teaching] and found out.

C.T.:   Has the image of black women in American literature changed in recent years?

WALKER:   I got this unpublished manuscript out for you because it addresses your question on images of black women in black American literature. Let me read some of it for you:

> The image of black women in American literature has rarely been a positive and constructive one. White American literature has portrayed the black woman as she is seen in society, exploited because of her sex, her race, and her poverty. The black male writer has largely imitated his white counterparts, seeing all black characters and particularly females as lowest on the socioeconomic scale: as slaves or servants, as menial, marginal persons, evil, disreputable and powerless. The status of women throughout the world is probably higher now than ever before in the history of civilization. Black women have as much status in this regard as white women (who really don't have much either).
>
> All black characters fall into typical and stereotypical patterns. Black people were portrayed in slavery and in segregated situations, equated with animals and having subhuman status: wild, savage, and uncivilized. This, in the face of great African civilizations and cultures, is shocking only if we do not understand why demeaning and dehumanizing roles have been assigned to blacks by whites in the first place. If we understand the underlying philosophy of white racism, and its development as a buttressing agent of slavery and segregation and if we see these social institutions as necessary for the development of Western world capitalism, then we would know why these subhuman roles have been assigned to blacks. But why blacks feel they should imitate such castigation of black characters is harder to answer.
>
> It is necessary as always when approaching Afro-American literature in any form—poetry, prose, fiction, or drama—to give a background of the socioeconomic and political forces and the historical context before proceeding to a literary analysis or synthesis. Then we will have the necessary tools with which to examine the strange phenomena found in American and Afro-American literature. Race is the subject of much of

American literature, but race is almost the entire subject of Afro-American literature. Character, setting, action, event, tone, and philosophy all partake of the American myth and ethos of race. This focus may seem particular to the Southern literature of whites, but is also characteristic of black literature wherever it is found. There are some blacks who debate this issue, who beg the question of black humanity by seeking to avoid racial subjects and claiming a broader theme of universal subjects. I do not wish to avoid the subject. I think it is a natural point of departure for a black writer. I do not, however, feel comfortable with the kind of treatment black women have received.

The plantation tradition is the source of female characters as the mammy, the faithful retainer, the pickaninny, Little Eva and Topsy, the tragic mulatto, conjure-woman or witch, the sex object, the bitch goddess, the harlot and prostitute and, last but not least, the matriarch. These are typical and stereotypical roles of black women in American fiction, poetry, and drama. Furthermore, black as well as white writers have worked within this tradition. It was on the plantation that the brutalizing of black women was at its greatest. Cooks, maids, wet nurses, forced mistresses and concubines were the most "refined" roles of black slave women. In that system it was "tit for tat and butter for fat." There were a lot of critics who tried to show that the field hand was the real black person, while the one in the house was treated more favorably. (They tried to do that with Vyry in *Jubilee*.) Miscegenation became a trite and hackneyed theme. . . .

Leslie Fiedler in *Love and Death in the American Novel* has made a brilliant study of the equating of black with evil and the black woman as portraying the loose, amoral, immoral harlot or slut, while the white, blue-eyed, blond woman was put on a pedestal and worshipped for her virtue and virginal purity. White was not only all right, but perfectly pure, while blackness and darkness meant evil. . . . John Pendleton Kennedy's *Swallow Barn* and Faulkner's *The Sound and the Fury* certainly had great influence on black writers. W. E. B. Du Bois in his *Dark Princess*—and even Sam Greelee's *Spook Who Sat by the Door*—tried hard to portray black women with sympathy. James Weldon Johnson wrote one famous novel during the span between Dunbar/Du Bois and the Harlem Renaissance, but in it we see the white woman is again favored over the black woman. Langston Hughes and Arna Bontemps did a little better. . . .

Black men seem better when portraying old women. Ernest Gaines does this exceptionally well. No one can deny that a strong theme in Chester Himes is hatred for the middle-class black woman, whom he believes castrates and destroys her black male lover. Richard Wright does a bad job on women, period; but his black women fare even worse than his white women. Violence in his novels is a pattern, and this violence is frequently wreaked on women. The black woman is, therefore, a stereotype in fiction. Rarely does she achieve humanity, at least in the hands of male writers.

Of course, the positive view of women in Afro-American literature is only portrayed by black women. The earliest novel—*Iola Leroy* By Frances Harper—created a woman who is intelligent, attractive, human, and forceful in her personality. Harper sees black women as she sees herself—having strength of moral character, an indomitable will, perseverance, and a determination to overcome all handicaps and obstacles in her path. Zora Neale Hurston created an immortal love story in *Their Eyes Were Watching God,* and her portrayal of Janie and her love for Tea Cake is recognized by black women as typical of their love for black men. . . . Black women have received such cruel treatment in the literature. Only when the author is a black woman does she have half a chance. With poetry it is slightly different. The brown girl was a beautiful subject during the Harlem Renaissance.*

I was distracted with *Roots.* I'm not distracted anymore. There's nothing that's going to happen, short of my health, that's going to keep me from my work.

You asked what advice I had to offer young writers. Well, I avoid giving advice because people don't want advice; they want sympathy. They want somebody to bolster and buttress them and say what they're doing is right. And I've found folks will not take your advice if you give it. They have to learn their own way.

I had a lot of people tell me I couldn't write. In fact, very few of my teachers encouraged me to believe that I could write. If I had believed them, I wouldn't still be trying.

---

* This excerpt is from a talk Margaret Walker gave at Purdue and at Texas Southern Universities in the late seventies, and is unpublished.

# · SHERLEY ANNE WILLIAMS ·

*L iterary critic and writer Sherley Anne Williams was born in 1944 in Bakersfield, California. She received a B.A. from California State University at Fresno in 1966 and an M.A. in 1972 from Brown University.*

*Williams began her career as an English teacher, but wrote for herself "anywhere and at anytime." She taught English at California State University at Fresno, her alma mater. Williams is currently a professor of literature at the University of California in San Diego.*

*Giving Birth to Brightness (1972) was Williams's first major publication. It defines a black aesthetic by providing the cultural background for the term "black," and by elucidating the political dimension of the black dialect. It also explores the notion of the hero by analyzing the protagonists of Amiri Baraka's The Dutchman and the Slave, James Baldwin's Blues for Mr. Charlie and Ernest Gaines's Of Love and Dust, and concludes that true black heroes are rooted in the black folkloric tradition. The Peacock Poems (1975) focuses on the black women blues theme, in which "the blues" is a term representing complicated despairing emotions out of which a catharsis may occur, giving rise to a new determination to survive with pride and dignity. Her most recent publication is Someone Sweet Angel Child (1982).*

*Williams frequently writes critical essays about the Afro-American literary tradition, especially the blues idiom and folk culture, and her poems appear in numerous national magazines.*

❖  ❖  ❖

SHERLEY ANNE WILLIAMS:  As I travel across the country, I'm hearing more and more that the people who were directly involved in the black movement feel they've been burnt out by the movement and its aftermath. I think the reason why so much attention is now being paid to black women writers is because as a group we are, in our individual ways, trying to say, "No, you can't stop now. Something was there, and you have to keep going on even in the face of the unknown." I see this much more in the works of black women writers as a group then anywhere else, even among the so-called movement leaders. When I listen to these leaders, I sense that they are out of ideas. I also sense, and this is scary, that they are not talking to anybody but themselves; but I don't feel that when I read works by black women writers or when I listen to them speak. There is still the same sense of commitment, that rock-hard will.

I heard Sonia Sanchez when she was at Cornell. Her work has matured; she's a much better writer now than she was ten years ago. She has continued to grow, but her will has not changed. I see that in almost all of the work by black women I read. They seem to be taking that will to survive outside of the framework of encounters with the white world. They've refashioned this will into an instrument for understanding ourselves among ourselves. In each of their works there is the white world as backdrop, its oppression, but the focus is on understanding the self, the family, and the community. The strength originates here. I think this has been generally true of black women writers over the years. Nella Larsen, Zora Neale Hurston and Ann Petry, among many others, wrote about black people trying to work out their own destinies, given this white backdrop. It was as if they were saying, "If we don't deal with ourselves, it doesn't matter how we deal with the white man." This issue over the years has constituted one of the main differences between black women writers as a group and black male writers as a group. Moreover, this issue is responsible for their not getting as much attention as their male counterparts. Black women writers don't deal with the so-called big subjects. Now, more so than at any time in our history, we see that the so-called big subjects—the themes Ellison dealt with in *Invisible Man*, the themes Richard Wright and James Baldwin etc., deal with—those themes are all well and good, but the question still remains: what are we going to do about the here and now, me and you?

CLAUDIA TATE:   A recurring question concerns the differences between black male and female writers in terms of selecting events, themes, characters. On several occasions the response has been that the women writers focus on the so-called small themes—the particular relationship, rather than the representative or the big subjects, as you call them.

WILLIAMS: I think that is true. Some writers try to do both. I think, for example, Toni Morrison does both in her work. That whole mythic element in *The Bluest Eye,* in *Sula,* and in *The Song of Solomon* addresses the big subjects: love, death, beauty, good and evil. I'm not sure if the mythic level really works because I think novels work best on the real, intimate level. For example, the relationships between Sula and Nel in *Sula* and that among Claudia, Frieda, and Pecola in *The Bluest Eye* are sharper than the notions of mythic evil. Morrison's attempt to unite the two kinds of subjects, big and little, is extremely important. Either that has to happen, or we're going to have to build into the audience's consciousness the idea that the small slice-of-life theme is also universal.

C.T.: How does being black and female constitute a particular perspective in your work?

WILLIAMS: I don't think I keep my being black and female self-consciously in mind. I just assume that whatever I write comes from that perspective. Whether it's there in an overt manner or not doesn't really change that source. What I do think about self-consciously is that I am a writer. That assumes, of course, that I must also be a person; and that, in turn, assumes that I must have some racial background and gender; I just go on from that starting point.

I feel that a writer ought to transcend his or her background to some extent. Background ought not to be the only source of creativity. On the other hand, I do know the reason I was first inspired to do a story was because I wanted specifically to write about lower-income black women. I didn't see them as dominant forces in any of the literature I had read; they were always incidental to a larger story. I felt that they had significance, that something could be learned from them. We were missing these stories of black women's struggles and their real triumphs. I wanted to see them in stories, and I felt that I was capable of writing them. That is the basis of the first writing I did. I didn't want to write about myself, a young, black, female college student. I wanted to write about them because they had in a very real sense educated me and given me what it was going to take to get me through the world.

My interest in black women writers grew out of my discovery of writers, not necessarily women writers, but writers who wrote about people and things I knew about from my own experience. It didn't matter that I was in Fresno, California, and Zora Neale Hurston, for instance, was in Eatonville, Florida. It was a deeper experience reading her work than that by Langston Hughes or Sterling Brown, though they are great writers. Zora Neale focused in on a situation in a very different way from them. Hughes wrote about the north, and Sterling is writing about farmers and sharecroppers. Zora Neale's society sits in between, which is precisely what my background is.

C.T.:    The blues perspective dominates your work. You are quoted in *The Black Scholar* in reference to the sexist debate as saying, "But until we know the blues intimately and analytically, we will not know ourselves."

WILLIAMS:    What I really believe is that we as a people must be consciously aware that we must perpetuate ourselves and some idea of ourselves. Western, white people do this through literature, but we black people don't have that: we don't emanate from a literate tradition. We do not have a literature in which we see ourselves perpetuated. What we learn from most literature concerns white people; but where we do, in fact, perpetuate ourselves is in the blues.

I use blues to refer to a body of continuous expression that encompasses popular Afro-American music, so that at any given time whatever is popular among black people can be found in that mass of songs and instrumentation. In blues there is some kind of philosophy, a way of looking at the world. When the black-consciousness people came along, they disavowed the blues expression, and put down whatever was popular at that time because of ideology, because it was supposedly "slavery time"; this disavowal made a rupture in the continuity of our preserved history in this art form. We, as writers, are not revealing what the philosophy is. The people who perform the songs do this. The blues records of each decade explain something about the philosophical basis of our lives as black people. If we don't understand that as so-called intellectuals, then we don't really understand anything about ourselves. Blues is a basis of historical continuity for black people. It is a ritualized way of talking about ourselves and passing it on. This was true until the sixties.

C.T.:    Is the blues idiom a natural posture for black women writers since they seem to concentrate on intimate male-female encounters?

WILLIAMS: The early histories about the blues speak about relationships between a man and a woman. You can, of course, write blues about other kinds of subjects, but generally the blues has dealt with intimate relationships. It does, therefore, serve as a natural way of focusing on intimate situations. It gives you form and a setting. It saves a lot of exposition. For example, the black male-female sexist debate needs to be placed into the blues tradition in order for us to understand it. People who care about one another argue, have disputes, but they still care. That we are having this debate now ought not to mean we no longer care about each other.

C.T.: How do you fit writing into your life?

WILLIAMS: I fit writing in any way I can. Before my years in administration, I never really had to think about fitting writing into my schedule. I would write anytime and anywhere. I could write in a room full of people; I could write on a train. I don't know if that was out of necessity, but I think it says I was comfortable enough to write anywhere. I could be at a party and would pull out my little sheet of paper and start writing. I could work with the TV on, with kids running around. I was happy I could do this. Prior to being an administrator I don't think I had any real consciousness of needing any special time to write; but now that I do, you can be sure I'm going to be really greedy.

C.T.: Would you describe your writing process? How do you select your topics?

WILLIAMS: My topics select me. Then I just go ahead and try to work with them. I really try not to push things. If it's going to come, it'll come. I've always had enough projects going, so that if one was not going well at one point, I could just go on to something else. I've never been on a schedule, and I don't want to get on one. I don't think that's the most fruitful way for me to work.

C.T.: What is your responsibility as a writer?

WILLIAMS: Basically, to be as good as I can be and to say as much of the truth as I can see at any given time. It's just as simple as that.

C.T.: Is there a transition between your critical and the creative postures?

WILLIAMS:   When I wrote *Give Birth to Brightness,* Toni Morrison said that the book was very masculine. I had never thought about that. It was a book of criticism about a given body of literature, and the fact that I was a woman looking at how the hero was characterized never bothered me. I was a critic, and I was looking at those writers. The fact that the works were by black men didn't concern me. If I had found women who fit my subject—a certain kind of heroic black character—I would have dealt with that, too. My approach wasn't divided up according to gender.

How I work with the language constitutes the difference between critical and creative writing. I have read a few books of criticism, though, which I consider to be in and of themselves like works of art. There is a kind of leap the writer takes that not only illuminates the particular subject he or she is writing about, but shows the reader how to get from A to Z in ways that weren't possible before. That kind of illumination is not any different for me than the kind you want to have happen in a poem, a story or any imaginative piece.

C.T.:   For whom do you write?

WILLIAMS:   I think writing is really a process of communication. I bore everybody to death when I'm writing—"I want you to read this; I changed a word since yesterday. Read it, see what you think." It's the process of reading to people and getting their feedback that's important to me. It's the sense of being in contact with people who are part of a particular audience that really makes a difference to me in writing. I don't think there's anything I've ever published that has not been seen by a lot of people, whether they gave me feedback, whether I acted upon it or not. Writing for me is really a process of saying, "Here, read this." It reinforces the fact that I'm in touch with somebody other than my own mind.

C.T.:   What determines your interest as a writer?

WILLIAMS:   It has to do with what is out there, where the gaps are, and do I have the wherewithal to fill in some of those gaps that ought not to be there. The imaginative work is wide open—whatever comes to my mind and whatever I think is going to be fruitful in terms of showing people something about themselves and their relationship to the world. I really believe writing has a purpose: to teach and to delight.

C.T.:    Have you written stories from the male perspective?

WILLIAMS:    I've done a couple of stories from that perspective, neither of which has been published. I think one ought to be able to do this as a writer; writers ought to be able to project themselves into another voice and from another point of view. In a very real way that's not very different from what I have to do when I create anyway. If I achieve that initial projection, then the character assumes a life of his or her own. At the time I wrote these stories, my approach wasn't, "Now I'm going to write a story about a man." It was, "Now I'm going to write a story that has to do with these things," and those things came with characters who happen to be male or female.

C.T.:    Does your work attempt to show the cohesion and meaning in life?

WILLIAMS:    For me writing is a process of ordering the world. It is a process of bringing insight, playing around with possibilities, solutions, in a way I could never play around with actual life. Just think of the differences between the "order" of a poem and a novel and the chaos of life. That can give you some insight in knowing that if the chaos cannot be ordered, at least it can be dealt with in a constructive way. It's this that I'm after.

C.T.:    Do you write from experience?

WILLIAMS:    For me that is not a meaningful question because whatever I'm writing about, whether it's drawn directly from my own experience or something imaginative, if the incident doesn't move beyond the initial observation, the initial imagination, then it doesn't work. No matter how close to autobiography any one piece happens to be, if all I can see is that this happened to the writer, then the writer has failed. The autobiographical thread must represent something else.

C.T.:    Do you have any advice for young, black, women writers?

WILLIAMS:    I think that we writers should get out there, even if we are wrong 99 percent of the time. That 1 percent would be enough to give us some insight, but it takes a lot to get out there. Somebody has to be first to take all the flak. We have to stop being afraid. I have to stop being afraid of being wrong; I can't wait until everything is perfect before the work comes out. I don't have that kind of time. That's not to say that the poem has not been attended

212 <small>BLACK WOMEN WRITERS AT WORK</small>

to, that it's not gotten to be the best it can. The poem or the story or the play doesn't just jump out there; it has been attended to; it's gotten to be the best it can.

C.T.: When did you first know you were a writer?

WILLIAMS: Know? I know I'm a writer now. I knew I was a writer last year. I knew that when I decided I was going to take my time with my writing.

I started writing short stories around 1966. I always wrote with the idea of being published, not just to slip it away in a shoebox somewhere. I do believe that writing is about communication. Once, to say *"I am a writer"* seemed to be a very presumptuous thing for me to say. In fact, it was a very hard thing for me to say. It's not something that I say lightly. It involves commitment. It says something about myself that at one time I wasn't sure I wanted to say.

When I said "I am a writer" to people, it didn't mean anything to them! It was harder for me to say than it was for other people to hear. They take it as a matter of course. Basically, people—and I didn't know this—will take you for whatever you say you are. Maybe if I had realized this, I would have been able to say "I am a writer" much more easily, but it seemed to me that if I said I was a writer, I needed to have something already in print. I would go out with people, and they would say, "What do you do?" I would say nothing, or, "I teach," but I would never say, "I am a writer." Even now I say it with caution.

C.T.: From a teaching perspective, does Afro-American literature fit into American literature?

WILLIAMS: One of the things I would like to see is *real* American literature taught in this country. I would like to see "American lit." defined and taught in such a way that you're teaching the literature of all the people in America, not teaching it from one point of view as in the past, which excluded everybody else except white men and a few white women from consideration. I'm talking about constructing a new kind of perspective. In some universities this is happening, though granted very slowly.

Culture is inculcated in people through the humanities, and nothing really addresses the new world as it really is. The phrase, "the new world," doesn't have any resonance for us, and it should, not just because the new world was such a driving force in history, but because it is indeed possible that we do live in a *new* world. In that way I see Afro-American literature as being intricately related to Anglo-American literature. In some ways you can't even understand one without having some knowledge of the other. At the same time I would like to see Afro-American maintained as a subset of American literature; that is, see it taught as a part of the vitality of the whole and yet recognized as having a vitality in and of itself, that it has a perspective and point of view in and of itself.

One of the things I like about my own work, both published and unpublished, is that I've not been afraid to experiment. There were no real barriers in the sixties and early seventies, and this was really exciting. Despite the strictures of the black-consciousness movement, there opened up new means of exploring ourselves that were not there before. This was very good. I'm not sure if this exists now. I say that because I haven't read a lot of younger writers to see if it's still there. I know it's still there in the writers of my generation. For instance, when I read Toni Morrison's and Alice Walker's novels, there is a sense of discovery, a sense that this is uncharted territory, and they are leading us through it. This is aside from sheer craftsmanship. It's their unique storytelling ability; it takes us somewhere in literature we may not have been before. That's great. Perhaps the absence of women as a force in black literature in the early twentieth century impoverished the literature to some extent because there was no dialogue.

AAB-9863

6/13/01
120—